# THE ADMIRABLE LIFE OF MADRE MARIANA DE JESUS TORRES [1]

**Fr. Manuel Sousa Pereira**

- 1790 -

Translation and Footnotes by
**Marian T. Horvat, Ph.D**

1. The complete Spanish original title of this work is *Vida Admirable de la Reverendissima Madre Mariana de Jesus Torres, Espanola y una de las Fundadoras del Monasterio Real de la Limpia Concepcion en la ciudad de Quito.* Its English translation is T*he Admirable Life of the Most Reverend Mother Mariana de Jesus Torres, Spaniard and One of the Founders of the Royal Monastery of the Immaculate Conception in the City of Quito.*

The devotion to Our Lady of Good Success has been approved by the Bishops of Quito since February 2, 1611, when the 8th Bishop of Quito, Salvador de Ribera (1607-1612) blessed the miraculous statue and formally installed her in the Abbess' chair of the Convent.

The process for beatification of Mother Mariana de Jesus Torres y Berriochoa was initiated by the Archbishop of Quito Antonio J. Gonzalez in April 1986.

Copyright © 1999 by Marian T. Horvat, Ph.D. for this English translation
All rights reserved. No part of this translation may be reproduced or transmitted in any form or by any means whatsover, including the Internet, without permission in writing from the translator, except that brief selections may be quoted or copied for non-profit use without permission, provided full credit is given.

ISBN: 0-9726516-3-2
Library of the Congress Number: 2005900988

First edition 2005 by Tradition in Action, Inc.
Second edition 2014.
Printed and bound in the United States of America
Cover by the TIA art desk.

The front cover shows the profile of the statue of Our Lady of Good Success. The back cover includes a close-up of a portrait of Mother Mariana de Jesus painted by Don Carlos Salas in May 1922.

**Tradition in Action, Inc.**
P.O. Box 23135
Los Angeles, CA 90023
www.TraditionInAction.org

Mother Mariana Francisca de Jesus Torres y Berriochoa
(1563-1635), one of the Founding Mothers of the Royal Convent
of the Immaculate conception in Quito, Ecuador.
This Spanish religious received many prophecies about the future,
especially about the crisis in the Church and society
in the 20th century.

Our Lady of Good Success told Mother Mariana that she would start to be known in the 20th century.
She promised her special help - both spiritual and material - to those who invoke her under this title during the great crisis the Church would be suffering in our times.

## Table of Contents

Foreword .......................................................................... 11

Chapter 1. Homeland, family and birth of Mariana de Jesus ............................................................................... 17

Chapter 2. First Communion of Mariana - Favors she receives from the Sacramental Jesus - Sweet ecstasy of the future religious of the Immaculate Conception ......... 20

Chapter 3. Religious vocation in the Order of the Immaculate Conception - Her heroic sacrifice - Taking leave of her parents and homeland - Leaving Spain to found the first Convent of the Order of the Immaculate Conception in the New World ....................................................... 24

Chapter 4. Voyage to Quito - Difficulties at sea - Terrible war the Devil wages against the Founding Mothers of the Royal Convent of the Immaculate Conception of Quito to impede its foundation - The Virgin beheads the infernal serpent ................................................................. 27

Chapter 5. Great difficulties beset the journey to Quito - Arrival in the Colony and foundation of the Convent of the Immaculate Conception ............................................. 32

Chapter 6. The novitiate, fervor, extraordinary graces and profession of Mother Mariana de Jesus ..................  34

Chapter 7. Probation period of Mother Mariana de Jesus - Her advancement in virtue - Our Lord gives her the penances she should practice throughout her life ........... 39

Chapter 8. Admirable penances of Mother Mariana de Jesus - Graces she receives from God ............................ 41

Chapter 9. Admirable behavior of Mother Mariana - Her Divine Spouse gives her daily subjects of meditation - Favors He grants her ........................................................  45

Chapter 10. Ardent love of Mother Mariana de Jesus for the Sacramental Jesus - The first death of Mother Mariana - She comes before the throne of the Most Blessed Trinity - Her miraculous resurrection ............................. 47

CHAPTER 11. Offices in the Convent held by Mother Mariana - Miracles she performs in executing her duties ...... 57

CHAPTER 12. Mother Mariana is named Novice Mistress - How she forms her novices - Special favors she receives from Our Lord ........................................................ 62

CHAPTER 13. Terrible desolation of spirit she suffers - The great sickness and humiliations she bears - Her second mystical death and her resurrection ............................... 66

CHAPTER 14. Mother Mariana is elected Abbess for the first time - In humility she renounces the office but is obliged to accept it under obedience - God confirms the choice of the young Abbess with a miracle - Forewarnings concerning relaxations of community life .............. 80

CHAPTER 15. How Mother Mariana prodigiously and wisely governs the Convent - Final illness of her aunt, Mother Maria Taboada, and her death and judgment - The grief of the Community ............................................ 87

CHAPTER 16. Suffering of Mother Mariana over the announcement of the separation of the Friars Minor - How her actions delay this separation - Consolations God gives to His spouse ................................................. 97

CHAPTER 17. The Holy Virgin of Good Success asks Mother Mariana for the first time to make a Statue of her so that she might govern the Convent - Second apparition of this queenly Mediatrix ................................... 103

Chapter 18. The election of Mother Magdalena de Jesus Valenzuela as Abbess - Mother Mariana humbly steps down and begins her terrible sufferings together with the other Spanish Founding Mothers - Separation of the Friars Minor - Obedience is rendered to the Bishop ....... 110

CHAPTER 19. The special graces God Our Lord concedes to His spouses imprisoned for love of Him - Celestial visits they receive in prison ............................................ 116

CHAPTER 20. The illustrious prisoners leave prison - God Our Lord vindicates the innocence of His spouses ......... 124

*Table of Contents*

CHAPTER 21. Mother Mariana de Jesus is again elected Abbess - Favors she receives from her Divine Spouse - The calumnies against her and her re-imprisonment .... 127

CHAPTER 22. Mother Mariana returns to prison - The other Founding Mothers join her - Sufferings they endure as prisoners - Another apparition of Our Lady of Good Success ........................................................................... 133

CHAPTER 23. The Bishop releases Mother Mariana and the other Spanish sisters from prison - She is led to the Abbess seat in triumph - Imprisonment of the guilty sister ................................................................................. 152

CHAPTER 24. The Abbacy of Mother Mariana - How she governs with admirable prudence and sanctity - Her sufferings and fourth imprisonment ............................. 159

CHAPTER 25. Mother Mariana leaves the prison in triumph - Miracle of the Virgin of Peace during the election of the new Abbess ................................................................. 168

CHAPTER 26. The Abbacy of Mother Magdalena de Jesus Valenzuela - The death and conversion of the rebellious "Captain"....................................................................... 193

CHAPTER 27. The Hell that Mother Mariana suffers to save the soul of the "Captain"- The terrible trials she endures for five years - She leaves Hell and Our Lord returns her heart ................................................................. 230

CHAPTER 28. Mother Mariana is elected Abbess for the third time - Special favors she receives from the Blessed Virgin - Our Lady of Good Success reprimands Mother Mariana because the statue has not been made ................................................................................ 248

BIBLIOGRAPHY ................................................................. 251

\* \* \*

# Foreword

The story and prophecies of Our Lady of Good Success are inseparable from the person of Mother Mariana de Jesus Torres, a Conceptionist religious who traveled from Spain to the New World at age 13 to help found a convent in the city of Quito, Ecuador. This saintly soul received apparitions of Our Lady with revelations regarding future events, especially the grievous situation of the Catholic Church in the 20th century.

Our Lady told her that in our lamentable times, heresies would abound, the corruption of customs would be almost complete, and the light of Faith nearly extinguished. To atone for the heresies, blasphemies, and impurity of our days, this 17th century nun was asked to become an expiatory victim. The vocation of Mother Mariana links her, therefore, to the crisis in the Church and society that we are experiencing today.

The publication of my two short works, *Our Lady of Good Success: Prophecies for Our Times* (1999) and *Stories and Miracles of Our Lady of Good Success* (2002), has generated a great interest in this admirable Conceptionist sister and these revelations. The broad acceptance for those revelations encouraged me to publish this biography of Mother Mariana, which is the source of the data used in my books.

Also, many questions have been addressed to me. Among other things, readers are asking: Is this an approved devotion? Why are we only hearing about Mother Mariana de Jesus Torres and her prophecies now?

*First*, let me assure my readers that this is not some new or questionable devotion. The devotion to Our Lady of Good Success has been approved by the Bishops of Quito since February 2, 1611, when the 8th Bishop of Quito, Salvador de Ribera (1607-1612) blessed the miraculous statue and formally installed Our Lady of Good Success in the Abbess' chair of the Convent. Every February 2 for the last 394 years, the Convent and the people of Quito have celebrated the feast of Our Lady of Good Success with the full approval of the ecclesiastical authority. In 1991, the Archdiocese of

Quito petitioned Rome for a canonical coronation of Our Lady of Good Success as *Queen of Quito,* a ceremony that took place on February 2, 1991. The same year, the Church of the Conceptionist Convent was declared an Archdiocesan Marian Sanctuary.

*Second*, the great virtue of Mother Mariana and the truth of the revelations she received from the Mother of God have been demonstrated by incontrovertible historical evidence. After examining extensive data on her life, Archbishop of Quito Antonio J. Gonzales issued an episcopal decree on August 8, 1986 to initiate her Cause of Beatification. He named Msgr. Luis Cadena y Almeida as postulator for the cause and established an ecclesiastical tribunal to begin the first phase of the process. This decree affirmed that Mother Mariana had practiced all the virtues to a heroic degree, and was distinguished for her devotions to the Passion of Christ, the Holy Eucharist, and the Mother of God. It also acknowledged her supernatural gifts and charismas during her lifetime.[2]

Since then, Msgr. Cadena y Almeida has compiled an impressive arsenal of documentation, testimonies, and works – many of which he published with ecclesiastical approval – that demonstrate the sanctity of life of Mother Mariana and the truth of the prophecies she received. I have cited material from these works in footnotes of this biography to provide some interesting details and background regarding her life, as well as to show how the prophecies she received have been fulfilled most accurately.[3]

Included in his compilation of evidence was the 571-page handwritten biography of Mother Mariana written by Fr. Manuel Sousa Pereira, O.F.M. in 1790. The work by Fr. Pereira has special value because he based it on primary sources from the Convent archives. Such sources included the *Autobiography* of Madre Mariana, written at the command of Bishop Pedro de Oviedo and

---

2. The decree and numerous other documents were published in a work written by the Postulator for Mother Mariana's cause, Msgr. Luis Cadena y Almeida, entitled *La Mujer y la Monja Extraordinaria* (Quito: Libreria Espiritual, n.d.).

3. Msgr. Cadena y Almeida dedicated one work specifically to the demonstration of how the prophecies of Our Lady of Good Success have been confirmed by History. It is entitled *Mensaje Profético de La Sierva de Dios Sor Mariana Francisca de Jesus Torres y Berriochoa* (Quito: Libreria Espiritual, 1989).

approved by him, as well as several other early biographies written by Franciscans who knew her.[4]

Volume I of Fr. Pereira's well-documented work is being presented here in its first English translation for the benefit of the growing number of devotees of Our Lady of Good Success in the United States.

*Third*, the reason why this devotion and these important prophecies only became known some 300 years after they were revealed is answered by Our Lady herself. On February 2, 1634, at the end of her life, Mother Mariana was praying, humbly beseeching Our Lady to hide her name and person. At that moment, the Mother of God appeared to her and assured her that only after three centuries of silence, in the 20$^{th}$ century, would her name and the truth of these revelations become known.

In those days of great calamity, a filthy ocean of impurity would inundate the world and the ingratitude and betrayal of religious souls would compel Our Lord to let His justice fall on a beleaguered world, Our Lady told Mother Mariana. In those difficult times when the Church would be so embattled and suffering from within, Our Lady told her, she wanted to sustain the faithful and be invoked under the title of Our Lady of Good Success. She promised to give good success to those who had recourse to her and fostered devotion to her under this particular title.

Just as Our Lady predicted, the prophecies only became known to the larger public at the end of the 20$^{th}$ century, when the devotion began to spread outside the borders of Ecuador.

Volume I of Fr. Pereira's work relates many details from the early life of Mother Mariana until the year 1594. In these pages, you will find a detailed account of the two deaths and resurrections she experienced, her four unjust imprisonments inside the Convent, and her heroic sacrifice of suffering mystically in Hell for five years to

---

4. Fr. Martin de Ochoa was assigned to write an account of the life of Mother Mariana shortly after her death. Fr. Francis de Anguita, her spiritual director and confessor, also wrote a work on her life. In 1650, 15 years after her death, at the mandate of the Royal Audience of Quito, Don Diego Rodríguez Docampo wrote an account of her life and prophetic gift she received. Fr. Pereira also referred to a biography written by Fr. Bartolomé Ochoa de Alcano y Gamboa in 1760.

ransom the soul of the "captain," the rebellious sister who led the non-observant faction inside the Convent. It also records the first three revelations of Our Lady of Good Success to Mother Mariana.

I believe that the reader will eagerly anticipate volume II, which Tradition in Action intends to publish as soon as possible. In it, Fr. Pereira completes the story of the marvelous life of Mother Mariana, recounts the history of the miraculous way the statue of Our Lady of Good Success was completed, gives many more prophecies of Our Lady of Good Success, many about our times, and leaves us the stirring Last Testament of Mother Mariana de Jesus Torres.

It seems to me an opportune time for the life of Mother Mariana de Jesus Torres to become better known to the English-speaking public. The prophecies she received from Our Lady of Good Success help us understand the enormous crisis the Church is suffering today with the introduction of the errors of Modernism at the turn of the 19th century, and the victory of Progressivism inside her walls at Vatican Council II in the early '60s. This victory marked the beginning of what has been called by its own partisans the "conciliar Revolution," which changed the face of the Catholic Church, her doctrine, her liturgy, her laws, her institutions and customs, and abolished her traditions.

Finally, I should remark that Our Lady of Good Success also gave a message of great hope. She promised her intercession at the very moment when the evil will seem to be triumphant and when the ecclesiastical authority will abuse its power. This would mark, as Our Lady said, "the arrival of my hour, when, in a marvelous way, I will dethrone the proud and accursed Satan, trampling him under my feet and fettering him in the infernal abyss." [5] These words harmonize perfectly with the message of hope Our Lady delivered to the three shepherd children at Fatima in 1917: "In the end, my Immaculate Heart will triumph."

\* \* \*

---

5. M. T. Horvat, *Our Lady of Good Success – Prophecies for Our Times*, (Los Angeles: TIA, 2000), pp. 57-8.

# Vida Admirable de la Rda. Madre Mariana de Jesús Torres, española y una de las fundadoras del Monasterio real de la Limpia Concepción en la Ciudad de Quito

Escrita por el Rdo. Padre Manuel Sousa Pereira de la Orden Seráfica de los Menores del Convento Máximo de S. Francisco de Quito en el Ecuador.

## Tomo Primero

# Chapter 1

Rev. Mother Mariana de Jesus Torres was one of the strongest pillars of this Royal Convent of the Immaculate Conception of Quito and the predestined daughter of the Queen of Heaven. To her, the Heavenly Queen confided ineffable secrets, disclosing to her the mercies of her loving heart toward this Convent, bequeathing to her daughters the precious treasure of the sacred statue of our Mother and Abbess, Our Lady of Good Success. The Rev. Mother Mariana de Jesus was the humble violet that hid its delicate fragrance in the very heart of Mary Most Holy, and she beseeched the Most Holy Virgin that her name be unknown, even in her own Community. And thus it would have remained until the end of time if the Virgin Most Holy had not revealed to her that, after three centuries of mysterious silence, the truth of the apparitions would become manifest in the 20$^{th}$ century, and, only then, would her name become known.

Until that fortunate time when the ineffable caresses of Mary Most Holy to her chosen daughter should be published, we write these lines for the glory of God Our Lord and in devotion to our Mother, Abbess and Advocate, the Most Holy Virgin of Good Success. Moreover, we offer this work in honor of our illustrious angelic sister, the Rev. Mother Mariana de Jesus Torres, and for the benefit, edification, and love of our successors.[6]

### Homeland, Family, and Birth of Mother Mariana de Jesus Torres

Mother Mariana de Jesus Torres y Berriochoa was born in Spain in the Basque province of Viscaya in 1563. She was baptized in one of the parish churches there, which was consumed by fire seven years later. She was the first-born child of Don Diego Torres

---

6. Manuel Sousa Pereira was born in 1751 in Sotomayor in the Diocese of Braga, Portugal. A young officer from an illustrious family, he was pursuing a promising military career when Mother Mariana appeared to him in his barracks. She told him to "leave this earthly army and enlist in the army of the Seraphim of Assisi to find a better army under his banner." He traveled to Quito and became a Franciscan priest, and was elected Provincial of his Order in Quito several times. Based on his conversations with the sisters of the Convent of the Immaculate Conception, records from the Convent archives, and the biographies written of the lives of all the Founding Mothers, he wrote the story of the life of Mother Mariana de Jesus Torres in 1790. This is volume I of that edifying work.

y Cádiz and Doña Maria Berriochoa y Alvaro, who gave her the name of Mariana Francisca.

The child was the delight of her parents, for Heaven had endowed her with rare beauty, quick intelligence, a sweet nature, and, above all, a strong inclination toward virtue. From infancy, she shunned all the childish games of youth. Instead, she would secretly retire to the church whenever she could, where her virtuous mother would find her prostrate before the Tabernacle.

For the Prisoner of the Tabernacle had already wounded the tender heart of His future spouse, who, unknowingly, was preparing herself in the fire of divine love to become the victim of His most pure flames.

A particularly noteworthy incident occurred in the life of this blessed family when the little girl was seven years old. A fire broke out in the church where she had been baptized. The parish priest was away, and the sacristan, in his carelessness, had left a good quantity of oil in the sanctuary lamp. A slight earthquake apparently caused the ground to tremor. The cords or chains that supported the sanctuary lamp broke, and the fire started. The old church was engulfed in flames. The family of the sacristan and the neighbors all hurried to the site, but it was impossible to extinguish the devouring flames.

### Our Lord in the Blessed Sacrament Is Rescued from the Flames

At the time of this fire, a priest named Fr. Luis Jayme de Berriochoa, the brother of Mariana's mother and the child's uncle, was visiting the home of his sister and her husband, Diego de Torres. Hearing the excitement and seeing the disastrous flames, he intrepidly entered the burning church, crying out, "My Lord Jesus in the Blessed Sacrament, I cannot allow these flames to consume Thee! Rather should the fire of my priestly love be consumed with Thee!" Taking the Ciborium and the Host used during expositions of the Sacred Species, he said, "We shall die together here!"

But the fire respected the minister of the Lord, and he was able to escape unharmed, carrying with him the Blessed Sacrament. As soon as he was outside the burning building, the altar and church collapsed behind him. The Torres family, unmindful of the danger to their own house, had followed the priest to the church. Rejoicing that he escaped the flames, they accompanied him to the neighboring parish church where the Sacred Species was safely deposited.

## "God Giveth and God Taketh away. Blessed Be His Holy Name!"

Since the house of the Torres family was adjacent to the church, it was also damaged by the fire. The family's vineyards were ruined, and the building was partly destroyed. Upon their return, the devout proprietors saw what had happened to their property, and, like holy Job, they knelt on the ground with their three children – Mariana Francisca, Diego, and three-year-old Santiago – to give thanks to God for taking their earthly belongings from them during their efforts to save the Sacred Species. They said, "God giveth and God taketh away. Blessed be His Holy Name!"

It grieved Mariana to see her virtuous parents suffer in the poverty to which they had been reduced. But the greatest pain that pierced her tender heart was caused by the absence of her beloved Jesus in the Blessed Sacrament. When He had been their neighbor in the nearby church, it had been easy to make her devout flights to adore Him in the Tabernacle. Now, distance did not permit these frequent visits. Desolate, she suffered greatly to be separated from her steadfast Beloved, Who thus began to habituate His beloved to these cruel absences and desolations, which, throughout the course of her life, this soul would have to suffer to become a heroine of the dolorous martyrdom of love.

\* \* \*

## Chapter 2

Thus, like a sunflower, Mariana opened her delicate face to follow the radiant light of Jesus in the Blessed Sacrament. Unable to adore Him frequently at the foot of the Tabernacle, she languished and, with agonizing love, longed for the Eucharistic union.

The loving lamentations of the child illuminated the sanctuary lamp like sparks of light, and the sacrifices of that loving heart pierced the Sacred Heart of Jesus. Her Divine Lover, unable to resist the clamors of the enamored virgin, thus disposed matters so that the young girl might have her Beloved in the Most Holy Sacrament.

### Mariana Hears the Voice of Jesus in the Blessed Sacrament

Because of family concerns, the parents of the young girl found themselves obliged to leave Viscaya and to relocate themselves and their three children to Santiago of Galicia. Once established there, Mariana was again able to seek out Jesus in the Blessed Sacrament.

On one occasion, prostrate at the foot of the Tabernacle, her heart was so inflamed with burning desires to unite herself to Jesus in Holy Communion that she exclaimed aloud, "Oh, my Love! When will that day arrive when I might unite myself to Thee in Holy Communion?" The next moment, she heard a voice coming from the Tabernacle that said, "Whatever day you desire, My daughter, for your heart is even now prepared." This was the first time that she sensibly heard the sweet voice of Jesus in the Blessed Sacrament.

The child was inundated in a sea of joy upon hearing the voice of her Beloved! Like a melodious lyre, she intoned sweet Eucharistic canticles. And like the spouse in the *Canticle of Canticles*, she asked herself if her ears had indeed heard the voice of her Beloved calling her from the hidden depths of the glories of the Tabernacle. And seeing her only Love so alone and hidden, the heart of this tender child poured itself out before Him in grief over His abandonment and her desire to be united to Him.

### THE OBSTACLES ARE REMOVED.
### MARIANA RECEIVES HER FIRST HOLY COMMUNION

Thus, from childhood, the life of Mariana was permeated by the highly refined myrrh of suffering. After this incident, she went and knelt before a priest of the Order of Saint Francis and unveiled to him her simple, innocent soul. This holy minister of God understood that she should receive Holy Communion and ordered her to prepare herself for this great day.

Filled with joy, Mariana went to communicate this happy news to her mother, but the illustrious matron told her that she was still too young to receive the Holy Host. For, at this time, children generally made their First Holy Communion between their 12$^{th}$ and 14$^{th}$ years, and Mariana was only nine. In face of this refusal, she returned in tears to her confessor to communicate to him her grief. The learned and virtuous priest consoled her, telling her that she would, indeed, soon receive Holy Communion, and that he himself would begin to prepare her, or, rather, to perfume the bed of fragrant lilies that Jesus Christ Himself had cultivated in the heart of this innocent virgin.

Finally, the day of December 8, 1572 arrived when Mariana received Holy Communion for the first time.

### THE FIRST VISION OF OUR LADY:
### MARIANA IS DESTINED FOR THE CONCEPTIONIST ORDER

Upon her first embrace with Jesus, the torrent of divine love in her heart overwhelmed her and she fainted in ecstasy. [7]

In this ecstasy she saw our Immaculate Mother who, captivating the child with her sweet presence, explained to her the grandeur of the vow of virginity. She showed her how she, the Queen of Heaven, had herself taken this vow in the Temple at the tender age of three. She taught the girl the meaning of such a vow and commanded Mariana to make it, for her Heavenly Queen had destined her to be a religious of her Immaculate Conception.

---

7. The prayer of ecstatic union adds the suspension of the external senses to the prayer of union, where the faculties of the soul and internal senses are intimately united with God. The intensity of the mystical union is so great the body cannot withstand it and falls into ecstasy (Antonio Royo Marin, *The Theology of Christian Perfection,* New York: 1987, pp. 483).

She told Mariana that she would give much glory to God by joining this order. From that moment onward, Mariana remained pledged to foster devotion to the ineffable mystery of the Immaculate Conception of her Mother, Mary Most Holy.

### Her Celestial Betrothal to the Only-Begotten Son of God

Then she saw in the Tabernacle the Three Persons of the Blessed Trinity, and she understood that the Second Person, the Divine Word, in the form of a Child in His Most Sacred Humanity, desired to be betrothed to her.

She also saw Saint Joseph, the most chaste spouse of the Blessed Virgin, and joyfully understood that Mary Most Holy and Saint Joseph were going to stand as witnesses for this celestial union.

She pronounced the solemn vow of chastity, repeating the words taught to her by Our Lady. When she had finished, the Eternal Father blessed the union of His Only Begotten Son with the child Mariana de Jesus.

### Mariana Leads a Life More Angelic than Human

This was her first ecstasy, for on her First Communion she enjoyed the delights of her Loving Spouse, Who asked her to walk the road of sacrifice and love. From that moment, she lived only to love the Sacramental Jesus, sustained, as she was, by the divine fire of love. She embraced a life more angelic than human, never losing her baptismal innocence. Her confessor wisely directed her, allowing her to observe in her home the austerities of the monastic life and permitting her to receive Holy Communion twice a week.

On one occasion her mother came upon her at the moment when her director was giving her Communion. This virtuous matron, moved by zeal and fearing that her child was approaching the celestial banquet without proper preparation, approached to reprimand her. But Mariana's confessor realized what the mother was thinking and prevented her from reproaching the child. Calling her aside, he revealed to her the rich reserves of graces and virtues that God, prodigious in His great mercy, had bestowed upon this angelic child.

## Her Frequent Communion, Prayer, Contemplation, and Mortification

Thus her mother's displeasure was transformed into admiration and thanksgiving to God Our Lord for the precious jewel that He had confided to her in the person of her daughter. From that time forward, she gave Mariana full liberty to receive Communion often and to practice all the virtues.

Her parents were, then, collaborators with and custodians of this innocent virgin, who began to fly in the ways of perfection in the seclusion and retreat of her oratory. In addition to the practice of the religious virtues, she dedicated herself to prayer, contemplation, and both interior and exterior mortification, transforming her house into a convent in the service of her parents and little brothers.

Carrying out her household duties, she imitated Martha, who prepared the food for Jesus. Like Mary, she found warmth and consolation at His Sacred Feet, where she presented to her Divine Lover the exquisite perfume of her love, her innocent heart being an alabaster vessel of purity and sacrifice.

This young child only knew sin to avoid it and to weep for the offenses of sinners, for, from her earliest childhood she led a life of innocence and penance. Indeed, the tears of this future spouse of Christ even then hastened the moment for the foundation of the Order of the Conceptionist religious in the city of Quito. For, from the moment when the Blessed Virgin communicated to her that she was destined to be a religious of her Immaculate Conception, Mariana's soul was inflamed with an ardent desire to carry out this mission. But, knowing neither when nor where this would take place, she abandoned herself to her fervent devotions, allowing herself to omit no sacrifices or prayers until such time as her desires were satisfied. God Our Lord, attentive to the sighs of His tender dove, was already preparing for her on the soil of Ecuador a nest where her love might find solace.

\* \* \*

# Chapter 3

It was the year of Our Lord 1556. The ladies of Quito, knowing that there was an Order of Religious of the Immaculate Conception of Mary Most Holy in Spain and moved by their love for Mary Immaculate, desired that such a Convent of religious sisters should be founded in their city. They understood the great glory this would give to God Our Lord and the immense good it would do for the people of the city.

Toward that end, the leading families of Quito, along with many of the inhabitants of the city, met with a group of friars to petition the King of Spain, humbly entreating him to found the first Convent of the Immaculate Conception of the New World in their colony.[8]

### THE KING OF SPAIN SENDS THE FIRST CONCEPTIONISTS TO QUITO

By the grace of God, their petition was heard, and the King himself sent from Spain the first group of founding mothers. He placed at their head the Rev. Mother Maria de Jesus Taboada, a descendant of an ancient and noble house of Galicia.[9] This illustrious, candid virgin was the aunt of Mariana, and she took her young niece on this venture along with the other Founding Mothers.

As soon as this innocent girl heard that a Convent of the Immaculate Conception was to be founded in the New World colony, she understood this to be the voice of her Beloved, which called to

---

8. Surrounded by mountains covered year round with snow, the City of Saint Francis of Quito was founded by Spanish conquerors of Emperor Charles V on December 6, 1534. In 1566, King Philip II issued the Royal Edict for the foundation of the Convent of the Immaculate Conception, dedicated *first* to the praying of the Divine Office, and *second*, to the religious education and formation of the Spanish daughters and *criollas* of the Spanish Colony.
The first convent in the newly founded city was formally installed on the corner of its main square on January 13,1577.

9. Mother Maria de Jesus Taboada was related to the royal family, and King Philip II himself chose and named her as Founder for the Conceptionist Convent he wanted to found in the city of Quito in New Spain. When the foundation was made, she was 33 years of age (Luis Cadena y Almeida, *Apariciones de María Santísima del Buen Suceso*, Quito, Libreria Espiritual, 1999, pp. 46-7).

her saying, "Leave your motherland and the house of your parents, for the King of Heaven has become enamored of your beauty."

How sweet that voice was to the ears of young Mariana, as her soul heard the call sounding the moment for her heroic sacrifice. She immediately communicated to her parents this divine call, telling them that she must separate herself from them forever on this earth.

### Apparition of the Divine Jesus

A few days before taking leave of her good parents, upon receiving Holy Communion, in her soul she saw the Divine Jesus at His perfect age. He said to her, "My Spouse, the time has already arrived for you to bid an eternal farewell to your motherland and to your paternal home. Eagerly coveting your beauty, I bring you to My house, where, behind strong walls, you will live far from flesh and blood, hidden and forgotten by all human creatures. For your inheritance and patrimony, you will have, in imitation of Me, the cross and great sufferings. Strength and courage will not be lacking to you. I desire only that your will be always prepared to do Mine."

Mariana accepted from Jesus Christ all that He asked of her and, following His footsteps, offered herself as a sacrifice of love.

### Mariana Leaves her Paternal House

The day of her departure arrived, a day most moving to all present, harsh and bitter for her parents and relatives, and also for the innocent child, for her candid heart dearly loved her parents and family. But it was also a sweet and satisfying day, for she was giving to her God an open demonstration of her love. At the same time, God gave her the ineffable consolations that He alone knows how to give to those who belong to Him in their hours of sacrifice.

Mariana was entrusted to the care of her aunt, Mother Maria de Jesus Taboada, who offered to act henceforth as mother to the child. Amid tears and embraces, that tender plant, who in America would become a verdant tree whose branches would provide shade and life for so many souls, left the Spanish world.

Oh! My God, how incomprehensible art Thy ways to the eyes of mere men, and how loving dost Thou show Thyself to be to Thy chosen ones! How painful a struggle for this loving child! Her parents wanted her to become a Carmelite sister in Spain. But to this she would reply, "I am called for the Order of the Immaculate Conception." But why, they argued, could she not become a Conceptionist sister in Spain? Why must her ties to family and homeland be completely severed?

But God desired that the holocaust be perfect! For this reason, the maiden would say, "I desire to cross the seas, and, in distant lands, far from flesh and blood, to consecrate myself solely to the love of my Jesus!"

How great the sword of sorrow that pierced the hearts of Don Diego and Doña Maria to be asked to sacrifice their daughter at so tender an age. And what appeared so cruel humanly speaking was, in fact, for the city of Quito the work of Divine Providence, which transplanted that Spanish lily to Ecuadorian soil at such a tender age. For this lily, with its exquisite fragrance, remindful of God Himself, would perfume the ambience of the Conceptionist cloisters, where delicate flowers and fruits of heroic sanctity would spring forth throughout the centuries.

Love and sacrifice having triumphed in the young girl, she heroically left her grieving parents and little brothers, and began her voyage to Quito. Only souls who have passed through this sacrifice can understand how Divine Love acts in such cases. Like a cruel dagger, He severs the hearts of both parents and child, leaving the victim in a living death so that she might suffer the martyrdom of filial love. With every beat of the heart of the spouse of Jesus Christ, at every moment of her existence, she renews her sacrifice. Immolating herself at the feet of the Tabernacle, she offers practical proof of her love for the Divine Spouse, thus earning for her cherished ones innumerable graces and favors.

\* \* \*

## Chapter 4

Mariana left Spain in the company of her aunt, Mother Maria de Jesus Taboada, and four other professed virgins, who wished to found this Order of the Immaculate Conception under the protection of the Seraphim of Assisi, according to the dictates of the holy Rule. [10]

### The Terrible Tempest at Sea

No sooner had they embarked than a tempest of unimaginable fury came over the ocean. The clear sky of day suddenly darkened, being transformed into a most disastrous night. The ship had already begun to sink, and the frightened sailors, their efforts rendered futile, cried out that this terrible tempest would bury them all in the ocean's bottomless tomb.

During this bitter trial, Mariana, weakened by her sufferings and confounded by the sense of her own misery, believed herself to be the cause of the terrible tempest.

She told her aunt, "My Mother, am I not the cause of this tempest, and, like another Jonas, should I not be cast into the sea so that it might become calm?"

"No, my daughter," said her aunt, clasping her niece to herself. "For this we should have recourse to prayer, that it might touch the merciful Heart of God."

---

10. The names of the six Spanish Founding Mothers were recorded in the Convent's Foundation Book as follows: Doña Maria de Taboada, or Mother Maria de Jesus Taboada from the noble house of Soloriego of Galicia, first Abbess of the Royal Convent; Catalina Rodrigues, called Mother Catherine of the Conception; Doña Francisca de Jaramillo, called Mother Francisca of the Angels; Maria de Torres, called Mother Maria of Saint John; Doña Aldonsa de Castañeda, called Mother Anna of the Cross; and Doña Lucia Jaramillo, called Mother Lucia of the Cross.

The six Quito ladies who were incorporated into the Convent from its founding included Maria Rodriguez, called Mother Maria of the Incarnation in religion, and the novices who later took their final vows: Doña Julia de Castañeda, Doña Magdalena de Valenzuela, Doña Juliana de Arce, Mariana de Torres, and Doña Leonor Tamayo. With the 13-year-old Mariana de Jesus Torres y Berriochoa, the number of the first inhabitants of the Royal Convent of the Immaculate Conception was 13. (Cadena y Almeida, *La Mujer y la Monja Extraordinaria,* pp 16-8).

### Apparition of the Infernal Serpent: "I Shall Not Permit this Foundation…"

Then Mother Maria and the young girl saw in the ocean a monstrous serpent with seven heads, which, stirring up the waters of the sea, was attempting to destroy the ship. Upon seeing this horrible sight, Mariana cried out and fainted in a deathlike stupor.

Mother Maria, frightened and fearing for the life of her young niece, directed to God this humble prayer: "Thou knowest, my God, that it is not by my own will that I go to make this foundation, but rather, in obedience to my Lord the King. If it is Thy will that the Order of the Immaculate Conception be founded in this Colony, make the darkness dissipate and this tempest subside."

God answered this entreaty most prodigiously. No sooner had Mother Maria finished her prayer than the young girl opened her eyes. At the same moment, it became day, and they heard a terrible voice that said, "I shall not permit the foundation. I shall not permit that it go forward. I shall not permit it to endure until the end of time, and I shall persecute it unceasingly."

This was the voice of the serpent crying out even as the tempest was calmed. For the Blessed Virgin, coming to the aid of her beloved virgins, had slashed his heads to pieces.

### Mariana Sees Our Lady in an Extraordinary Vision

The storm having subsided and the daylight returned, Mother Maria turned to embrace her young niece, saying to her, "My daughter, what happened to you?"

"I will tell you when we are alone, my mother," she replied.

At the first opportunity that presented itself, they retired and spoke about what had occurred during that terrible storm. Mother Maria realized that her niece had experienced a remarkable vision when she had fallen into that deathlike stupor. Therefore, she questioned her carefully: "My daughter, tell me what you saw?"

"I do not know in what world I was, my mother, but there I saw a horrible, writhing creature."

"And what was this creature?" asked Mother Maria.

"It was a serpent," replied the child, "larger than the sea. I also saw a Lady of incomparable beauty, clothed in the sun and crowned with stars, carrying a beautiful Child in her arms. Over the heart of this Lady was a monstrance with the Blessed Sacrament. In one of her hands she carried a large cross of gold, which at its end took the shape of a lance. With this she subdued the enormous serpent with its two-edged tongue. The Lady, who wielded the cross with the help of the Blessed Sacrament and the hand of the Child, struck the head of the serpent with such force that it was slashed to pieces. At that moment, this monstrous serpent cried out that it would not permit the foundation of the Order of the Immaculate Conception."

Mother Maria understood the profound significance of this vision. When the opportune moment came, she ordered a picture drawn out of this scene of the Blessed Virgin in accordance with this admirable vision. It was made into a cloth medallion, which the Conceptionists wear on the breast of their habits.

Mariana also communicated to her aunt the countless difficulties and sufferings that would be endured so that this foundation might be made in the city of Quito. After its foundation, the Community would suffer even more persecutions and great tribulations throughout the centuries because of the hatred of the serpent; this God would permit for the glory of His Most Holy Mother.

### THE GIFT OF PROPHECY

Mariana was also made to understand many future events that would take place in the Community. She saw the saintly religious who would blossom in this Convent and also the unfaithful souls who would fail to correspond to the grace of their vocations.

Mother Maria, frightened and distressed upon hearing this account, said to her niece, "My daughter, if so much is to be suffered in this foundation, and so much opposition will arise against this Community of Conceptionists, let us not make this foundation. Let us instead return to Spain."

"No, my mother," replied the unconquerable child. "It is true that we will have much to suffer and that there will be unfaithful souls, but there will also be saintly religious who, by their interior lives, sufferings, and humiliations, will give glory to God and to His Immaculate Mother, thus preserving this Convent until the end of time."

"My daughter," questioned Mother Maria, "will you be one of these souls?"

The young girl, with angelic candor and profound humility, replied, "Yes, my mother, and the day will come when the Queen of Heaven herself will speak to me."

Without manifesting her admiration, Mother Maria continued her questions: "And will I see that day?" The child responded, "You will witness the first favors that Our Lord and Our Immaculate Mother will grant to me, but, my dear Mother, it will not be for you to see them all."

And thus was this prophecy later fulfilled.[11]

It is believed that during these grievous trials suffered while still at sea, God Our Lord granted to Mariana the gift of prophecy. Since the age of nine, her soul had been imbued with a sublime degree of the prayer of quiet.[12]

During this blessed conversation with her aunt, the Angels must have awaited in suspense the *fiat* of Mother Maria for the foundation of the Convent, so that they might carry it aloft to the throne of His Most August Majesty. At the same time, how the demons waged their furious battle to prevent so great a good from occurring!

Convinced by these explanations of her niece, Mother Maria resolved to proceed with the journey to make the foundation in Quito, offering herself as a sacrificial victim of love to her Divine Spouse Jesus and her Immaculate Mother. Then the angels crowned

---

11. Mother Maria witnessed the first and second deaths of her niece and miraculous returns to life in 1582 and 1588, before she died on the Feast of Saint Francis on October 4, 1593. The first apparition of Our Lady of Good Success to Mother Mariana was one year later on February 2, 1594.

12. The gift of prophecy is one of the most important of the *gratiae gratis datae* [charismas]. It is an intellectual miracle whereby God communicates to an individual the knowledge of future contingent events, although properly speaking, any type of knowledge could be the subject matter of prophetic revelation. The prophetic mind can be instructed by God by either explicit revelation, which gives the prophet absolute certainty about the things revealed; or by a mysterious prophetic instinct, unaccompanied by certainty whether the knowledge is from God or his own mind. The prayer of quiet is a type of mystical contemplation in which the soul experiences an intimate awareness of God's presence which captivates the will and fills the soul and body with ineffable sweetness and delight. The prayer of quiet begins to give the soul an actual possession and joyful fruition of the Sovereign Good (A. Royo Marin, *The Theology of Christian Perfection*, pp. 474, 568).

the heads of these two triumphant virgins, while the celestial choirs sang a hymn of love to Mary Immaculate.

Mother Mariana de Jesus was the shield of fortitude that sustained Mother Maria during this difficult battle. She is the honor and glory of the Order of the Immaculate Conception and the strongest column that supports this Convent, which was persecuted by the infernal serpent from the very beginning of its foundation.

The demon caused the ship carrying the acts of the foundation to be shipwrecked so that these documents would not reach Toledo. But, saved by the hands of the Angels, they were nonetheless delivered to Mother Beatrice da Silva, Mother and Founder of the whole Conceptionist Order.

\* \* \*

## Chapter 5

The trials at sea having come to an end, the travels continued by land. There they hoped for some respite, but new trials lay ahead for them. Again the devil attempted to prevent this foundation, for it was found that there were not enough horses for the journey. It is impossible to express the sufferings of those delicate virgins as they traveled along those rough roads.

The Divine Spouse, who asked these labors from His spouses, thus presented them with sufferings and crosses in order to provide a firm foundation for the beautiful edifice of the Order of the Conceptionists.

### The Foundation of the Convent

The illustrious founding sisters arrived in Quito on December 30, 1576. They were received by the Royal Audience and the ecclesiastical government with great manifestations of joy. The noble and pious ladies of Quito showered every kindness on them, lodging them in houses reserved for them. Because the walls of the cloisters had not yet been completed, they were obliged to remain in these quarters living in great poverty for more than a year. However, the Franciscan friars fortified their spirit, instructing them in the religious virtues and angelic poverty. When the preparations were finally completed, the date for the foundation was fixed.

On January 13, 1577, the Convent was founded, the spiritual and temporal government of the religious being entrusted to the hands of the Rev. Father Antonio Jurado, O.F.M. Since the details of this ceremony are recorded in the foundation book and in the chronicles of the Order;[13] let it suffice to say that on this day the Vicar Provincial of the Franciscan Order received the vows of obedience of the Founding Mothers. Mother Mariana de Jesus was

---

13. The four houses that occupied the site of the first Royal Convent were donated by the Quito families of Diego Mondragón and Alonso Paz, who purchased the property in 1575 from Lorenzo de Cepeda y Ahumada, the brother of Saint Teresa of Jesus of Avila. The proper arrangements for a monastic establishment were made and a provisory Chapel was constructed on the site of the present-day Church (Cadena y Almeida, *La Mujer y la Monja Extraordinaria*, pp. 35-6).

not yet able to make her profession because of her young age, for at that time she was only a few months past her thirteenth year.

### The City Celebrates the Foundation

The whole city of Quito came together to partake in this solemn celebration. In those times, on the occasion of great festivities, the people would celebrate with bullfights, and a wealthy landowner provided a large number of bulls for the games as a token of his joy for the foundation of the first Convent in the Colony.

The inhabitants of the city thus rejoiced in their celebration of this happy event, honoring, loving, and bestowing gifts on these spouses of Jesus Christ.

\* \* \*

## Chapter 6

After the foundation was established and the Founding Mothers had made their professions, the virgins of Quito, like zealous bees, flew to the garden of the Conception to nourish themselves upon the sweet nectar of the first religious flowers.

These noble and virtuous maidens began their novitiate in the Convent as the first stage of their cloistered life. From the moment she stepped foot on that blessed ground, Mariana redoubled her fervor. Because of her young age, she was separated from the other novices, and, for a year and a half, she helped her aunt in domestic duties and setting up the Community workrooms. In this way, in the temporal as well as spiritual spheres, she became the strongest and most beautiful column of the Convent.

Mother Maria de Jesus used this time to strengthen, or, rather, to perfect her niece in the practice of the religious virtues, wherein Mariana shone as a model of the most perfect observance, for she seemed like an angel nourished solely by divine love.

Since the ongoing construction of the Church and the Convent exhausted its funds, the Community often lacked money for food, and the Divine Spouse exercised them in the practice of angelic poverty. At times, the fare was quite poor and meager, and Mother Maria suffered greatly in her concern for the delicacy and youth of her niece. On one occasion, the young girl sweetly told her aunt, "My mother, do not worry about the younger ones, for our youth sustains us; rather be concerned about those who are older." As this incident demonstrates, she was the consolation of her aunt.

### Novitiate and Profession of Mariana

On completing her 15$^{th}$ year, Mariana entered the novitiate, beginning her year of probation under the guidance of her aunt and the direction of the Friars Minor.

Her director acted with great discernment in guiding this candid and innocent soul. Seeing the great progress she made in virtue, he considered himself unworthy to direct her. Her companions in the novitiate admired her fervor and would allow themselves to be guided by her counsel; often they witnessed her totally absorbed in the prayer of quiet.

During the spiritual exercises that she made in preparation for her profession, God Our Lord granted her many graces. On the day before her profession, she passed the whole day in a deathlike state.

The frightened sisters summoned Doctor Sancho, who, after examining her, could only remark in admiration, "I can assure you that this is no natural illness. Leave her be, for I am certain that her state is a supernatural one, and there is nothing I can do for her."

For the doctor understood that she was receiving extraordinary graces from God on this special day, the eve of her profession.

When she returned to her senses, Mariana was questioned by Mother Maria: "What happened to you, my daughter?"

"My mother," she replied, "Our Lord has promised to receive me as His spouse. I was given to understand the difficult times through which our Order will pass. However, throughout the course of time, in this Convent there will be holy religious and, at all times, hidden and unknown souls, who by their sacrifices and sufferings will sustain the Community.

"But there will also be ungrateful and false religious who will be unfaithful and will leave the Convent. Every fifty years Our Lord will purge the Community, separating the chaff from the good wheat. At the end of the 19$^{th}$ century, a religious will suffer from a kind of leprosy, and once again, sanctity will return to this Convent. She will end her days in a place set aside for those dying of this disease.[14] I saw the immense glory she will have in Heaven.

"As long as sacrifices and sufferings are made in this Convent, it will not disappear."

On the long-awaited day of her betrothal, Mother Mariana de Jesus made her religious profession at the hands of her Abbess and aunt, the Rev. Mother Maria de Jesus Taboada.

---

14. Msgr. Cadena y Almeida notes that this sister was an expiatory victim so that the Convent would be protected from the anti-Catholic corruption of that century. *Madera para Esculpir la Imagen de una Santa* (Quito: Libreria Espiritual, 1987), p. 31.

The act was most solemn, with the friars teaching the ceremonies and procedures of the profession.[15] Mother Maria directed a short sermon to the novice, the same sermon which even today [in 1790] is given to the novices of the Community, after which Mariana made her profession.

As she finished pronouncing her vows, she was transported to heaven in ecstasy. Thus, at the same time Mother Maria accepted her profession, Mariana heard the Eternal Father repeating the words of her aunt: "If you are faithful in this, I promise to you eternal life."

She then saw the Person of the Divine Word, the Most Holy Humanity united to the Divinity, the God-Man, as a handsome youth in the very fullness of His Manhood at the perfect age of 33. With ineffable majesty and sweetness, He espoused Himself to her, placing on the finger of her right hand a beautiful ring with four precious stones. On each stone was written both in Latin and in Spanish one of the four vows: poverty, obedience, chastity, and cloister. In the center of the ring, set most exquisitely, was a star engraved with the name of Mary.

At this indescribable betrothal, the Blessed Virgin and her chaste spouse Saint Joseph stood as witnesses. Then her Divine Spouse Jesus presented to her His Cross – with all the pains and sufferings that He had endured in His mortal life.

He addressed her, saying, "My Spouse, I desire for you a life of immolation. Your life will be a continuous martyrdom." He made known to her all the diverse tribulations, temptations, and persecutions that she would have to suffer, promising to preserve her only from temptations against her angelic purity. He told her that she would suffer terrible persecutions from her fellow creatures, even from some who were good, just souls. She saw the spiritual desolations, the abandonment and absences of her Beloved, in short, the prolonged and cruel martyrdom of her life of crucified love. With profound humility, she responded to her Spouse, "I accept with pleasure and with gratitude, as a precious gift, the sufferings with which Thou art presenting me. I willingly offer myself to imitate

---

15. Mariana de Jesus, age 17, made her vows on October 4, 1579 at the hands of her aunt, and in the presence of the officiating Franciscan priest Fr. Antonio Jurado (Cadena y Almeida, *Apariciones*, p. 72).

Thy life; but I am only a miserable creature, and, although my spirit is willing, I fear that my nature will weaken, and I beseech Thee to help me with Thy grace."

Her Divine Spouse promised that assistance and let her glimpse the graces He had prepared for her. Once again he gave her to understand in a veiled way that she would receive an apparition of the Blessed Virgin of Good Success. As the days passed, she better understood the significance of all that she had seen in this indescribable ecstasy.

### Our Lady Severs a Vein of Mariana's Heart

The Blessed Virgin spoke to her words of maternal sweetness, "My daughter, my most favored one, you shall live protected not only under my mantle, but also hidden in my heart. So that you are purged of all earthly affections and reserve your love only for my Most Holy Son and for me, I am severing this vein of your heart." And, extending her hand to the heart of the new spouse of Christ, she cut it. At this, Mariana experienced a pain more acute than she had ever known; this pain remained with her until her death.

Then her heavenly patron, the glorious Saint Joseph, approached her and placed in her heart a white lily. At the same time he told her that she would never have even a thought or inclination against the angelical virtue of purity.

The love of Mother Mariana, severed from all earthly affections, was thus reserved only for God and for her neighbor.
As she returned from this ecstasy, she felt as if the Divine Spouse were removing the ring from her finger, causing her such intense pain that it seemed as if her whole finger were being wrenched from her hand.

During the whole time of her ecstasy, her body remained flexible and active, allowing her to carry out all the ceremonies of her profession. Her face was rosy, illuminated at times with great joy and, at other times, flooded by torrents of tears.[16]

---

16. Although normally a person in ecstasy is insensible and completely immovable, there have been mystics who spoke and described their contemplative visions during the state of ecstasy or who have moved around during the state of ecstasy, as Mariana did on the date of her profession into religion (A. Royo Marin, *The Theology of Christian Perfection*, pp. 484-5).

Upon returning to herself, she was called by the Abbess, who said to her, "Now that you have made your profession at my hands, I ask you to practice your vow of obedience for the first time. I hereby order you to relate to me all that has happened to you today."

The recently professed sister responded, "Oh, my Mother! How harsh is the persecution of the just and of one's fellow man!" And she proceeded to relate to her what she had seen and what God had communicated to her during that admirable ecstasy which she had experienced at the moment of her profession.

Who can imagine the incomprehensible secrets of divine love that were revealed to this innocent virgin who had just celebrated her betrothal to the Divine Lover! And with what immense stores of graces did He prepare His spouse for her life of immolation and sacrifice!

This heroic Conceptionist virgin received the habit on September 8, 1577, and made her solemn profession on October 4, 1579. May God be praised and glorified for all that He does in His saints!

\* \* \*

# Chapter 7

Following her profession and after taking the name of Mariana de Jesus, she continued to lead a life more angelic than human. She took flight in the exercise of all the virtues, diligently carrying out all that her Divine Spouse asked of her.

### The Abbess Exercises Mariana's Humility

The Abbess, who was also the Novice Mistress, entrusted her niece to help her direct the other novices. The young assistant discharged this command with perfection, for the duties involved therein provided her the opportunity to better practice the virtue of humility.

The Rev. Mother Maria, who desired that her niece progress in virtue, would severely chastise and humble her in public, even when she was not at fault. In the refectory, she gave her severe penances and reprimands. Seeing Mother Mariana accept this treatment with so much sweetness and tranquility, the Abbess would be unable to contain her tears and would go to prostrate herself before the Blessed Sacrament. With her forehead on the ground, she would pray: "My Lord, I act thus with this creature because I desire to see her one day raised to the altars, for I know her merits and virtues."

During the two years of her initial period, she was a model religious in the practice of all the virtues and in following the most strict observance of the Rule. On December 8, 1579, the feast of Our Immaculate Mother, Mother Mariana ended her initial period. With profound humility, she prostrated herself in the refectory before the Community to confess her faults and ask pardon for the infractions she had committed during that time. She thanked the sisters for the charity with which they had borne with her, and, with seraphic love, she kissed their feet.

For this innocent dove believed herself laden with faults and imperfections. For this reason, she told her sisters with all sincerity, "Although my initial period has ended, I shall always be the least of all." And, in reality, she was.

### Her Divine Spouse Gives her Another Ecstasy

After this act of humiliation, Our Lord again drew her into ecstasy, leaving her on earth as one dead. This time, however, the religious were not so alarmed, for they knew that she was resting in the arms of her most sweet Spouse.

In this ecstasy, God Our Lord told her the practices she should carry out during the free hours of the Community and the penances she should perform each week; He even gave her the subjects upon which He desired her to meditate.

When Mother Mariana returned to herself, Mother Maria again ordered her to tell her what had occurred. "For all that you do should have my blessing and permission," she explained. When she heard the prayers Our Lord had asked of this soul, she said, "My daughter, do all that God asks of you." But, taken aback by the excruciating penances, she added, "Tell Our Lord that your Abbess fears that you will lose your health from the rigor of these penances."

### Our Lord Fortifies Mariana's Spirit

Mother Mariana obediently delivered this message to her Divine Spouse on the tenth day of December, on which occasion she was again favored by the Divine Majesty. Not wishing His spouse to do anything without the permission and blessing of the Abbess, He kindly responded: "Your health will not suffer from this, my daughter. Performing these penances, you will appear fresh and exuberant like an April rose."

Then the Celestial Spouse, Who appeared to her on this occasion more beautiful than the Heavens at His perfect age of 33, took from His holy Side a drop of crystal clear water. Placing it on the lips of His beloved Mariana, He said, "This will fortify you throughout your life of penance."

Savoring this divine liqueur, Mother Mariana tasted a drink of unimaginable sweetness and her soul experienced unspeakable celestial delights. Only those souls who receive such graces can understand or describe the gifts that God Our Lord gives to those who sacrifice themselves for His love. In this way her body was fortified to practice the excruciating penances asked of her by her Beloved.

## Chapter 8

The rule of the Conceptionists does not prescribe austere penances, for few young women would want to embrace such a life. However, it permits its loving aspirants to practice such penances according to divine inspiration.

Mother Mariana de Jesus was truly a heroine in the practice of atrocious penances. She wore a hairshirt that covered her whole body, and she placed small iron tacks even on her tongue and in her ears, leaving free only her face and hands, which all could see.

### Her Severe Disciplines

On every day except Sunday, she used to take the discipline three times, once with a whip made to raise blood. During Advent and Lent, she used to apply the latter discipline three times a day, and the former six times. During Holy Week, she would take nine scourgings a day, and every Friday of the year she would mortify her taste, placing something very bitter in her mouth.

Not satisfied with this self-inflicted rigor, she had herself scourged by the hands of another. For this, she chose a strong, robust woman, Martina Ceferina de la Vega, who lived in the Convent. This young woman, who was taught and catechized in our faith by Mother Mariana de Jesus and received Holy Baptism in the Convent at age 12, was her *confidante* in these severe penances.

### Apparition of the Holy Family During the Way of the Cross

On Friday nights she would make the Way of the Cross, carrying her large wooden cross through the lower cloisters until the break of dawn. One night, as she entered the lower choir carrying the cross, she saw the Holy Family of Jesus, Mary, and Joseph. During this apparition, the Child Jesus presented her with flowers.

On Fridays, she would consume absolutely nothing, for her food passage would close. When the Abbess ordered her to eat something, in obedience she would put food in her mouth, but she was not able to swallow it. Her confessor, a Franciscan, also ordered her to take some nourishment. Seeing that she could eat nothing, he brought Doctor Sancho to examine her. After a careful examination, the doctor found that her food passage had closed.

He said nothing in the presence of Mother Mariana, but only shook his head. After leaving her, however, he told the Abbess and the confessor, "This is a supernatural thing. Leave her be."

And so she continued her life of sacrifice and penance. Most undoubtedly, the violence of sharing in the Passion of Our Lord prevented her from taking any food on Fridays.

On Saturdays, she felt so keenly the sorrows of the Holy Virgin that nothing could console her. Only with great difficulty could she take even a little water.

Every day she crucified herself for a quarter of an hour on a large cross that she guarded in the privacy of her cell, where she also kept all the instruments of penance and martyrdom that she used on her innocent body. During these crucifixions, she would hang on the cross supported only by some ropes.

Every Friday of the year, after Vespers and Compline, she would lock herself in her cell and wear a hairshirt for one hour, thus accompanying Our Lord when He was scourged at the pillar. She would then spend long periods in imitation of His Crucifixion.

## More Excruciating Penances

After she had descended from the cross, she would take a scourging or practice such penances as walking on her knees, continuing her martyrdom even during the hour of afternoon rest. It thus falls to some chosen religious to appease Divine Justice by the rigor of their penances.

Mother Mariana, an innocent victim, would close herself up in her cell and share the torments of her Beloved. She would accompany Him as Pilate sentenced Him to be scourged, entering the Heart of Our Lord and sharing the grief He had experienced then.

This loving spouse, filled with compassion for her Lord so weakened by suffering, would scourge herself with three types of most atrocious disciplines in imitation of Jesus, Who was scourged with three of the cruelest of scourges.[17]

This innocent dove, her body mutilated and bathed in blood, would spend the whole hour of silence in the highest contemplation of the torments of Jesus. At the tolling of the Vespers bell, she would leave her cell for the choir, her face glowing with happiness and with the spirit of such profound recollection that even the Angels of Heaven looked at her in admiration.

How many chaste embraces and tender kisses this enraptured soul gave to Jesus Christ present in the Sacrament of His Love! Only souls that have savored the delights of mortification can express the richness of the love that Jesus Christ showers upon them!

### HER FASTING AND SENSE OF ABANDONMENT DURING HOLY WEEK

The fastings of the Church and of the Rule were rigorously observed by Mother Mariana. On Sundays she would eat everything that was served to her in the refectory, including the fruit that was customarily served on that day, for she rejoiced on that day in the Resurrection of Our Lord. In the same manner that He communicated to her the suffering and afflictions of His Passion, He also allowed her to share the joys of His Resurrection.

During Holy Week, this loving heroine asked her Divine Spouse to take from her all spiritual consolation and leave her abandoned so that she might share in the abandonment and agony that He suffered on the Cross. This favor was granted her, and she spent those days annihilated and weakened by the violence of the sorrow that Our Lord shared with her.

She slept only three hours each night on a hard bed covered with a thin lambskin, for she never knew the comfort of a soft bed and treated her body as if it were her worst enemy. To imitate her

---

17. According to revelations of the Our Lady to Blessed Mary of Agreda, the torturers of Our Lord first scourged the innocent Savior with hard, thick cords, followed by a scourging with hardened leather thongs. The third pair of scourgers beat Our Lord with tough rawhides, afflicting him more cruelly because they were cutting into the wounds already produced by the previous scourgings. Their fury was further incited by the devils, who were filled with new rage at the patience of Christ (*The City of God: The Transfixion*, trans. by Fiscar Marison, Washington NJ: Ave Maria Institute, 1971, pp. 606-7).

crucified Beloved, she would wear a crown of thorns on her head and chains around her neck, thus captivating God Himself, Who, in His mercy, granted her whatever she asked of Him. Thus does He reward the sacrifices of those who love Him.

The life of Mother Mariana de Jesus was one of continuous prayer. She prayed four hours each day in addition to the two hours of daily prayer prescribed by the Rule: from midnight until one in the morning; from 3 to 4 a.m., and during various other free hours. Our Lord told her that those who foster the devotion of praying at midnight will receive many graces, for they will be accompanied in their prayer at that hour by the Divine Majesty Himself.

\* \* \*

## Chapter 9

In the ecstasy Mother Mariana experienced during the second year of her profession, Our Lord instructed her to make the following meditations for each day of the week:

- On Mondays, the washing of the feet of the Apostles by Our Lord and the institution of the Sacrament of the Holy Eucharist.
- On Tuesdays, the prayer of Our Lord in the Garden of Olives and the imprisonment of the Savior.
- On Wednesdays, the presentation of Our Divine Redeemer before the Pontiffs and Judges, and the scourging He suffered for love of us while bound to the pillar.
- On Thursdays, the crowning of thorns, the *Ecce Homo*, and how He carried the cross on His shoulders to His crucifixion.
- On Fridays, the holy mystery of the Cross of Our Divine Redeemer, the seven last words, and His death.
- On Saturdays, the piercing of His Side after His death, the grief and tears of His Most Holy Mother, and His burial.
- On Sundays, how the soul of Our Divine Redeemer descended into Limbo, His glorious Resurrection, His apparitions to Our Lady, Mary Magdalene, and His disciples.

Mother Mariana meditated on these points throughout the week, beginning anew each Monday. In this way, she paid homage to the Holy Passion of Our Lord, to which she was so strongly devoted.

Our Lord gave her these afternoon meditations to exercise each day of the week:

- On Mondays, the knowledge of self, the memory of her sins and their gravity.
- On Tuesdays, the condition and misery of human life.
- On Wednesdays, death.
- On Thursdays, the Final Judgment.
- On Fridays, Hell.

- On Saturdays, the blessed happiness of Heaven.
- On Sundays, the divine favors received, both general and particular, and the infinite debt of gratitude owed to Our Most Loving God.

### HER PROFOUND INTIMACY WITH HER GUARDIAN ANGEL

Mother Mariana meditated on these points with angelic fervor. God Our Lord also granted to her a great intimacy with her Guardian Angel, who appeared to her as a shining youth of 18 years of age. On his breast was a reliquary imprinted with the holy names of Jesus and Mary. The divine rays radiating from it communicated to Mother Mariana celestial lights of understanding. The Angel appeared as one armed for battle, and the sight of him fortified her against the terrible serpent, who would visibly persecute her. Writhing beneath her feet, this hideous monster would threaten her saying, "I shall not leave you alive!"

The innocent virgin would smile, and her Angel would come to her defense. Often the Devil, in the figure of a serpent, would torment Mother Mariana, but her Guardian Angel always ensured that she emerged victorious in combat, for she fought with the weapons of humility and the practice of the virtues, as well as prayer and penance, which were the swords under which the serpent writhed and recoiled.

As will be seen later, her love for Jesus in the Blessed Sacrament wounded the infernal monster.

\* \* \*

## Chapter 10

Mother Mariana's dominant passion was her love for Jesus in the Blessed Sacrament. Not content with spending the hours of common prayer before Him, she would hasten there in her every free moment to soothe her enamored soul near her Beloved, confiding to Him all her interior and exterior sufferings. Even her work she would bring to do in His Holy Presence so that in those things also, her Beloved might instruct her.

### She Confides her Sufferings to Our Lord

This holy religious suffered insults and persecutions from her sisters without ever opening her lips to justify herself or protest. Only at the foot of the Tabernacle did she confide her secret sorrows to her Beloved.

One day, after a particularly bitter incident with one of her sisters, which Mother Mariana suffered in silence, she went to the feet of Jesus Christ, communicating to Him her torment and begging Him for fortitude.

He replied to her, "On the day when I betrothed Myself to you, I carefully tested your will. Your sufferings are reaching their apex."

To this, the innocent virgin responded, "My Lord, my will is ready, but the flesh is weak..."

Our Lord returned, "Strength will not be wanting to you, as nothing is lacking to the soul who has recourse to Me."

At that moment, she heard an overwhelming sound, and saw that the whole Church had become immersed in darkness, as from dust and smoke. Fearful that the building would collapse and uncertain what had happened, for she had not felt the tremors of an earthquake, she asked herself, "What is this?"

Examining her conscience, she could find no fault for which she could accuse herself. Nonetheless, in her profound humility, she believed that she must be guilty of something that was causing this disorder.

### Apparitions of Our Lord, Our Lady, and Saint Mary Magdalene

In the darkness of the Church, Mother Mariana looked up and saw the main altar very clearly, as if it were illuminated by full day. Suddenly, before this humble, kneeling virgin, the Tabernacle opened, and Christ Himself emerged, suffering as He had at Golgotha. The Blessed Virgin, shedding tears of pearls, along with Saint John and Mary Magdalene, were at His feet.

The suffering Christ, still without the wound in His Side, began His death agony.

Seeing this, the humble virgin, believing herself to be at fault, prostrated herself on the ground with her arms extended in the form of a cross, exclaiming, "Lord, I am the guilty one. Punish me and pardon your people."

Her Guardian Angel made her rise, saying, "No, you are not to blame. Arise and approach, for God desires to reveal to you a great secret."

She arose, and seeing the tears of the Most Holy Virgin, she addressed her, saying, "My Lady, am I to blame for thy sadness?"

She replied, "No, it is not you, but the criminal world."

Then, as Our Lord agonized, she heard the voice of the Eternal Father saying, "This punishment will be for the 20th century."

Then she saw three swords over the head of Christ. On each was written, 'I shall punish heresy, blasphemy, and impurity.' Then she was given to understand all that would take place in that century.[18]

The Holy Virgin continued, "My daughter, will you sacrifice yourself for the people of this time?"

Mother Mariana replied, "I am willing."

Immediately, the swords moved away from the agonizing Christ and buried themselves in the heart of Mother Mariana, who

---

18. In later apparitions, Our Lady of Good Success described the great crisis in the Church that would occur in the 20th century. In those lamentable times, she said, heresies would abound, the corruption of manners and customs would be almost complete, purity would be lacking in the clergy and laity, and the light of the Faith would be nearly extinguished. See M. T. Horvat, *Our Lady of Good Success, Prophecies for Our Times* (Los Angeles: TIA, 2000), www.TraditionInAction.org.

fell dead from the violence of the pain.

## The Death of Mother Mariana

As she was always the first one at all the Community acts of prayer, the religious went to search for her when she did not appear. They found her body cold and, to all appearances, lying dead in the lower choir. The sisters carried Mother Mariana to her bed, exchanging her lambskin for a soft mattress. Seeing that she did not show any sign of life, the guilty sisters who had persecuted her so cruelly that morning surrounded her bedside, kissing her hands, beseeching her, "Forgive us, Mother Mariana, for we knew not what we were doing."

The holy religious, however, did not respond. The worried sisters summoned the physician, Doctor Sancho. He examined her, distressed, for he could find no sign of life. After he had tried various methods to revive her, he announced, with tears in his eyes, "Mother Mariana is dead. Her beautiful soul has left the lovely abode of her body. Call an artist so that her portrait might be painted before she is buried."

Before taking leave of the Community, he approached the dead sister with profound grief, saying, "Holy virgin, remember those who were devoted to you who yet remain pilgrims on this earth." The doctor then left, making public throughout the city the death of Mother Mariana.

Upset by this news, the people began knocking at the doors of the church, clamoring to be allowed to kiss the hands of their precious treasure. The highest theologians of the Franciscan Order, along with the spiritual director of Mother Maria, hurried to the Convent. When the artist arrived, however, he could not enter, prevented by an inexplicable force.

The Friars Minor, approaching the bed of the deceased religious, tried several tests to see if any life remained in the body of the nun. But she showed not the least sign of life. The guilty sisters also entered to confess their faults. The Father Provincial reprimanded them severely, imposing a heavy penance on them.

While all this was going on, Friar Diego, who had accompanied the Franciscan entourage to the Convent and had gone to pray in a corner of the cell, fell into ecstasy. The Father Provincial harshly reproved him for this, ordering him in the name of holy obedience to return to himself. Then he commanded the friar, "Leave this Convent and return to your monastery." Friar Diego humbly complied, after first kissing the hand of his superior.

### Mariana Goes Before the Throne of the Most Holy Trinity

Oh! incomprehensible judgment of God, which accepted the sacrifice of this innocent virgin! In fact, Mother Mariana had died, presenting herself before the judgment seat of God. Finding no fault in her, He said: "Come, beloved of My Father, receive the crown that We have prepared for you since the beginning of the world, for in your tender years you heard My voice, and, leaving your fatherland, you traveled to distant lands to sacrifice yourself for My love."

Then she prostrated herself before the throne of the Most Blessed Trinity, and was given to understand something of that ineffable mystery. The Eternal Father rejoiced for having created her, the Divine Son for having redeemed her and taken her for His spouse, and the Holy Ghost for having sanctified her.

In Heaven, the soul of Mother Mariana thus enjoyed those ineffable delights of that blessed place, even while on earth fervent prayers were being made for her life. In particular, Mother Maria implored God's mercy, for she had no one else who could form her novices, and she had placed her hope for the prosperity of the Conceptionists in her young niece. She implored God to restore the precious life of so holy and illustrious a religious.

The sisters were joined in their prayers by the Franciscans, who would not leave her bedside. They placed hot vapors at her feet to try and revive her. Seeing that she did not respond, they redoubled their prayers, especially Friar Diego.

### Our Lord Presents her with Two Crowns

Our Lord, Who heard the humble entreaties of His servants, permitted Mother Mariana to see the prayers for her life ascending to the throne of God. He then presented her with two crowns: one of immortal glory of indescribable beauty; the other of white lilies surrounded by thorns.

He spoke to her, saying, "My Spouse, choose one of these crowns."

With this she understood that if she chose the crown of immortal glory, she would remain in Heaven. If she took the other, she would return to suffer in the world. In response to her Beloved, the humble virgin asked that her Divine Majesty choose the crown that He so desired for her.

"No," Our Lord replied. "When I took you for My spouse, I tested your will. Now, I do so again."

That blessed soul, ecstatic with the happiness of Heaven, was then given to know all the Conceptionist religious who would inhabit her Convent throughout time – even to the last day of the world. She saw their names and the offices they would exercise, the graces they would receive and how they would correspond to them until the last day of the world. She saw that some would hold offices contrary to the will of God and that these religious, lacking the graces to fulfill their duties well, would commit many faults, and she prayed for them.

She also saw the ones who would be unfaithful, and she trembled for them before the throne of God. She saw that some of the Novice Mistresses would be condemned not for their own personal sins, but because of the poor formation they gave to the novices. It was revealed to her that if she returned to the world, she herself would hold this difficult office.

She saw that the Franciscans would be removed from the government of the Convent and all the sufferings the Community would undergo as a result of this.

Thus absorbed in ecstasy, this happy soul was faced with choosing one of the two crowns that Our Lord had presented to her.

Oh! difficult choice, so grave and of such great importance to the Order of Conceptionists!

The obvious choice would be for Mother Mariana to remain in Heaven, thus assured of her salvation, enjoying the reward she had merited by her sufferings on earth, including having endured the persecutions and insults of her own sisters. Why should she expose herself to new battles and sufferings in this miserable world when she could enjoy the caresses of her Spouse for eternity?

Why should she again be reduced to see her Beloved hidden behind His earthly veil in the Eucharist, when she might contemplate Him face to face in the ineffable delights of the mystery of His Love?

### "I Left the Glories of Heaven and Descended to Earth to Protect My Children"

Oh! sweet heroine! How, then, could you descend from Heaven, dying anew to so much bliss? This seraphic victim, who, drawn by her love for her Conceptionist Order and given to know these ineffable secrets, was thus torn in battle.

To prepare her for this struggle, her loving Mother, the Immaculate Conception, approached her, and said: "My daughter, I left the glories of Heaven and descended to earth to protect my children. I desire that you imitate me in this and return to life, for your life is most necessary for the Order of my Conceptionists.

"Woe to the Colony in the 20th century! If, in Ecuador, already so guilty, there are not souls who by their lives of immolation and sacrifice will appease Divine Justice, fire will rain from Heaven, consuming its inhabitants and purifying the soil of Quito. Until the end of time, one of these sacrificial souls will inhabit this, my Convent, and, imitating you, will appease Divine Justice."

Knowing this to be the will of God through the message of His Immaculate Mother, the humble religious replied: "My Lady and Mother, may the Divine Will be accomplished in me. Oh! how my soul trembles to see itself again exposed to the imminent danger of being lost by returning to life and carrying out the critical offices of Abbess and Mistress of Novices. As Abbess, I must be a tender Mother as thou art. But, at the same time, I must practice fortitude in not permitting transgressions from the regular observance, which preserves convents, especially the strict silence ordered by the holy Rule. I must do this maintaining unity and charity, which at times will demand even heroism.

"As Mistress of Novices, I ask Thee to help me know the formation I must give to each soul confided to me, as I study each soul and pray incessantly to understand the degree of virtue to which it is called both here and in Heaven beneath your blue mantle. Let me know which place is right for each one. For this, let me be firmly molded in thy most profound humility, which thou, Queen of Virgins, provided for our example.

"I know that I must practice the virtues - from the lowest to the highest - with each novice according to the spiritual needs of each one, so that, without stain of sin, they might be worthy imitators of their Heavenly Mother.

"So that holy religious might be formed for the preservation of my beloved Convent, I shall pray and offer sacrifices that another of my sisters might hold this office, for they are all better than I. Because of my lack of virtue, I do not consider myself capable of carrying out this office. How, then, Virgin most chaste, shall I form these young souls who have pledged themselves to virginity whom thou will place in my charge as spouses of Our Lord, Who takes His delight amongst the lilies and irises?"

### "You Will Not Be the Mistress, but, indeed, I Shall Be..."

To this, the Immaculate Virgin replied: "Daughter of My Heart, be not fearful, for you will not be the Mistress, but, indeed, I shall be. Using you as my instrument, I shall transform your novices into holy religious. Treat, educate, and form this young woman X, whom Christ has called to His enclosed garden, as you do the others, for she has already wept for her sins, and, like a loving Magdalene, she has thrown herself at the feet of her Divine Master. This soul is well founded in humility and will be a holy religious, one whom my Divine Son loves dearly. Later, when he takes her from earth, He will raise her to Heaven to be reunited with her Conceptionist sisters."

After hearing these words, Mother Mariana chose with humility and resignation the crown of lilies surrounded with thorns, and returned to the world to suffer.

At that very moment, her spiritual director, inspired by God, approached the bedside of Mother Mariana and said to her, "Mother Mariana, should you be dead, in the name of holy obedience, I order your soul to return to its body so that it might live and that you render to us an account of what has happened to you."

At that very instant she breathed a light sigh, opened her eyes still glazed by death, and said, "Father! Why did you send

Father Diego away in such disgrace at the very moment in which we were communicating with each other?"

### THE RESURRECTION OF MOTHER MARIANA

Doctor Sancho was summoned. Entering the room, he asked, "What has happened here?" Mother Maria replied, "Mother Mariana is alive."

"No, she is dead," he returned. Hurrying into the cell, he found her alive with her usual rosy complexion. Frightened, he stepped back, thinking it was an illusion.

The Friars Minor, however, encouraged him, saying, "Mother Mariana is alive. Draw near and see." Approaching her bedside and examining her, he shook his head in wonder, saying, "My Fathers, there is nothing I need do for her. For her return to life had nothing to do with me, but rather with your prayers." He only prescribed a fresh drink to cool her parched throat, then took his leave.

Her spiritual director remained alone with Mother Mariana, asking her for an explanation of what had happened while she lay dead. She humbly related all that had occurred. When she reached the subject of how she would one day hold the office of Novice Mistress, she begged the director to forbid her under obedience to tell this to Mother Maria. "For, my Father," she said, "I fear that this might be an illusion." In her humility, she feared to bear such a critical office.

The Father granted this request, and he himself told Mother Maria that Mother Mariana would tell her everything save one point that he had forbidden her to reveal under obedience.

Then Mother Mariana addressed the Franciscans, saying, "My Fathers, I thank you greatly for your assistance and all that you did for me. But it is no longer necessary for you to remain here. Return, then, to your monastery."

The Franciscans immediately took their leave, edified by the delicacy of conscience of this holy religious.

### FATHER DIEGO SEES THE GLORIFICATION OF THE SAINT

As soon as they arrived at their monastery, the Provincial went to look for Friar Diego and found him working in his cell.

Again he severely reprimanded the friar, asking him how he dared to drift off to sleep in the cloisters, causing scandal to the sisters.

The friar replied, "My father, this was no natural sleep, but a mystical one."

The Provincial only sharpened his reprimand, insisting that it was only a dream. But, in fact, this was no ordinary sleep, for this simple brother was a saint.

Then he imposed a penance on Friar Diego, commanding him to eat bread and water in the refectory and kiss the feet of the religious. This he did with holy joy, being rewarded for his humble obedience with great favors from Our Lord.

The Provincial, who wished to know what the friar had seen in this ecstasy, questioned him further, "Brother, what did you dream about when you fell asleep in the Convent?"

With holy simplicity, the friar replied: "I was pleading with God for the health and life of Mother Mariana. I saw, however, that she had died and that her soul had presented itself before the judgment throne of God. The Lord, finding her pure and stainless, said to her, 'Come, beloved of My Father, receive the crown that We have prepared for you since the beginning of the world, for in your tender years you heard My voice and, leaving your fatherland, you traveled to distant lands to sacrifice yourself for My Love.' Hearing this, she prostrated herself before the throne of the Most Blessed Trinity. The Eternal Father rejoiced for having created her, the Son for having redeemed her, and the Holy Ghost for having sanctified her.

"I saw also the immense glory that this happy soul would enjoy because of her sacrifices and the insults of her sisters that she had borne in silence. In this she imitated Jesus Christ, her Spouse, Who suffered in like manner before the tribunals during His sorrowful Passion.

"I saw the prayers of the Community beseeching her life, especially those of Mother Maria de Taboada, rise to the throne of God. Then I saw Our Lord present her with two crowns: one immortal and most splendorous should she choose to remain in this celestial glory, and the other with white lilies surrounded by thorns should she return to life. The Lord asked her to choose, but, at that very moment, Your Reverence called to me, so I do not know what happened next."

Upon hearing this, the Father Provincial was further assured of the sanctity of Mother Mariana.

As soon as the Franciscan fathers left the Convent, the religious went to embrace Mother Mariana. She extended her arms to each one with a love so ardent that it seemed to have descended with her from Heaven, releasing itself in this fraternal affection she displayed toward her sisters.

Mother Maria then asked to speak with her niece in private. But that prudent virgin replied: "My Mother, before all else, we should give thanks to Our Lord at the foot of the Blessed Sacrament."

They prostrated themselves before Jesus in the Blessed Sacrament and made their act of thanksgiving. This concluded, Mother Mariana then retired alone with her superior to give an account of all that had occurred. When she had finished, the Abbess asked, "My Daughter, have you told me everything?"

"Yes, my Mother, save for one matter, which, through obedience, I cannot tell you," she answered.

Distressed, Mother Maria said, "My daughter, a thorn is lodged in my heart, for I fear that I may be lost forever because of my lack of capacity to govern. Perhaps this Convent should close, and we should take steps to return to our native country of Spain."

Mother Mariana smiled, saying, "No, the matter [upon which I am ordered to silence] has nothing to do with this. It is something pertaining to myself alone, and which you will know when God so desires it."

To comfort her further, she added, "My Mother, do not worry about the situation of this Convent or allow yourself to think of returning to Spain. For this Convent will never be destroyed."

\* \* \*

# Chapter 11

After returning to the world for love of her sisters, she dedicated herself with even greater zeal to the practice of the monastic life of sacrifice and charity. She carried out the duties to which obedience bound her with extraordinary promptitude, burning with the fire of her seraphic love.[19] She was given the office of nurse, and, in discharging these duties, she served the sick as if Our Lord Jesus Christ Himself were suffering in each one.

On a certain occasion, one young sister had an accident in which half of her face and all of one arm were scorched. Doctor Sancho arrived to examine the patient, and quickly realized that the burns were mortal, for they had penetrated to the bone. With tears of compassion, Mother Mariana nursed this patient on her knees. Seeing this, Doctor Sancho said, "This woman's life will be saved only if Mother Mariana works a miracle."

In fact, after one month, the burned sister was completely healed and healthy. Even before this miracle, Doctor Sancho had exclaimed: "Mother Mariana is a saint! If the people of Quito realized this, they would take her to the hospitals filled with patients suffering from the plague, and she would cure them all. For just as the shadow of Saint Peter cured the sick, so also would the shadow of Mother Mariana cure all those who drew near her."

Doctor Sancho was well acquainted, indeed, with the virtues of this fragrant lily, for he had witnessed the ecstasies that this angelic creature had experienced since she was but a child. Thus he appreciated the sweet fragrance of her innocent and suffering soul.

Fearing that her young niece might become vain because of this miraculous cure, Mother Maria told her, "How clever Doctor Sancho is in the practice of medicine to have worked this cure!"

---

19. Mother Maria de Jesus Torres carried out the office of Nurse from 1581 to 1583, Bursar from 1583 to 1585, Sacristan from 1585 to 1587, Porter from 1587-1589, Choir Mistress from 1789 to 1791, and Novice Mistress from 1591 to 1593. In 1593 she was elected Abbess for the first time, and also served for the terms of 1599-1601, 1610-1613, 1616-1619, 1622-1625, 1625-1628, and 1629-1631 (Cadena y Almeida, *La Mujer y la Monja Extraordinaria*, pp. 39-40; 205).

Smiling, Mother Mariana replied, "It was the mercy of God that accomplished this cure."

### OFFICE OF BURSAR

Mother Mariana prodigiously carried out the office of bursar. When there was not enough bread for the Convent inhabitants, what they had would be multiplied by her hands. Because of the early poverty of the Convent, the sisters often lacked what was necessary for their sustenance. Then Mother Mariana would prostrate herself at the feet of Jesus in the Most Blessed Sacrament, drawing from His abundant wealth what was needed for her Community. Arising from the feet of Jesus Christ, she would always find donations from the populace of the food they needed.

With what gratitude, joy, and humility Mother Mariana received these gifts that her Divine Spouse provided for her sisters! She herself would distribute the food, and, passing through those hands created by God to be an instrument of His mercies, the amount would be sufficient to satisfy all.

Oh! blessed cloisters, witness of so many marvels! Blessed workrooms, sanctified by the heroic virtues of Mother Mariana! Blessed religious, whose hunger and needs were so often satisfied through the miracles obtained by the prayers and penances of their holy provider!

### OFFICE OF SACRISTAN

She carried out the office of sacristan like a seraphim.

With what ardent affection, lively faith, and profound humility she served the Prisoner of her love. When she found her angelic enthusiasm burning low, with the confidence that love inspires, she would say to Him: "What do you require of me, my Love? Why do You seem to sleep? For how long? What a deep and heavy sleep it is! Rouse yourself, for You have been sleeping for a long time. I am drowning in an ocean of tribulations, and You are sleeping. Rouse yourself, my Love, and give me succor."

At other times, at the foot of the Tabernacle she would say, "Do you no longer have need of me, my Love?" With this filial confidence she would address the Sacramental Jesus.

When the oil lamp of the Holy Eucharist would go out, she would beg her Guardian Agnel to light it, and he would promptly comply. At times when the enamored virgin was sleeping, her Angel would wake her, saying to her, "My sister, the lamp of your Love has gone out." Reproving him, she would say, "Instead of waking me, why do you not light it with your great resplendence?" Then she would hurry to the choir where she would find her Love in darkness, and she would ask her Angel to light the oil in the lamp.

How this humble religious made amends to Our Sacramental Lord! How her heart grew faint from the lamentations of seraphic love that consumed it, and how many sweet soliloquies the Divine Prisoner would have with His beloved spouse!

What happy nights He passed in unspeakable delight within those choir grilles with the humble Conceptionist virgin! Well, indeed, can one exclaim with St. John of the Cross: "O night that has united the Lover with his beloved. O night more lovely than the dawn."

### OFFICE OF TURN-BOX KEEPER

She carried out the office of porter like an apostle of divine love. The sinners who came to the turn-box attracted by the benevolent magnetism of her words would leave in compunction and remorse, wounded by the timbre of the words of that charitable virgin, and be converted.

Who can comprehend the miraculous conversions that Mother Mariana worked at the turn-box. The souls that approached there improved. For if the heart of the porter was a burning furnace of divine love, it is not strange than the lukewarm souls that drew near it should become warm, and the ones already afire should increase their ardor.

The holy Porter was all charity. When there was no one to send out to bring what the sisters needed, she would pray to her Guardian Angel to obtain what was necessary. Then the serpent, who would always persecute her, would coil itself up next to the turn-box. Mother Mariana would say to it, "Lazy creature, because you do not have anything to do, you are here contorting yourself." Or she would send it away with other humiliating words, "Get away from here!" Then she would shut the door, leaving the serpent screeching horribly. When her Holy Angel returned, bringing what was needed, he would tell her where the sisters were who needed the things so she could take it to them.

It is not difficult to understand the peace, charity, and unity in which the Community lived during those blessed times, when all was followed according to the letter of the holy Rule and with Mother Mariana as a model to be imitated in all the offices she exercised.

### OFFICE OF CHOIR MISTRESS

Mother Mariana carried out the office of choir mistress with a zeal for Divine Worship that incited the admiration of the Angels. What recollection, humility, and fervor she exacted in the praying of the Divine Office! What punctuality in the recitation of the Hours! For having seen in Heaven how the Angels praised God three times holy, she imitated on earth their divine psalmody.

Once, as she was cleaning the choir stalls in the Convent, she saw various deceased religious who were suffering their purgatory there, atoning for having broken the silence in choir, for succumbing to various distractions in the recitation of the Office, or even for their laxity in prayer. By her entreaties and supplications, Mother Mariana was able to relieve them of their sufferings.

She was a model of perfection in the praying of the divine worship. The Friars Minor taught the religious the music and Gregorian chant, and Mother Mariana, gifted with a melodious voice, would alternate with her sisters in singing and playing the organ. Words cannot describe the loving affection with which this seraphic swan sang to the Sacramental Jesus and His Holy Mother, for this virgin was a most worthy instructress of the divine worship.

This humble religious, who had said that she would always be the least of all, made true her word. On Saturdays, the day reserved for general cleaning, she would sweep as much as four other religious. When Mother Maria protested that she should not work so hard, she humbly replied, "My mother, it is better to work one day in the house of the Lord than to spend many years in the service of the world."

She preferred to sweep the lower cloisters, for it was there that she did her hidden penances by night. The demons, who wanted to frighten her, would scatter enormous quantities of repulsive worms on the floors she had swept. When she would see these swarming masses of creatures, she would make the Sign of the Cross, and all would disappear, leaving the floors once again clean.

On one such occasion, Mother Maria saw Mother Mariana still sweeping, even though the floor already appeared clean. She asked her, "Is it not already clean?"

Mother Mariana made the Sign of the Cross, and the worms disappeared with a loud roar. Frightened, the Abbess asked, "What was that?"

Mother Mariana, however, responded only with a smile.

Oh! happy cloisters, battleground of so many struggles and victories of this heroine! Oh! rooms made holy by her terrible penances!

In carrying out these various offices of the Convent, from the most humble to the highest, that of Abbess, Mother Mariana always acted with humility and docility, as if she were the least of the novices. Her manner of dealing with others was sweet and smooth, and so prudent, discrete, and affable that the very religious who tormented and persecuted her came to realize the precious treasure that they had in her.

Mother Maria, who knew how much the others had come to esteem Mother Mariana, became quite concerned, and asked Our Lord that her beloved niece not be deprived of persecutions and sufferings, for she understood the immense reward awaiting those souls who suffer united to the Passion of Our Lord. In fact, her Divine Spouse did not fail to bestow on His bride rich treasures of humiliations, sufferings, and abandonment.

\* \* \*

## Chapter 12

The years of her mortal life flew swiftly by, and Mother Mariana de Jesus, like a valiant warrior, continued to fight the battles of Our Lord, accruing triumphs and laurels in each combat. She lived dead to the world and hidden with Christ in God. Her virtue grew continuously, reaching the height of perfection to which God called her.

After the Blessed Virgin had revealed to her in Heaven that she would be the Novice Mistress, the humble Mariana, like a lovely violet, seeing in herself only her lowliness and unworthiness, never ceased to cry out to her Divine Spouse with touching fear, "My Love, take from me this most bitter chalice."

### Mother Mariana as Novice Mistress

But Christ remained deaf to these pleas, and the time chosen by God having arrived, the religious unanimously elected Mother Mariana de Jesus as Mistress of Novices. Ignoring the sad and plaintive protests of this humble dove, they placed on her shoulders the heavy cross, for this seems to have been the greatest sacrifice to which God had yet subjected her. Having no will other than that of her Divine Spouse, she submitted, repeating His very words: "Not my will, but Thine be done."

On the eve she received into her care the novitiate - three novices and four postulants - she prostrated herself before them, as if to confess her faults, saying with her great humility: "My little sisters, the Community has charged me with this office not because I have merited it, but so that I might come to learn with you the practice of the virtues. I ask that you look to me as a sister and treat me as such, for, indeed, I am your elder sister and thus you can have confidence in me. It falls to me to form your souls so that you will be holy religious.

"However, the day will come when you will see that it is not I who act as Mistress, but rather it is the Most Holy Virgin Herself Who holds this office. I am but her feeble instrument, and I will do only that which She disposes."

Based on this humble rationale, she began to govern the novices, being completely dedicated to each of them, directing each soul to practice the degree of virtue to which it was called. The number of postulants multiplied prodigiously.

She was careful, however, to open her novitiate only to chosen souls, and not permit the entrance of any who did not have a true vocation. Mother Mariana formed her novices in such a way that all of them became excellent religious and, many of them, saints. Thus did this holy Mistress form a generation of religious of such good spirit that even today the precious seed of that fruitful tree of virtues has not been dissipated.

Oh! blessed time when this holy Mother made of her novitiate a paradise of delights wherein the Divine Spouse and His Blessed Mother took their pleasure, served in spirit and in truth!

### She Understands the Soul of Each Religious

When it came time for the novices to make their profession, the holy Mistress carefully prepared each one, giving advice that suited the spirit of each. On the eve of their profession, she solemnly forewarned each one all that she would have to pass through in accordance with the designs of Our Lord.

She also informed each one how and when she would die.

To those who would leave this earthly life before her, she would say, "My daughter, I shall not leave your bedside until I have delivered your soul into the hands of God Our Lord."

And to those who would die after her, she would say, "My daughters, when my death approaches, do not forget your Mother." In this way she foretold to her daughters what would come to pass, having first exercised them in the practice of the virtues, for she understood the interior of each one.

At times, a sister would conceal from her the faults she had committed during the day. Then Mother Mariana would call her aside, saying, "My daughter, you committed such-and-such a fault today, you broke the silence in such-and-such a place, saying these words ... Let us go now and do penance."

Then she would kneel down together with the novice and ask pardon of Our Lord for the fault. The novices could hide nothing from her. For this reason, they loved her like a mother and venerated her as a saint.

Oh!, happy novitiate, antechamber of Heaven, or, better said, sweet Heaven here on earth, where adoration, praise, and love was given to God through faithful adherence to the observance of the Rule and the practice of a life of sacrificial love! For the saintly Novice Mistress strictly observed even the least rules and practiced holy observance to the Rule of the Community.

Her novices were usually the first to rise in the morning, arriving early with Mother Mariana for the praying of the Little Office of Our Lady at 4 a.m.[20] One morning, when the novices were reluctant to rise so early, Mother Mariana went alone to pray before the others arrived. It was her custom, as she drew near the building that housed the choir, to stop and discipline herself for all the Poor Souls. When she finished taking this discipline, she directed her steps to the choir.

As she began to advance, she found herself impeded by a deep and terrible pit that opened up before her. From its depths, she heard terrible cries. Frightened and confused, Mother Mariana had the sense that she was no longer inside the Convent, and she cried out, "Oh my God! Where am I? Oh! my beloved Convent!"

### INFERNAL HATRED FOR THE LITTLE OFFICE OF OUR LADY

She then saw the head of a terrifying dragon, as large as the novitiate house, which opened its mouth revealing therein a multitude of souls. This monster cried out in a hideous voice, "I have swallowed all these souls and they are mine, and you also shall be mine!"

Her fright was so great that she fainted. When she returned to herself, she felt herself being supported in the arms of her Guardian Angel, who said, "Spouse of the Lord, why do you fear? You saw Hell! The devil did this to try to impede the recitation of the Little Office."

---

20. The Little Office of Our Lady (*Officium parvum Beatae Mariae Virginis*) was an accretion to the Brievary prayed in religious orders. By the 13th century, it had become a favorite prayer also of lay persons everywhere and was included in a separate prayerbook called *The Book of Hours*.

Then she heard another voice that said, "Bitter times will come when the Little Office will be left aside, and the spirit of the Convent weakened! Woe to those who shall have a part in this!"

She realized then that her Angel was transporting her through the air to the choir room. On the step ascending to the choir, she again heard that hideous voice, which cried out: "I shall use all my power to prevent the praying of this accursed Little Office, for, by it, my forces are weakened and I am destroyed."

Advancing several steps, she saw a light that illuminated the whole Convent. Raising her eyes toward the ceiling of the Church, she saw a most beautiful star with the name Mary shining on it. She entered the choir, and the Blessed Virgin met her to congratulate her for her victory and to restore her interior peace.

For when she saw the abyss in the ground, Mother Mariana had become disturbed, losing her customary peace of soul as she asked herself why Our Lord had permitted this and why her Guardian Angel had hidden himself. However, upon reaching the choir, her normal serenity returned when she saw the Blessed Virgin.

The other sisters then began to arrive to pray the Little Office. At that blessed time, the whole Community would rise for this prayer that was recited at 4 a.m. The prayer was obligatory only for the novices and the newly-professed sisters until their sixth year of profession. The others would pray it if they so desired from devotion. The extraordinary fervor with which Mother Mariana prayed the Office that morning can well be imagined.

Since her director, Father Jurado, had ordered her to make known to her Abbess all that happened to her so that posterity should not be deprived of these rich treasures, she went to inform Mother Maria of what had taken place as soon as the Community prayer ended. Both Mothers grieved sorely for what was to come to pass in the 20th century.[21]

Through the centuries, the religious have continued to recite the Little Office of the Most Blessed Virgin, which has never ceased to be prayed in this Convent and thus ensures the happiness of this Community of Conceptionists.

---

21. Mother Mariana received many more revelations about the great crisis in the Church in the 20th century, which are recounted in detail in Volume 2.

## Chapter 13

There are facts so stupendous and extraordinary in the life of Mother Mariana de Jesus that except for the fact that they were testified to under oath by the Friars Minor, the doctor, and other sisters, they would not be believed by some people. These include, for example, the prodigious trials and sufferings which God Our Lord gave to her and by which He tested His beloved spouse.

### Mother Mariana Receives the Wounds of Our Lord

On September 17, 1588, Mother Mariana, who had 28 years of age, was saying her customary prayers at midnight, prostrate on the floor in her room. Suddenly, her whole body shuddered so violently that she could not help but cry out. Mother Maria immediately came to see what had taken place.

"What has happened to you, my daughter?" she asked.

"We must leave here immediately, my Mother, for the whole house is falling down. It is an earthquake," she replied.

The Abbess embraced her and, trembling in fear for her niece, carried her to her bed. The other Spanish sisters also arose. Mother Francisca of the Angels, who was the Convent nurse, examined her hands and saw that on each palm was something similar to a hole into which something had been driven.

The same was present on the soles of her feet, in the very place where the spikes had been driven into the feet of Our Lord. Upon her heart was a purple bruise and red mark, as if it had been wounded by a sword. Her heart was beating so loudly it could be heard from a distance.

It is believed, because of this, that Our Lord interiorly imprinted upon her His Most Sacred Wounds. During this time, her body was stiff and rigid as a rock; only her eyes and mouth could move. In this state she passed the night in a veritable martyrdom.

### She Becomes Ill as a Result of her Penances

With the morning came the Convent physician, Doctor Sancho, who examined her carefully. Because of her life of penance, he said, she was completely debilitated, the marrow of her bones dried up, her body paralyzed. The only movement he could find was the beating of her heart.

Mother Francisca said to the Abbess, "My Mother, the Rule requires that we take her to the infirmary."

But Mother Maria responded, "My daughter, how can the dormitory be deprived of its sunshine? Let all of us, then, stay with her in the infirmary."

"No, my Mother," replied the nurse, "for the Rule ordains that the Abbess should sleep in the dormitory."

During the transferal of the patient and her bed, they found a rough hide scattered with bloody tacks that served as her mattress. The Abbess took and treasured this penitential cloth. She wanted to replace it with a soft mattress, but the doctor opposed this, warning her that when persons accustomed to such strong penances changed to a soft bed, they often became worse. Instead, a straw mattress was placed on her bed.

The doctor ordered a warm, spiced bath, but it was to no avail. Mother Mariana remained consumed by the strange illness. Her customary rosy complexion had changed to that of ash. Her face would still become red, however, when they would clean her or apply treatments following the doctor's orders. Then she would weep copiously in humiliation.

Mother Francisca of the Angels would console her on these occasions, saying, "Why are you embarrassed, my dear sister? For we are all sisters of the same Father and daughters of the Seraphim of Assisi. What I do for you now, you will do for me later. Do not suffer, my little sister."

With these and other sweet words, she comforted her patient.

Mother Maria would also vie to perform these services for her niece.

"This work belongs to me, as Abbess," she would say, "for I should be the servant of my subjects."

But Mother Francisca would counter, "This service belongs to me as nurse."

Thus they would lovingly dispute to serve this body that had become an open wound. They would turn her stone-like body to bathe it and try to relieve it with various powders. She could no longer swallow food, and had to be sustained only by liquids.

During this terrible sickness, she was the victim of atrocious mental trials. Her patience was tested by her Divine Spouse throughout the five months the sickness lasted. During this time, Her Divine Majesty withdrew His heavenly light and consolations and appeared to abandon her to suffer the punishment of a condemned soul.

### "ALL THOSE THINGS WERE ILLUSIONS, TRICKS, AND LIES…"

In the figure of a serpent, the devil would approach her when she was alone, for even her Guardian Angel was lost to her sight. He relentlessly tormented her, saying, "All those things of the past were illusions, tricks, and lies. You are mine." Then he would appear as a terrible cock, threatening her with his cockscomb that appeared as a sharp saw: "With this, I will tear you apart." He would glare at her with his horrible beady eyes, hopping about the cell.

When the exhausted patient would wake from a sleep, she would find the serpent attempting to climb onto her bed.

The sight of this monster caused the holy patient unbelievable torment. When the Abbess visited her, she would ask, "My daughter, is the serpent here?" (for she could not see him).

When Mother Mariana responded, "Yes, Mother, he is writhing over there," Mother Maria would become frightened and call for another religious to join her.

In this dark night of tribulation, Mother Mariana never abandoned her midnight and 3 a.m. prayers. At the same time, she suffered more and more each day from interior desolation. She was convinced that she had been deceived, tricked, and lied to her whole life. She saw herself condemned for all eternity. She would look to the Passion of her Beloved, yet it would seem that He was justly condemning her; she would call to the Star of the Sea, her Mother, Mary Most Holy, but since this Moon had hidden herself in the dark night of suffering, it seemed that She also, in Her justice, had condemned her.

## Chapter 13

**THE DARK NIGHT OF THE SOUL IS INTENSIFIED**

Feeling herself forsaken by Heaven and earth, Mother Mariana suffered without relief. The Friars Minor would enter, celebrate Holy Mass in her cell, and oblige her to receive Hoy Communion. Whenever her director would approach her with the Sacred Species, he would find her lips tightly sealed, unable to open. He would then order her, in the name of holy obedience, to open her mouth and receive Communion. Only then and with the greatest pain would she do so.

These Communions increased her torment, for she became convinced that with each one, she had committed yet another sacrilege. The serpent would dance about merrily, taunting her, "I have yet another sacrilege for Hell," which inflicted more suffering on the innocent victim.

At times her director would exorcize the cell so that the serpent would withdraw. Seeing her sufferings, he would weep for her, powerless to relieve her, for when God wants to purify a soul, He alone can give it relief. Because of the high degree of perfection to which God was calling Mother Mariana, she was subjected to great sufferings and trials during this dark night of the soul.

Amid these atrocious sufferings of soul and body, she would call out to God. However, at times, she could not even speak because of the intensity of the torments. Only her tears gave witness to her martyrdom. When she was alone, she composed these verses expressing her cruel desolation:

> My love's delight, Jesus of my soul,
> Why do you leave me in such bitter pain?
> Like a solitary dove do I weep
> In the full night of sorrow enchained.
>
> In the depths of my ardent love
> I find neither peace nor repose,
> Return, I beg, and be with me again,
> Oh! Spouse of my soul, sweet Host.
>
> If it is reparation for my faults Thy justice demands,
> Then Thy pardon now I humbly implore,
> Oh! sweet Lover of the heart that loves Thee,
> Like the dust of the earth, I do Thee adore.

Thou hast placed in my soul this emptiness,
My life is but a graveyard dark and vast,
Where buried inside it, My Love, is
Thy memory, Thy beauty, and Thy goodness past.

And although by the light of my ardent faith
Thy immense goodness I still ascertain,
My soul is parched like a withered flower,
Lacking, as it does, Thy life-giving rain.

Amidst this pain comes an alluring hope
Like a messenger bearing Thy love divine.
And hastily turns toward me
To succor me in my sorrows of brine.

Oh! fire of charity, my hidden God!
Let my soul be consumed in Thy divine love.
For neither my sorrows nor Thy apparent forgetfulness
Can estrange me from Thou Who art my love.

I live prostrate on my bed of sorrows,
Awaiting the charity of my sisters' touch,
Oh! Thou Who lives under this one same roof,
Bless these daughters whom Thou lovest so much.

And when I am freed from this burdensome body,
My happy soul to Thee will take flight.
Then open to me, Oh! Beloved of Mine,
The doors of Thy mansion of heavenly delight.

And then, Oh! Mother of Love most sweet,
Oh! then, my celestial Maria of love,
Then Thou Thyself shalt present my soul
To my beloved celestial Spouse above."[22]

    Mother Maria instructed the saintly nurse, Mother Francisca of the Angels, to write down these touching verses, for Mother Mariana could not so much as move even her fingers. She would recite these plaintive verses aloud, then together they would sing them, for despite her extreme weakness, she still retained her melodious voice. Thus they wounded the Heart of their Beloved, for Mother Francisca was also of a proven holiness, and when she sang with the afflicted victim, it was like a celestial concert.

22. Oh! encanto de mi amor, Jesús del alma!
Por qué me dejas en amarga pena?
Cual tortolilla solitaria lloro,
En plena noche de dolores llena.

Allá en el fondo de mi amor activo,
 No encuentro calma, ni el menor reposo,
Vuélvete, dice, a estar conmigo,
Oh! de mi alma celestial Esposo!

Si de mis culpas tu justicia clama,
Yo, ya humillada, tu perdón imploro;
Y confundida con el polvo yo te adoro,
Oh, fino Amante del corazón que te ama!

Tu puesto en mi alma está vacío,
Mi vida es un vasto cementerio,
Do se hallan sepultadas, Amor mío!
Tu recuerdo, tu hermosura y tu cariño.

Y, aunque la luz de mi ardiente fé,
Me hace entrever Tu bondad immensa;
Mi alma se seca cual una flor marchita,
Faltando el riego del que le dió vida.

En esto viene la esperanza bella,
Cual mensajera del amor Divino,
Y presurosa hacia mí se inclina,
Para alentarme en mi amarga pena.

Oh! fuego de caridad, Dios escondido!
Se abrasa mi alma en Tu Divino ardor,
Ni mis dolores, ni Tu aparente olvido
Me alejarán de Ti que eres mi amor.

Postrada vivo en doloroso lecho,
Esperando la caridad de mis hermanas,
Oh! Tú que vives bajo un mismo techo!
Bendice aquellas a quienes tanto amas!

Y cuando libre del pesado cuerpo,
Mi alma feliz tienda hacia Tí mi vuelo,
Entonces, ábreme, Amado mío,
De tu mansión las puertas del Cielo.

Entonces, Madre del Amor hermoso!
Oh! mi bella y celestial María!
Presenta Tú misma el alma mía,
A mi amado y celestial Esposo!

At times Mother Maria would enter and hear these two sacrificial victims singing melodious lamentations, and her heart would dissolve with tenderness. For she was powerless to alleviate the relentless diabolical siege that her holy niece was undergoing. Despite her natural fear of the serpent, this loving Abbess would go and stay with Mother Mariana during all her free moments. Let the readers imagine what passed between these two angelic hearts during those sweetly sorrowful meetings.

It was February 2, 1589. The sun had risen, but the dark night of Mother Mariana had not abated. The charitable nurse had rendered her services and left the patient to assist at Holy Mass and receive Communion, in conformance with the regulations of the Holy Rule. Mother Mariana remained in the company of her Guardian Angel and her Seraphic Father Saint Francis, and under the care of her Heavenly Mother.

Unable to move on her bed of pain, she suddenly heard a dreadful clamor in her cell. Mother Mariana, who had been praying and suffering a great interior bitterness, opened her eyes and saw a hideous serpent writhing and twisting in her cell, crawling frantically on the walls, as if pursued by someone trying to drive him away.

At that moment, the pain of this unconquerable virgin increased and her spirit was overwhelmed with despair. All the heroic acts of her life seemed criminal to her. Her good works appeared as works of perdition, her very vocation an illusion and sham by which she had delivered herself to eternal damnation. In this woeful interior state, when it seemed to her that her soul would detach itself from her body from the violence of her suffering and sink like lead into Hell, she mustered all her strength, crying out:

"Star of the Sea, Mary Most Immaculate, the weak vessel of my soul is sinking. The waters of tribulation are drowning me. Save me, for I am perishing!"

### Our Lady Appears and Hurls the Serpent into Hell

Before she had pronounced the last word, she saw a celestial light around her and felt a loving hand touching her head. At the same time, she heard a sweet voice that said, "Why do you fear, My daughter? Do you not know that I am with you in your tribulation? Rise up and look at Me!"

The humble religious raised herself up in her bed and saw a Lady of great majesty and grandeur who breathed sweetness and love. She asked, "Who are you, beautiful Lady?"

"I am the Mother of Heaven whom you invoked. I have come to dissipate the darkness of the night of your soul. You see now what Hell is, for you have experienced it, but you shall remain there no longer. I will place you in Purgatory so that you might finish purifying your soul, for your Lord and God has destined for you great and auspicious things during your lifetime.

"Tell your Mother on earth to prepare herself for her journey to eternity, for the time has arrived when, leaving this earth, she will receive her reward for the many sacrifices and sufferings she has endured over the foundation of this Convent, which I love with all my Heart.

"This Convent will be severely persecuted in the centuries to come, with the persecution reaching such an extreme that attempts will be made against the lives of my daughters.[23] Not succeeding in this, they will strive with infernal tenacity to destroy it, making use of the religious within it and the authority of their superiors. However, man can do nothing against the works of God, and I will have in this house daughters worthy of my love, martyrs of the spirit, who, despised by the world and by their own, will be most beloved by God and the firm columns that will sustain the then-agonizing Community.

"Now, I will impart life to your nerves, veins, and arteries, and I will dispel the infernal serpent. You will be left in the sweet tranquility that the souls in the place of expiation enjoy."

---

23. In 1912, 1916, and again in 1918, the Convent of the Immaculate Conception faced threats from the liberal, anti-clerical government directed exclusively against it, whose property the government wanted. Under the pretense of offering another site on the outer periphery of the city, they tried to evict the sisters and usurp the property. Several times, the lives of various sisters who offered valiant resistance were threatened by civil authorities, who were chastised for their aggression in sudden and unexpected ways, which the Sisters attributed to the hand of God.

In 1918, the inhabitants of Quito made a large penitential procession imploring the protection of Our Lady of Quito and spreading leaflets exposing the government's plan to raze the holy building. This had the desired effect of halting the liberal offensive against the Convent (Cadena y Almeida, *Mensaje Profetico*, pp. 46-61).

As she finished speaking, the enormous serpent emitted a horrible scream of despair and hurled himself into Hell with such a great roar that it caused the earth to tremble throughout the city and the Convent.

Mother Mariana remained lying as if she were dead. She was found in this state by Mother Francisca and the Abbess, who, feeling the earthquake, had rushed to assist her. Praying near her, they saw Mother Mariana coming back to consciousness.

Opening her eyes, she found she was again able to move all the members of her body, which had been dry and lifeless for five months. Directing her gaze toward the two sisters, she said, "Mothers, my whole body can now move. How good is the Queen of Heaven, who has cured and saved me. Let us pray the holy Rosary."

As Mother Mariana began to pray, her soul was in a profound sadness. At the same time, she had the deep peace and tranquility of the just soul who suffers united to God, without fear of falling into His disfavor.

After they finished reciting the Rosary, they sang the Litany of Loreto. Mother Mariana led with the intonations, while the other two religious responded filled with joy. After this prayer of thanksgiving to the Heavenly Queen, they brought Mother Mariana a bowl of soup with bread and meat, which she was able to eat by herself with no need of assistance. Again, she gave thanks to Our Lord Who gives all good things. Then Mother Francisca retired and she was alone with Mother Maria to give her an account of all that had passed in her soul.

After the Abbess heard all that had taken place, she went to her Father Confessor, telling him, "Father, my earthly sojourn will soon end. Help me to prepare my soul for the great wrenching it will experience as it is taken from time to eternity."

Her confessor asked how she knew this, but she remained silent.

Later, he went to speak with Mother Mariana. Afterward, he told Mother Maria: "Courage, my daughter, courage. Your Reverence will soon see Heaven. When you are under the blue mantle of our Immaculate Mother, do not forget your sisters and brothers of St. Francis, those who, throughout time, will assist this Convent of the Immaculate Conception."

### "Jesus Christ Suffered Much More than I Suffer…"

Mother Mariana still remained in her bed, suffering indescribably in soul and body, but now with the tranquility of a just soul. She had, moreover, the consolation of being able to move. Throughout the period of this Purgatory, she provided a practical example of how a religious should receive interior trials and physical illness for the edification of our neighbors in the spirit of sacrifice and by the exercise of the virtues of faith, hope, charity, patience, tolerance, and silent resignation.

Although Our Lord had freed her hands, allowing her movement to attend to herself, she continued to suffer the acute pains of her sickness. Doctor Sancho did not know what to prescribe for her, even though he was the most illustrious doctor in the country, sought out by sick persons far outside the city. He told Mother Maria that there was no hope regarding the illness of Mother Mariana, whose condition worsened day by day. He insisted that her death was inevitable and that they would then have a friend, a sister, and a mediator in Heaven.

The physical strength of this angel of sorrow continued to wane with every day that passed. Even after she reached the point where she could no longer swallow any liquids, she never lost her sweet and saintly tranquility of soul.

When the Abbess and her sisters inquired how she was feeling, she would respond with a celestial smile, "Very bad. I believe that my time of exile is coming to an end, but Jesus Christ, the Beloved of my soul, suffered much more than I do, and in Him lies my happiness."

### The Second Mystical Death of Mother Mariana

Mother Mariana remained in this state until September of 1589. On the second Wednesday of that month at 9 o'clock in the morning, her agony began. That morning Holy Mass was celebrated in her presence and she received Extreme Unction with edifying fervor and the immense joy of one who sees herself at the end of her sufferings. Upon hearing the mournful tolling of the bell announcing the last agony of a member of the Convent, the Community and the Franciscan friars surrounded her bed to pray and accompany her. There they remained until noon, when they all retired for their midday repast, leaving only the holy nurse at her side.

In the afternoon, the sisters and friars returned and prayed at her side until the bell of the Hail-Mary's rang. Then she was ordered, in the name of holy obedience, not to die except in their presence. Assured of the obedience of this exemplary religious, they passed a peaceful night of sleep.

On the next mornings, they found her as before, still agonizing. On Friday at noon, her body was seized by convulsions. Her beautiful face became disfigured, taking on the pale hue and coldness of death.

Seeing her great suffering, Mother Maria and the friars said, "Sisters and Mothers, let us pray fervently that, if it be the will of God, He release this blessed soul from its body, for none of us have the heart to see her suffer like this any longer."

And they began to pray, recommending her soul to God.

At 3:30 in the afternoon, Mother Mariana raised her eyes to heaven, then let her gaze fall to the crucifix that she held in her hands. She clasped it to her heart, shedding tears that fell on it. She inclined her head slightly toward Christ, and breathed her final breath.

Weeping, the friars mourned her passing, saying, "She was our angelic sister; unhappy are we who still remain in this earthly exile."

When they were convinced that she had indeed died, the sisters also began to weep. After intoning the final responsorial over her body, the friars called Doctor Sancho, who testified to her death and left the Convent. The sisters laid out her cold body for burial, arranging flowers around it on the litter they used to transport it, and then carried the body to the lower choir.

The noble and the poor of the city arrived in droves to keep vigil over her body on Friday and Saturday. The people wept and cried to see the body of their Mother, saying, "She died a saint, for she was truly an angel on earth for us." The religious prayed day and night by the burning candles set around the litter to illuminate her body. They feared that her body might begin to decompose, but when they approached and touched her, they were convinced that no corruption had yet begun in her cold body.

On Saturday night, Mother Maria said to the sisters, "My daughters, our sister no longer has need of us. We are all worn out by our mourning and are tired. Let us take some rest, leaving her under the care of our Sacramental Spouse Who resides alone in the Tabernacle, Whom our sister loved so dearly. Let us regain our strength so that tomorrow we might pray the Little Office, which will always be the mainstay of regular observance and the preservation of the religious spirit for the daughters of the Immaculate Conception. This would be the desire of our holy sister, whom we will bury on Monday."

Sad and tearful, the religious left the lower choir. Overcome by weariness, they fell into deep sleep.

### Her Resurrection

The next morning, they awoke and directed their steps to the choir to pray the Little Office. When they arrived, they saw Mother Mariana praying there. She rose to embrace them, greeting them with the Alleluia. Frightened, the sisters began to take flight, but Mother Mariana called out to them, "My little sisters, I am alive. Why do you fear, you who have loved me so dearly?"

But they all fled, running to the dormitory to relate this startling news to Mother Maria. Together, in Community, they returned to the upper choir. The Abbess, who found Mother Mariana still praying there, thought that it was her spirit. She addressed the figure sternly, saying, "In the name of God and holy obedience, I command you to tell me what you need."

"Mother, do not be afraid," the figure responded. "I am alive and want to be with my sisters and live among them."

After saying these words, she approached Mother Maria, who was quivering with fear.

Mother Mariana insisted, "Look at me, Mother, it is truly I, who am sound and healthy."

Still fearful of Mother Mariana, the Community began the prayers of the Little Office. Then they all processed to the lower choir to see if the cadaver was there. They found only the empty litter, the shroud, and the candles, which convinced them that she had indeed been resurrected.

The friars who had seen her die were told the news, and they were astounded by this marvel. Mother Mariana received Communion, then gave an account to Mother Maria and her director, Father Antonio Jurado, of everything that had happened to her.

She told them that after her death, God Our Lord had placed her soul through another purification, where she saw what seemed to be her body suffering a mystical Purgatory. She remained in this state of suffering until 3 a.m. on Sunday. At that hour, the same at which Our Lord resurrected, her soul returned to her body, communicating to it all of her former vigor and health.

She rose, descended from the litter, and extinguished a candle, which, because of a tremor in the earth, had fallen and was threatening to set the Convent afire.

After extinguishing the candle and freeing herself from the burial shroud, she went to the upper choir to await her sisters in order to greet them with the *Alleluia*. Our Lord had restored her to life, she told them, because it is sweet and meritorious to endure and suffer for the love of Christ.

Hearing all this, they marveled, for they saw that Mother Mariana, who had been a pallid and weak invalid for more than a year, was now robust and restored, her cheeks as rosy as they had ever been.

They sent news of what had happened to Doctor Sancho and asked him to come immediately. At first, he was reluctant, thinking them mad from exhaustion. Instead, he went to the Franciscan monastery to ask the friars to bury the cadaver of Mother Mariana soon, for the sisters were succumbing to madness.

Finding the friars gone from their monastery, he went to the Convent. There he found Mother Mariana, alive and healthy. Startled and amazed, he marveled at the miracle, saying, "How incomprehensible are the ways of God!"

He, along with the Franciscan priests who were present and the Community of sisters, made a solemn statement under oath of what had taken place. These testimonies are preserved in the archives of the Convent.[24]

Mother Mariana thus resumed her penitential life in the Conceptionist Convent. Who can adequately describe what took place within the soul of this saintly creature, who returned to life in order to suffer? Nor can one express the happiness of the Community, who rejoiced to find the treasure that they had mourned as lost.

God most great, how admirable Thou art in Thy saints!

\* \* \*

---

[24]. The solemn sworn oaths of the Priests, the doctor, and circumstantial observers testifying to the two extraordinary deaths and resurrections of Mother Mariana de Jesus are contained in the Chronicles of the Monastery of the Conception of Quito, attests the Postulator for the Cause of her Beatification (Cadena y Almeida, *Apariciones*, pp. 79-80).

## Chapter 14

Three years passed, and the heart of Mother Maria, worn out by her sufferings, became increasingly weak. In 1592, Doctor Sancho told the Friars Minor that the Founder Mother needed tranquility and rest.

Hearing this, the Father Provincial of the Seraphic Order called an assembly of the Friars Minor to discuss the matter. They resolved to call a chapter meeting at the Conceptionist Convent to elect a new Abbess so that the life of the Founder might be prolonged. Having arrived at this decision, the friars set off for the Convent and called the Community together.

The Provincial addressed the religious, advising them of the medical prognosis of Mother Maria. He explained that it would be best for her to step down from the Abbacy and a new Abbess elected. The election would take place the next day after Holy Mass. He enjoined the sisters to pray fervently to God Our Lord to bless the outcome of this election and gave a loving sermon on the importance of the event.

Then, in the presence of her Franciscan brothers, Mother Maria asked to speak. With these words, she stepped down from the office she had held since her arrival in New Spain 15 years earlier:

"Beloved daughters and my sisters, the loving goodness of God to these lands caused me to come from Spain to found this Convent of the Immaculate Conception of Mary Most Holy.

"How sweet are the memories of the time I spent in my Convent in Spain, where faithful monastic observance reigned. I found myself tranquil and content there in my advancing years. Nonetheless, when I least expected it, obedience commanded me to cross the oceans and come to make this foundation. Tears, pleas, attempts to avoid it – all were in vain.

"I surrendered myself to the heavy yoke of obedience, and, turning my face to the Holy Cross, I embraced it with a spirit prepared to endure every bitterness. From the moment that we sailed the open sea, when the infernal serpent caused that torment, until today, the heart of your Founder has been the victim of cruel

## Chapter 14

martyrdoms. How many sacrifices, hardships, and renunciations to provide you with what you have needed! ...

"Now the hour of my final farewell to this earth has arrived! I will await you in Heaven. But, before parting, I want to confide to you a secret: I am dying of sorrow because I see your rapidly growing defiance against submitting in obedience to the Franciscan Friars and the reckless deviations you are making from the path on which I have directed you.

"My daughters, if you only realized the gift of God that you now have! Tomorrow your Franciscan Friars will be shedding tears of grief that will reach the throne of the Lord. I beg you yet one more time that you consider this grave matter under the light of eternity.

"Finally, your Mother, prostrate on the ground before you, asks pardon for her bad example and lack of virtue. As a pledge of my maternal love, I leave you my niece, Mariana de Jesus, and a blessing. Finally, I ask your prayers for me."

When she had finished speaking, the tears of the religious were flowing in torrents. All embraced the Founding Mother. So touching was this last scene between mother and daughters that it seemed to these grieving children that their hearts were being wrenched from their breasts. As each sister embraced her, she promised to submit faithfully to the Friars Minor. However, when the four discontent religious who had instigated the campaign to put the Convent under diocesan rule embraced their Mother, they remained silent, promising nothing.

Amid her tears, she told them: "My daughters, how I long to give you my heart as a pledge of my love!"

It was a moving and tender scene. Bewailing the loss of their Founder as Abbess, the sisters begged the Provincial to leave them their Mother some time longer and implored him not to call a chapter meeting. But the Father Provincial made them see that this was impossible and that a new Abbess would have to be elected the next day. The fathers then took their leave. It is not difficult to imagine how the Community passed that night, invoking their Divine Spouse to illuminate them to elect a Abbess in accordance with His Holy Will.

## MOTHER MARIANA IS ELECTED ABBESS

God did indeed hear their prayers and inspired them to see who should occupy the place of the Founder.

On the next day after Holy Mass, the Friars Minor opened the chapter, and, on the first vote, Mother Mariana de Jesus Torres was elected Abbess by a unanimous ballot. There was general rejoicing among the religious when they learned that God had given them an Abbess so worthy and holy, the niece of their Founding Mother.

Confused and embarrassed, this humble dove did not consider herself worthy of such a high dignity and wanted to refuse the office. Weeping inconsolably, she seemed like a sad child in the arms of Mother Maria.

The Holy Founder comforted her, telling her that she herself would help her discharge this office and offering other kind words of consolation. Seeing that her niece would not accept her arguments, Mother Maria addressed her with an air of authority, "My daughter, is this how you should act as a religious?"

Then, vesting her in the large cloak of the Abbess, she obliged Mother Mariana to carry this heavy cross. But Mother Mariana continued to renounce the office before the Provincial. She insisted, amid tears, that she did not have the age requested by the Rule and that there were others who were better and more worthy religious.

Hearing this, the Provincial asked her, "Do you also renounce your religious vocation?"

"Not that, my Father," she replied. "Never will I do that."

The Provincial continued, "If you have a love of obedience, then, in the name of our Seraphic Father Saint Francis and holy obedience, accept the office of Abbess."

With this command, she submitted, weeping as she received the office. Sitting in the abbatial chair, she received the obedience of all the religious. The first to kneel before her to render her obedience was the Founder, who, embracing her, said, "My daughter, now you are my Mother, and you will close my eyes in death."

After her, each religious rendered her obedience. At the end of this moving ceremony, the Provincial gave an eloquent sermon explaining the significance of the ceremony and how the Abbess should be reverenced and esteemed. At the end of the address, the sisters entered the cloisters in procession, and the Friars Minor sang the *Te Deum laudamus*.

During the procession, the face of Mother Mariana, which was always so rosy, became ashen and pale, although preserving its great beauty. The ceremony completed, the friars congratulated the sisters on the successful election in the chapter hall, then left the Convent.

At midday, at the very moment when the sisters were going to the refectory to take their meal, the bell at the door rang. It was the Franciscan friars, who had sent a meal to their sisters. For such was their love for the Community, and especially the Founding Mothers, that they had begged alms to prepare a special meal for the new Abbess and her daughters.

The Founding Mother, the new Abbess, and the other sisters received this offering from their Seraphic brothers with great joy and gratitude. They understood that their Franciscan brothers desired not only to provide spiritual sustenance on this happy day – offering themselves to help the new Abbess to serve and protect the Community howsoever God desired, but also to offer them a delicious repast for their bodies.

Great, then, was the rejoicing of the Community in celebrating their new Abbess in these blessed cloisters. In Heaven, this union and charity shone resplendently, and the Immaculate Conception was glorified to have as Abbess the select daughter of her love. She chose to manifest her content in a very special manner.

## Our Lady Sends Mother Mariana a Celestial Gift

On the evening of the same day, a stranger rang the bell at the turn-box. Mother Maria answered the call and received this message, "The Lady, knowing that Mother Mariana de Jesus was elected Abbess, sends her this meal and tells her that She has her present in her heart."

The gift was so exquisite and plentiful that the Founding Mother had to call other sisters so that they might help her carry it in. When she inquired to know the name of this Lady who had sent such a fine offering, she received no response.

Mother Maria joyfully presented the grand gift to Mother Mariana, saying," My Mother, see this exquisite present that was sent to you," and she delivered the message from the Lady.

"Who was this Lady?" asked Mother Mariana.

"She did not give her name," responded Mother Maria.

"Undoubtedly it was the Marquesa," said the saint.

With a sweet smile, Mother Mariana fixed her attention on the offering. The food was distributed among the religious, and, marvelous to see, it seemed to multiply itself, with each one receiving so much that it would have sufficed to satisfy the greatest of hungers. The sisters all testified that they had never eaten food so exquisite.

Without doubt the Blessed Virgin had sent this celestial food to her daughter, and Mother Mariana had smiled for this reason, for she understood that it was her Heavenly Mother who had sent her this gift.

### The Marquesa Denies Sending the Gift

The following day, Mother Maria again went to the turn-box to receive the plentiful food sent by the Marquesa, as well as some sterling pounds she gave for the support of the Community. The Marquesa, who knew that Mother Mariana had been elected Abbess, wanted to see her personally in order to congratulate her. However, Mother Mariana, who had become ill, was unable to receive her that day.

The Marquesa replied that she would return on the following day. She asked that Mother Mariana be assured that so long as she held the office of Abbess, the pantry of the Convent would always be provided for.

Mother Maria then thanked the Marquesa for all that she had sent, especially for the exquisite food they had received the day before.

"No, Mother," said the Marquesa. "You are wrong. I sent nothing yesterday. I am embarrassed about this, but the produce from my lands had not yet arrived and I could prepare nothing yesterday."

When Mother Maria insisted, the Marquesa asked her to describe the gift. She listened carefully to the description, then responded, "This was neither prepared in my house nor served on my table."

Then Mother Maria clearly understood that the Blessed Virgin had presented this gift to her niece as her first demonstration of love and mercy for this Community.

On the first night after she was elected, Mother Mariana remained five hours as if she were dead. The other religious, frightened, wanted to call the doctor, but Mother Maria told them that this was not necessary and they should leave her be. When the new Abbess returned to consciousness, she shed a torrent of tears.

The sisters, perturbed at this behavior, met together and decided to speak with Mother Maria, their Founder Mother. They beseeched her to continue governing them since Mother Mariana's health was so precarious, and they feared she would become ill again from so much weeping.

"No, my daughters," she responded. "This will pass, for this is the will of God."

When she was alone with her niece, she addressed her on her knees, "My Mother, for you are my Mother and Abbess, but I am the Founder Mother and you are my child. Therefore, I have the right to ask you to tell me what has happened to you."

### MOTHER MARIANA RECEIVES NOTICE OF MOTHER MARIA'S APPROACHING DEATH

Mother Mariana took the hand of Mother Maria, and pressing it to her heart, she kissed it. Then she spoke: "Mother, I saw you dead, leaving me alone when I would have most need of you. I prostrated myself before the throne of God, offering my life in place of yours, but this offering was unworthy of acceptance, for the fruit is now mature and ready to be harvested for Heaven."

Trembling, Mother Maria asked, "When will this be, my daughter?"

"Very soon, Mother," responded her niece, "and I wish that I might accompany you!"[25]

"No, my child," she responded. "When I reach Heaven, I will prostrate myself before God's throne and implore Him to give

---

25. This prophecy was soon fulfilled with the death of Mother Maria Taboada on October 4, 1593.

you a long life so that you might maintain the holy observance of our Rule and govern my Convent."

"Alas, my Mother," returned Mother Mariana, "the Friars Minor will soon be separated from the Convent. You could not withstand this suffering. It remains, then, for me to bear it."

Then she communicated to her aunt the sufferings that she would have to bear, for she had seen all this in ecstasy. "I will be persecuted, imprisoned, and tormented," she told Mother Maria.

Mother Mariana saw the face of her aunt transformed by a profound sorrow, and she felt a secret inspiration to tell her no more of her future sufferings so as not to aggravate her already delicate state of health. Thus she said no more about what she had seen.

## FOREWARNINGS ABOUT RELAXING THE COMMUNITY LIFE

Mother Maria told her niece, "My daughter, I know that the common life will be relaxed, and I beseech Our Lord that this will not take place in your lifetime."

"No, my Mother," said Mother Mariana. "This will not occur in my time, and even when this takes place, there will still be souls who, with their sacrifices, will hold back the divine anger."[26]

Mother Maria then gave her niece rules for governing the Community and confided to her various secrets regarding the great sufferings that had been endured for this foundation.

After embracing her niece, she left her and went to speak with the Father Provincial. Weeping, she told him, "My Father, I greatly fear the relaxations in holy poverty that are taking place among the Franciscans. Hold them in check and strive to eliminate all such abuses."

"My daughter," responded the Provincial. "What you say is true, but it is difficult to remedy this evil. I fear that some catastrophe in ahead for us." He knew of the powerful intercession of the Founding Mother before God, and he enjoined her to implore God's assistance in this serious matter.

---

26. This prophecy of Mother Mariana was fulfilled. Common life lasted 118 years after the foundation of the Convent, long after her death.

## Chapter 15

From the moment she accepted the cross of Abbess, the government of Mother Mariana was peaceful and sweet, with strict observance to the Rule required. She imitated her Divine Spouse with supreme diligence and heroic fortitude to guard the honor of her Beloved and to foster divine worship. In a word, the Holy Virgin was governing the spirit of Mother Mariana.

In all the problems that arose, she consulted with her holy aunt, Mother Maria, her only consolation, in whom she could confide her doubts and tribulations. But since Our Lord wanted the soul of this young Abbess to climb Calvary all alone, He permitted the death of the Founding Mother in order to purify the soul of Mother Mariana.

Thus, alone and destitute, she was the victim of the Convent of the Immaculate Conception.

### Mother Maria's Condition Worsens

As the year 1593 progressed, the health of Mother Maria became noticeably worse. Such was her weakness that she had to exert great effort to assist in the routine life of the Community. Her daughters begged her to rest a little, for her infirmity would excuse her from following strict observance.

"My daughters," responded the Mother, "I am the Founder of this Convent, and I want to leave as foundation this violence I inflict upon myself so that the Rule might always be faithful observed here. I will allow myself no rest except in Heaven, for this earthly life is the time for us to labor."

In effect, this pure victim was offering herself on the sacrificial altar of charity for her daughters – both present and future. On September 17, the feast of the Stigmata of the Seraphic Father Saint Francis, during the second Vespers, she was struck by a strong seizure of pain. Supported in her chair and sustained by Mother Mariana, she remained until the end of Vespers. At its conclusion, she found herself in the arms of her Abbess and niece, who helped her out of the choir and into the infirmary.

There Mother Mariana told her, "My Mother, this is the first order I have given you. Under obedience, I am telling you to rest in bed and not to assist at the Community activities."

Mother Maria accepted the order from her Abbess. With tears streaming from her eyes, she kissed the scapular of her niece, and remained in bed for some days.

On each of the nine days of the novena before the feast of Saint Francis, Mother Maria was dressed and carried to the choir. Her bed was always surrounded by her daughters, who wanted to be close to their Founder Mother. During one of the days of the novena, her condition became violently worse. Her very bones and nerves quivered. She closed her eyes as if in her last agony.

This agony lasted three hours and the religious cried inconsolably, thinking that she had already died. But Mother Mariana consoled them, "Do not cry. Mother Maria will still remain with us for some days."

Some days before this crisis, Mother Maria had addressed the sisters who gathered round her bedside, "My daughters, as Founder, I would like to request a favor of you. In the days preceding my death, will you permit the Mother Abbess, my niece, to remain always at my side, while the Vicar Abbess presides over the Community in her place?"

All her daughters readily acceded to this request. Therefore, in these last days, Mother Mariana never left the bedside of the dying Founder Mother, who gave her guidelines and advice for correcting those who committed faults.

"My daughter," she said on one occasion, "never let your zeal lead you to correct a sister too harshly if she is not calm and willing to admit her fault. Instead, prostrate yourself at her feet, begging her to amend herself. This is what I have done."

Mother Mariana spent these nights praying with her holy patient and offering her consolation even during the morning's light repast. When she prayed, she asked Our Lord to spare the life of her Mother and avert the bitter chalice of her death, offering herself in her stead.

However, in her interior, she felt that this was not the will of God. Then, echoing the words of her Divine Spouse, she would say, "Let Thy will, not mine, be done."

## Chapter 15

### Prophecies of the Founding Mother Regarding the Order

After her violent attack, Mother Maria was stronger for several days. On one of these days, Mother Mariana de Jesus, finding herself alone with her aunt, ordered her, "My Mother, I have confided my innermost thoughts to you, but now you will tell me what happened to you."

"My daughter," replied the Founding Mother, "soon the Friars Minor will no longer govern my Convent. Alas! Some unworthy sisters will refuse to submit to the sons of the Seraphic Francis. The Order of the Immaculate Conception is a part of the tree of our Father Saint Francis, and he himself will shake this tree to make the rotten and withered fruit fall from it. He will prune it so that the flowers will blossom, and this will occur in the 20$^{th}$ century. This strong and verdant tree of the Immaculate Conception will be shaken from time to time by Saint Francis so that its buds will flower and ripen into the mature fruit of virtue. There will be unworthy souls who, refusing to submit to the Friars Minor, will lose their vocations."

In this vision she recounted, the Founding Mother had seen all that would take place in her Convent in the centuries to come. She told Mother Mariana many things that are not possible to reveal here, for these two souls were deeply united by the spirit of prophecy communicated to them by God.

Again Mother Maria's condition took a turn for the worse. When they called Doctor Sancho, he only looked at her, shook his head, and said, "Mother, remember your friends when you are in Heaven." Then, leaving her cell, he told Mother Mariana, "Mother Maria is dying," and expressed his most profound sorrow.

On October 4, the feast of our Seraphic Father, the holy patient awoke quite invigorated and full of life. The sisters thought that their father Saint Francis had heard their prayers and would cure their holy Founding Mother, and a great happiness spread throughout the Community.

The Father Provincial entered Mother Maria's cell, celebrated Mass there, and gave her Communion. Afterward, he approached her bedside to feel her pulse, and told Mother Mariana, "The pulse is going, for our Mother is dying."

### Last Words and Blessing of the Founding Mother

Mother Mariana approached her and asked, "My Mother, what is happening to you?"

"Farewell, my daughter, I am leaving you," she responded.

For the last time she received Extreme Unction. Then the Provincial Father asked for a blessed candle. Placing it in her hand, he said, "Mother Maria, your Divine Spouse is awaiting you in Heaven. Now, as Founder of this Convent, bless your daughters and speak to them your last words."

Mother Maria sat up. All trace of infirmity disappeared from her face. She appeared most beautiful, like a living rose, as if she were again 33 years of age, the age she had been when she had founded the Order in Quito. Her gaze ran over her daughters with sweetness and affection. She asked for a crucifix and lovingly took it from the hands of the Provincial Father. Then she began to make her farewell to all her daughters. She asked their pardon for all that she might have done to cause scandal or suffering. Turning to the four non-observant religious, she tried to make them see how her firmness in demanding subjection and obedience to the Franciscans was for their own good. To the others she spoke more words of unction and love. Meanwhile, the Community sobbed and lamented, and the Friars Minor surrounded her bedside, grieving with the sisters.

"My daughters," Mother Maria told them, "remember how much this foundation has cost me." And she strongly exhorted them to the holy observance of the Rule. "Do not forget your Mother," she concluded. "Farewell, my daughters. I will watch over you from Heaven, and from there I will also chastise you."

The sisters assured her that she had been blameless in her governance. Instead, they asked her to pardon them for all they had done to offend her. When Mother Mariana, as Abbess, approached to receive her blessing, the Founder blessed her with the crucifix. Afterward she blessed each religious, extending to each sister the cross she carried to kiss the Sacred Wounds. Then, she extended her own hand for each one to kiss.

After blessing all of the Community, she called for her niece, saying, "Let the Mother Abbess approach."

For her she had these words, "My daughter, farewell. For your inheritance, I leave you my courage, my spirit, all my sufferings, and the Passion of My Divine Spouse. I entrust to you my flock for you to guard most diligently. I must make a strict account for the souls of each one of my daughters. I sustained myself with fortitude by the fulfillment of the holy Rule."

The Founder spoke other lofty and edifying words, blessed Mother Mariana once again and entrusted her daughters to her. Then she showed her the crucifix, saying, "My daughter, kiss the Wound in the Side." As Mother Mariana complied, it seemed as if she were entrusting her niece to the Sacred Heart of her Divine Spouse. The Founder then gave her one final embrace.

Mother Maria then raised the crucifix and said: "I bless my Community here present. I bless all my future daughters who will be faithful to their vocations in these Convent walls. I know them all, their faces, their characters, their virtues and defects, and I see all that will happen to them in the centuries to come. I bless this Convent, I bless these holy cloisters that have cost me so dearly. I bless these walls and I bless this room. These things I say now will remain written in the hearts of all my daughters present here. They will transmit them to my successors, who, knowing and reading this, will love me. From Heaven I will give them a special blessing.

"And this will become known when my Community will be agonizing in the $20^{th}$ century, like a weak branch being tossed to and fro by furious waves, for in this time I will have daughters worthy of their vocation.

"During this difficult and anguished period, the Star of the Sea, Mary Most Holy, will save them from shipwreck, and the breath of the Holy Spirit will calm the fury, leaving them in tranquil peace, serenity, and harmony."

With this, she gave her final blessing with the crucifix to all those who would come after her. She also gave a special blessing to the Seraphic Order, saying, "Many times blessed by God be the Seraphic Order, my mother, under whose shadow I have lived and in whose arms I die tranquil. I place all of my daughters under the blessed protection of Mary Most Holy until the end of time. My daughters should be under this same blessed shadow until the last day at the end of time. Thus will they be safeguarded from the infernal Devil and his plots and suggestions. May those who love the Franciscan Order be blessed by God, and those who despise it or separate themselves from it be accursed. My Father Saint Francis, always guard your Conceptionist daughters and keep them in your seraphic heart!"

This, then, was her last élan of burning love for God and the Seraphic Order. Her trembling hand let the crucifix fall, and the Provincial placed the blessed candle in her hand. Her death agony began.

### The Last Agony of Mother Maria

Even now, her voice was sonorous. As her agony began, she gave a sigh and lovingly prayed the ejaculations that the Father Provincial or Mother Mariana would suggest. "Jesus, Mary, Joseph and Francis," she would sweetly repeat. When the Provincial and Mother Mariana fell silent, the dying religious would continue to repeat these words.

Her beautiful eyes had been raised toward Heaven. As the end approached, Mother Mariana slowly closed them with her own hands. When they were completely closed, she heard Mother Maria's last word, which she could barely make out: "Francis!"

### Her Death and Burial – The Judgment of God

The friars prayed the prayers for the agonizing and, while they were singing the Credo, Mother Maria expired with a sweet smile, as if she were seeing some celestial vision. At that moment her precious soul separated itself from her virginal body and Mother Mariana saw it present itself before the terrible judgment seat of God. It had the aspect of a beautiful white mist, with only the slightest bit of obscurity.

At the same time Mother Mariana saw the majestic throne of glory in Heaven that would belong to Mother Maria. It was in a special choir occupied only by the Founders of religious orders. Her throne was most exalted and resplendent because she was the Founder of the Convent of the Immaculate Conception of Quito.

God Our Lord allowed Mother Mariana to see that her aunt would spend eight days in Purgatory. There she would not suffer the pain of fire, but only that of loss. She saw all this at the very moment when the Founder died with all the Friars gathered around her bed.

When they saw that she was dead, they wanted to sing the responsorial, but the sisters were opposed to this. Undoubtedly they were hoping that she was only in a state of ecstasy, for her face was most beautiful. Her cheeks were red and her lips like roses – with her mouth outlined in a sweet smile, half-open as if she were going to speak. For this reason, they thought she might still be living.

From the beginning of the agony, the Friars also feared for the life of Mother Mariana because of her extreme suffering. But God strengthened his spouse, who was undergoing a double martyrdom: one, at seeing her Mother die; and the other, at seeing her in the prison of Purgatory. She knew that Mother Maria was already dead, but she did not say a word. She only kissed the forehead, hands, and feet of her beloved Mother. The Fathers insisted upon singing the responsorial, but again the sisters resisted. Thus they all remained gathered around the bed of their treasure.

Finally, Doctor Sancho came. They had sent messengers to find him, but he was not at his home or office. So, they had resorted to sounding the bell that the religious used to call the doctor. After examining the Founder, he informed the Franciscan Friars, "My fathers, Mother has been dead for two hours." With this confirmation, the responsorial was finally sung. Their hearts pierced with sorrow, the friars left, leaving behind an inconsolable Community bewailing the death of their Mother.

Mother Mariana permitted no one to prepare the corpse for burial. She herself, with the love of a niece, the devotion of a daughter, and the reverence of a saint, prepared the holy body.

When it was ready to be moved, the sisters covered it with flowers and carried it to the lower choir to keep vigil over it there. Her face was beautiful, as if in ecstasy, and her cheeks like roses. The body had not decomposed even after three days nor did it give out the odor of death. Her daughters, unwilling to separate themselves from their Mother, passed day and night with the corpse, kissing it, and at times became convinced that she was still alive.

Mother Mariana, who knew that she had been judged, said nothing and permitted them to relieve their anguish at the feet of their Mother.

On the third day, they saw that a vein on her hand had swollen. Even though the body was still flexible and the face beautiful, it was necessary to bury her. They buried her in the lower choir with a nameplate stating that she was the Founder. The obsequies and funeral services were performed by the Friars Minor.

Her own heart pierced with pain as the body of her aunt was buried, Mother Mariana gave full vent to her grief. She shut herself up alone to weep at being left an orphan, and to pray to Her Divine Spouse, telling Him she could not bear to see her Mother in Purgatory.

## MOTHER MARIANA FREES THE SOUL OF MOTHER MARIA FROM PURGATORY

"My Love," she implored, "if Thou hast taken my Mother from this earth, let me see her in Heaven. Deliver the soul of my Mother, and thus will I know that Thou dost love me. Blot me out from the Book of Life so that her soul may soar to Heaven."

To these amorous prayers, Our Lord from the Tabernacle responded, "My daughter, continue your prayers and penances, and do everything with this intention for five days, and the soul of your Mother will soar to Heaven."

With what fervor did Mother Mariana offer all her actions of the next days to deliver the soul of her beloved aunt from Purgatory!

On the fifth day, after she had received Communion, the Abbess went into ecstasy during Mass. When the priest elevated the Sacred Host, she saw a most pure and beautiful dove rise up to Heaven. It was the soul of her aunt, Mother Maria, who said to Mother Mariana, "Thank you, my child, I am going to Heaven, where I will bless and help you."

Then she soared to Heaven, leaving Mother Mariana below to thank her Divine Spouse for having freed the soul of her beloved aunt from Purgatory. She also saw the immense glory she was now enjoying. From this day forward, God allowed the blessed soul of the Founder to communicate with Mother Mariana, who in her difficulties would consult the Founder, the consolation of this sad orphan who helped and consoled her from Heaven.

How abundantly God Our Lord recompenses the sacrifices made for His love! Also, how strictly he judges! When the soul stands before the Divine Presence, the slightest blemish calls for purification in order for it to be united with God!

Mother Maria was an extremely pure soul but she had greatly feared death. Mother Mariana had questioned her about this fear, asking if perhaps she still had an attachment to some earthly good.

"No, my daughter," she replied. "For having left my country and all that I had in Spain, I have neither longings for nor attachment to any earthly thing. I fear death because I know the great pain the soul feels upon leaving the body, and I fear that I lack the great strength needed at that hour." This was the temptation and suffering of this seraphic soul, for which she was purified in Purgatory.

After the death of her aunt, Mother Mariana was alone. Her sense of loss was indescribable, but her magnanimous soul supported this burden in silence. Instead of seeking solace, she was the consolation of the other sisters, who went to her to lament the loss of their Founder. She also offered consolation to various residents of Quito who mourned the death of their saintly Mother.

For all of them, Mother Maria had been the balsam that soothed the wounds of their hearts. In her seraphic charity, Mother Mariana did all that she could for everyone; she alone suffered in silence the immense void she felt at the loss of her Mother and Founder. The virtues of Mother Maria and the immense good she did for the Convent and the city of Quito are related in the chronicle and biography of her life.[27] Here we note only those things that relate to the life of Mother Mariana.

---

27. After the death of Mother Mariana de Jesus in 1634, the Franciscan Fathers undertook the responsibility of writing the biographies of all the Founding Mothers. The biographer of the first Abbess, Mother Maria of Jesus Taboada, was written by Fr. Michael Romero, who was her confessor and spiritual director. The Father Provincial Fr. Jeronimo Tamayo, wrote about Mothers Magdalena of Saint John, Maria of the Incarnation, and Catherine of the Conception. Fr. Louis Catena, who also held the office of Provincial in 1625, wrote the lives of Mothers Lucia of the Cross and Anna of the Conception. Fr. Martin de Ochoa related the lives of Mother Francisca of the Angels, and Mariana de Jesus Torres.

After the death of this illustrious Founder, Mother Mariana continued to govern the Convent with prudence, sweetness, and discernment. At the same time, she firmly demanded strict observance of the Rule in its first rigor. She was a victim of love for her Convent, the heroine who preserved the fervor and spirit of the Founder in her Community.

Mother Maria de Jesus Taboada, Founder, died on October 4 in the year 1593, 16 years after the foundation of the Convent.

\* \* \*

---

These biographies were preserved in a large volume of records, entitled el *Cuardernón* [the Grand Notebook], to which Fr. Manuel Souza Pereira had access when he wrote this biography of Mother Mariana de Jesus (Cadena y Almeida, *Madera para Esculpir la Imagen de una Santa*, pp. 173-5).

At the present time, the whereabouts of the *Cuadernón* is unknown, because it was hidden in some secret closet in the Convent for safekeeping during times of political unrest at the end of the 19th century. Mother Mariana de Jesus predicted its loss and also that it, along with other items, would be found in a miraculous way during the time of restoration of the Holy Church.

## Chapter 16

After the death of the Founding Mother, the plots of the rebellious sisters to separate the Convent from the rule of the Friars Minor started up again. During this epoch, the Monasteries and Convents, especially the Orders of the Preachers [Dominicans] and of Saint Catherine, had somewhat relaxed their rules. There were some lapses among the Franciscans who had slackened in the practice of angelic poverty and religious observance, but not to the same degree as the ones mentioned above.

The Friars Minor who governed the Convent of the Immaculate Conception were religious of great learning, virtue, and sanctity. Since they could not restrain the relaxation of the Conceptions, they prudently decided to step away from the direction of the Convent. They did not, however, renounce their complete jurisdiction in order to allow a return when the hour of God would come.

Indeed, there was a faction of sisters who were opposed to the strict observance of the Rule. They strove to put the Convent under the Bishop of Quito, and no longer the Franciscans, who led them in the right direction according to the spirit of the conventual life. This faction caused the Friars Minor to unwillingly make the decision to leave the government of the Conceptionist Convent.

Because of the opposition of this faction, the Friars Minor judged it prudent to reluctantly resign their direction of the Conceptionists. They did not, however, completely renounce their jurisdiction over the Convent so that they could maintain the holy freedom to return when the hour of God would arrive.

During this epoch, the Church was suffering greatly from excesses and irregularities in its ecclesiastical government. Discord reigned between the Bishop and the canons, and the suffering of the religious who were subjected to the Ordinary was indeed great.

The day feared by the daughters of the Immaculate Conception finally arrived. The announcement of the separation of the Franciscan friars broke the hearts of the faithful religious. On this woeful day, even Heaven seemed to commiserate with the grieving Conceptionists, for it sprinkled the whole day. Mother Mariana had the appearance of a corpse walking on thin air. She spoke with various officials in attempts to postpone the day when the Friars Minor would separate from the Convent. We will not refer to the details of this here, for we do not want to agitate the hearts of our newest religious who will read these lines.

What a terrible suffering for the innocent doves who had made their nest in the wounds of the Seraphim of Assisi!

### "THE FRANCISCAN FRIARS WILL RETURN"

On one of those bitter nights before the separation, Mother Mariana rose from her poor bed and went down to the choir where she prostrated herself on the sepulcher of her aunt, Mother Maria, as if, like another Eliseus, she would raise up the Founder. "I can no longer bear it, my Mother!" she pleaded. "Arise and support me!"

Then the Founder spoke these words to her: "My daughter, for a period of time this separation of the Franciscan Friars is necessary. Our Father Saint Francis dearly loves his Order, which is so beloved of God that He will never permit the great deviations that will be made in other Orders to occur in it. A golden era will arrive when the Friars Minor will return to govern my Convent. In those days to come, many holy religious of the Immaculate Conception will rise up. Suffer, my daughter. Through the course of the centuries, many will suffer in this Community, for the inheritance I have left my daughters is suffering and the summit of sorrow.

"The time will come when the religious will be stripped of all their temporal goods. During this epoch, the Community will receive many graces from Christ Our Lord directly through the Friars Minor and also through the Company of Jesus.[28]

"There will be a member of my Community who will steal away the crown [of glory] of the religious. Because of her imprudence and unenlightened spirit, she will be like one who is blind,

---

28. On June 25, 1902 the Law of the *Manos Muertas* [Dead Hands] was passed by the liberal, anticlerical government of President Eloy Alfaro. Under one of its provisions, the property of the clergy and religious was confiscated by the government. This law left cloistered Convents like the Conceptionist in a disastrous condition of begging their daily bread to survive. The majority of the religious communities, including the Conceptionist Convent, put up a heroic and sacrificial resistance to the pretensions of this Masonic government (Cadena y Almeida, *Mensaje Profetico*, pp. 46-56).

unable to see the things of God. With feigned virtue and misdirected zeal, she will make the Community suffer much and will take her complaints to the Bishop.[29] She will glorify herself for this, but the hour of God will arrive. For this religious will have a heart that is not spiritual. The religious under her rule will be mystical martyrs.

"The Franciscan friars will separate themselves from this Convent at a time when you will no longer be governing it, and the Abbess under whom this takes place will remain in Purgatory until the Day of Final Judgment.

"You should share your concerns with the other Founding Mothers, for they will also receive celestial visits. Speak especially to Mother Francisca of the Angels, for she will be your successor and will help you in everything. Now, rise up and continue to fulfill your obligations as Superior."

Mother Mariana rose and went to prostrate herself before the Most Holy Sacrament, where she prayed to be united to her Mother, asking Our Lord to take her from this earth. A refulgent light issued from the Tabernacle, and she heard these words, "My daughter, it behooves Me to not allow the Friars Minor to separate themselves from the Convent during your time as Abbess." [30]

Mother Mariana then asked Our Lord to not take Mother Francisca to join their Founder in Heaven. For this religious had been praying to Our Lord to permit her to die rather than live to see the Convent's separation from the Friars Minor. Our Lord responded, "Command her under obedience not to ask me for death."

Mother Mariana left the choir. Finding Mother Francisca, she ordered her as her Abbess, "I command you, under obedience, to no longer ask for your death from God Our Lord, for you must stay here and assist me in all that takes place."

---

29. Msgr. Cadena y Almeida proposes that this sister is the rebellious non-observant sister called "the Captain," who caused the Community to suffer much by the division of its members, the scandal caused inside and outside the Convent, and her mendacious and calumnious complaints to the Bishop about Mother Mariana and the Spanish Founding Mothers (*Mensaje Profetico*, pp. 39-40). However, it is quite possible that this prophecy could be referring to a sister who instigated a great spiritual damage in times more recent, for it would appear that she had a position of command inside the Convent, which the captain never officially had.

30. The separation of the Friars Minor took place in 1601 at the time that Mother Magdalena of Valenzuela was exercising her first term as Abbess.

Mother Francisca bowed her head, kissed the scapular of the Abbess, and accepted this command. Mother Mariana then spoke to her of the sufferings that they, united in spirit, would endure as victims of seraphic love.

### SATANIC ONSLAUGHT AND THE APPARITION OF SAINT GABRIEL

One night, as was her custom, Mother Mariana was making the Way of the Cross, carrying the cross and wearing a crown of thorns and an iron chain in order to imitate her Divine Spouse. Suddenly, in the lower cloisters that leads to the choir, a sea of fire surged before her, a terrible bottomless fire with an incommensurable width that prevented her from taking another step.

Shocked at this terrible sight, the innocent virgin then heard horrible voices issuing from the ocean of fire, saying, "This is the place we want to bury this wicked Convent. But these miserable sisters hold us back, especially that one heinous sister whom we will bury here." At that moment, two enormous black mastiffs jumped out of the flames. With one on each side of Mother Mariana, the huge creatures tried to suffocate her.

But she called out, "Star of the sea, Most Holy Mary of Good Success, help me!"

"At that very instant," the Abbess later recounted, "I saw a star as large as the choir ceiling, refulgent and diffusing great rays of light. In the center of this star the name Mary was inscribed. From it came a golden canoe imbedded with emeralds and precious stones. An Angel guided this small vessel to my side and told me, 'I am the Archangel Gabriel, sent by your Mother, Mary of Good Success, to help you.' Then he set me, along with the cross I was carrying and all the symbols of the Passion, into the canoe. He added, 'This canoe signifies your long life.'"

The Archangel steered their small vessel through the ocean of fire. As they proceeded, Mother Mariana underwent the same sufferings and combats she had experienced on the ocean coming from Spain. After crossing this ocean, the Archangel placed her on the firm ground of the cloister, where he knelt and prayed a Hail Mary.

"Mortal man can never even begin to understand all the grandeur contained in the angelic salutation," said Saint Gabriel.

Then he disappeared, and with him, the sea of fire, and all returned to normal. Mother Mariana went to the upper choir to await her sisters for the recitation of the Little Office.

How all of Hell wars against the recitation of the Little Office of Mary Most Holy! And what marvels that great Queen works so that it might continue to be said!

The holy Founding Mothers, who suffered so much to preserve that practice, guaranteed that this early morning psalmody is what preserves the Convent. When it would no longer be sung, then the religious spirit would be lost.

Woe to this Convent if, when our newest sisters read these lines, they do not preserve this holy devotion and custom! We beg all who follow us to sacrifice their sleep in order to rise and pray this Office at 4 a.m. with the devotion and the fervor of the Founding Mothers. Then, they will see how the spirit of the Community, perhaps dying, will be restored!

### Mother Mariana Hears the Voice of Our Lord

On another night, the holy Abbess was praying in the upper choir when she heard a frightful roar and terrible sounds that seemed to demolish the very foundation of the chapel. Frightened, she felt herself being overtaken by a terrible despair, and she ran to prostrate herself at the foot of the Tabernacle. With her forehead on the ground, she begged mercy from her Divine Spouse. "What terrible thing is this that I am hearing?" she asked.

From the Sacrarium, Our Lord replied, "My child, what you are hearing in the spirit is what your successors will suffer materially. For the time will come when the devils will try to demolish this Convent, availing themselves of both good and evil persons to achieve that end. But they will not succeed so long as the spirit of sacrifice remains. To maintain it, interior victims are needed.

"Now, my daughter, you should prepare yourself to receive a visit from my Most Holy Mother, a visit that I desire to bestow upon you."

Mother Mariana was so filled with joy that morning at choir that Mother Francisca asked her, "What has happened to you, my Mother, to give you such happiness?"

Then Mother Mariana related the great favor she would receive, and the two seraphic souls conversed together, assisting and supporting each other in the accomplishment of the divine will.   Later, Our Lord made Mother Mariana know how holy poverty was relaxed among the Franciscans. "Speak with the friars, my daughter," He told her, "and try to remedy these abuses by your sacrifices."

Mother Mariana did this and increased her sacrifices for these intentions, for truly she was a victim of love for her Seraphic Order.

\* \* \*

## Chapter 17

At this time, the state of the poor Colony was one of sadness and affliction, primarily because the ecclesiastic and civil governments were the target of many bad rumors. The incursions of the Spanish into the South caused chaos and crimes too horrible to relate.

The Church and the Country had a great need for heroic souls who, by their practice of solid virtue, would stand between the sinful Colony and Divine Justice, thus preventing these lands from being covered by a great deluge as just punishment for their crimes. For even the religious communities, and especially the orders for men, were not as observant and holy as the religious and sacerdotal state demands.

The cause of this relaxation in the monasteries of the friars was due to the fact that Spain, like other countries, was sending their undisciplined and disruptive friars to the Colony. These insubordinate men would not subject themselves to the monastic rules of their monasteries and were sent overseas as punishment. It is easy to imagine how members of such communities might act.

Such was the state of affairs in the Colony at this time when, in silent recollection in the cloisters of the Immaculate Conception, truly holy souls lived. Without these heroic souls, Quito would have already ceased to exist. Standing out eminently among these sacrificial souls was Mother Mariana de Jesus Torres, who, hidden behind those four walls like a humble violet, perfumed with her sufferings the corrupt ambience of the Colony.

She suffered for the offenses made to the Divine Majesty, for the loss of so many souls, and for the internal turmoil in her own Convent, where some few members were antagonistic to the Seraphic Family. Since the death of their Founder Mother Maria de Jesus Taboada, these non-observant sisters had been persistently striving to throw off the yoke of holy obedience.

This was the state of affairs in the year 1594, when Mother Mariana de Jesus Torres was at the head of the Community, governing it with as much discernment, prudence, and charity as an

Abbess of much greater maturity and experience.[31] For this young religious had received the gift to govern directly from God and from His Immaculate Mother! One could say that Jesus and Mary were presiding over this Convent so beloved by Divine Goodness, this Convent which will always be persecuted and calumniated until the end of time.

In face of these bitter sufferings that weighed like incandescent shackles on the holy Abbess, she was a strong branch of the Seraphic Tree. Even when she was whipped by terrible gales, she did not waver, firmly embedded on this trunk with its life-giving sap. During the turbulent storms, she would have recourse to Jesus, Mary, and her Father, the Seraphic Stigmatic, to find light, consolation, strength, perseverance, and relief.

Thus, on the morning of February 2, 1594, with a heart filled with bitterness and pain, Mother Mariana was praying prostrate on the ground in the upper choir of this blessed Convent.[32] She was beseeching Our Lord, through the intercession of His Blessed Mother, to stop these trials through which her beloved Convent was passing and for an end to the many sins being committed in the world.

### FIRST APPARITION OF OUR LADY OF GOOD SUCCESS

During this long penitential act, she perceived the presence of someone before her. Her heart was perturbed, but a sweet voice called her name. She rose rapidly and saw before her a most beautiful Lady, who carried the Child Jesus in her left arm and, in

---

31. By this time, the number of Convent inhabitants had risen to 300: 120 professed religious, and 180 others – *donadas* (a kind of third order sister), daughters of Quito inhabitants who were there for education and formation, and servants. Among such a large number, it is very easy for factions to form, which is what had happened. Some of the native sisters were resentful of the strict observance of the Rule that the Spanish sisters insisted upon, and wanted to introduce relaxations into the monastic life in the Convent. Knowing this was impossible so long as the Convent was under Franciscan rule, they sought to change its jurisdiction and put the Convent under the Bishop Ordinary (Cadena y Almeida, *Mensaje Profetico de la Sierva de Dios Sor Mariana Francisca de Jesus Torres y Berriochoa*, Quito, 1989, p. 34).

32. The place chosen for the apparition was the upper choir, where the whole community of professed sisters congregate to fulfill their primary obligation of praying the Divine Office.

her right, a polished gold crosier adorned with precious stones of unearthly beauty.

Her heart was filled with an indescribable and holy happiness and such an immense love of God that it seemed insupportable and she thought she would die of joy, she later told her spiritual director. In this holy transport of joy and happiness, she asked the Lady, "Beautiful Lady, who art thou and what dost thou want? Dost thou not know that I am but a poor sister, filled with love of God, most surely, but also overflowing with pain and sorrow?"

To this the Lady responded: "I am Mary of Good Success, the Queen of Heaven and Earth. It is because you are a religious soul filled with love of God and His Mother that I am speaking to you now. I have come from Heaven to console your afflicted heart. Your prayers, tears, and penances are most pleasing to our celestial Father. The Holy Ghost Who consoles your spirit and sustains you in your just tribulations formed from three drops of the Blood of my Heart the most beautiful Child of mankind. For nine months, I, Virgin and Mother, carried Him in my most pure womb. In the stable in Bethlehem, I gave birth to Him and lay Him to rest on the cold straw.

"As His Mother, I carry Him here, in my left arm, so that together we might restrain the hand of Divine Justice, which is always so ready to chastise this unfortunate and criminal world.

"In my right hand, I carry the crosier that you see, for I desire to govern this Convent as Abbess and Mother. Soon the Franciscan friars will no longer govern this Convent, which is why my patronage and protection are more necessary than ever, for this difficult trial will last for centuries. With this separation, Satan will begin to try to destroy this work of God, making use of my ungrateful daughters. But he will not succeed, because I am the Queen of Victories and the Mother of Good Success, and it is under this invocation I desire to be known throughout time for the preservation of my Convent and of its inhabitants.[33]

---

33. Thirty years later, on February 2, 1634, the miraculous statue of Our Lady of Good Success was christened with holy oils and placed on the Abbess chair in the upper choir. She will remain Abbess and Mother of the Conceptionist Convent in Quito, offering consolation and assistance to her daughters there until the end of time. She foretold that she would become known under this invocation in the 20th century, and would offer her assistance to those who invoked her under

"In all times until the end of the world, I will have holy daughters, heroic souls in this Convent who will suffer persecutions and calumnies within the very bosom of their Community. They will be the object of the complaisance and love of God and His Mother. We shall personally console them, for they are destined to be familiar with us by means of their external manifestations.

"Like strong, stout columns, they will sustain the Community in troubled times. Their lives of prayer, self-denial, and penance will be most needed during each period. After having lived on this earth unknown, they will rise to Heaven to occupy high thrones of glory and receive the palms and crowns of virgins and martyrs of penance and love of God.[34]

"Now I desire to give you strength and encouragement. Do not allow suffering to discourage you. For you will live a long time on this earth for the glory of God and His Mother, who speaks to you now.[35] My Most Holy Son desires to give you every type of suffering. And to infuse you with the valor that you will need, I take Him from my arms. Receive Him in your own. Hold Him to your weak and imperfect heart."

The Most Holy Virgin placed the Divine Child in the arms of the happy religious, who embraced Him next to her heart and caressed him fondly. As she did so, she felt within herself a strong desire to suffer.

---

this title. For more on the prophecies of Our Lady of Good Success concerning the crisis in the Church in the 20th century, see Marian T. Horvat, *Our Lady of Good Success: Prophecies for Our Times*, (Los Angeles; TIA, 2000).

34. Our Lady promised Mother Mariana that there would be at least one faithful sister in this Convent throughout time. These faithful sisters, she foretold, who would suffer greatly – even by the hands of their own sisters, would sustain the Community in the bitter times ahead. The life of Mother Mariana and the Founding Mothers are examples of this. For this reason, the Community recorded the names of favored sisters and extraordinary incidents in the Convent chronicles. To the disgrace of History, large lacunas appear in these records due to the lack of care of Abbesses and religious responsible for the execution of this order. (Cadena y Almeida, *Mensaje Profetico*, pp. 61-65).

35. Mother Mariana de Jesus died at age 72 on January 16, 1635. As Our Lady foretold, she suffered much during her long exile on earth as an expiatory victim for her own sisters and Convent, and also as a victim soul for the 20th century, a time when heresies, blasphemies, and impurity would abound in the spiritual and temporal spheres.

This visit from the Queen of Heaven lasted until three o'clock in the morning.[36] Throughout the apparition, lights emanated from Mary Most Holy, the true Dawn, and from the Sun of Justice, her Son, resplendent with an unearthly brightness. When this Dawn and Sun had gone, everything around her was again darkness and night.

Mother Mariana rose from the place where she had been praying, walked through the grille gates of the upper choir, entered to the right, and took her seat as Abbess to watch over her daughters who were coming to pray the Little Office, so pleasing to Mary Most Holy.

The sisters arrived and began their morning prayers, but they noticed the transformation of their Abbess. Without understanding why, they felt their hearts inflamed with love of God and Mary Most Holy, and they prayed with greater than usual fervor.

As she prayed, Mother Francisca of the Angels was given to understand that her Mother had just received some important grace, and she gave thanks to the Divine Goodness. Later that day, she asked the Abbess if she could know this great privilege. Mother Mariana de Jesus told her briefly what had occurred. Then these two seraphic souls conversed together, thanking Our Lord for this manifestation of His great love for their Convent.

From that happy day of February 2, 1594, when this apparition of the Mother of Good Success to her chosen daughter took place, Mother Mariana de Jesus felt herself reinvigorated and inflamed with the love of God. She enjoyed an imperturbable interior peace, with both her soul and body reflecting the grandeur of the grace she had received.

The time was arriving when her three-year term as Abbess would end, an office she had exercised without ever having committed the least fault. For she had meticulously observed and

---

36. After this apparition in 1594, Our Lady of Good Success often favored Mother Mariana de Jesus with visits on February 2 until the end of her life. The Postulator for the Cause of her Beatification, Msgr. Cadena y Almeida, counts the number of visits as 40, for in some years she would receive more than one (*La Mujer y la Monja Extraordinaria*, p. 40). Many of these visits and the prophecies of Our Lady of Good Success will be related in Volume II of this work by Fr. Sousa Pereira. See also Horvat, *Our Lady of Good Success: Prophecies for Our Times*, passim.

enforced strict monastic silence, exact observance of the Rule and vows, and especially the rule of perfect enclosure.

### Mother Mariana Hears the Voice of the Holy Ghost

Nine days before the election of the new Abbess, Mother Mariana began a novena to the Holy Ghost, begging Him to enlighten souls to make the right choice. On the seventh day, during her fervent prayer, she felt a strong wind, like the one on the day of Pentecost when the Holy Ghost descended upon the Apostles. She saw refulgent rays illuminating the whole room.

A voice emanating from this shining light said: "I am He Who gives My seven gifts and twelve fruits. I take my repose in pure souls as on a bed of roses and lilies. Now, I come with the gift of fortitude to give new strength to your soul, for the time of your great sufferings is at hand, when, step by step, you will imitate the life of your Crucified Spouse. The sufferings awaiting you are so great that without the gift of fortitude to support you, your life would end. For soon the Franciscan friars will surrender their government over the Convent of the Immaculate Conception, and you will be persecuted, slandered, and imprisoned."

Saying this, the refulgent light dissolved, and Mother Mariana fell to the ground in a faint.

When the religious saw that their Abbess did not appear, they looked for her everywhere. Not finding her, they became quite anxious until Mother Francisca of the Angels found her lying on the floor of the balcony as if she were dead. The vision had taken place in the lower choir where the Abbess customarily made her penances and prayers. After her first swoon, she had managed to rise and had reached the balcony before she again fell to the ground senseless. It was there that the religious found her.

The sisters asked Mother Francisca, the nurse, to administer to their Abbess. Mother Francisca applied some aromatic oils to try to bring her back to consciousness. But she sensed that this mysterious illness was not of a physical nature. To herself, she was thinking, "I do these things to no avail. For Mother is suffering from something supernatural."

When Mother Mariana did not regain consciousness, the sisters became increasingly upset. Concerned about the growing disturbance, Mother Francisca beseeched God Our Lord to bring the Abbess to herself. Immediately, Mother Mariana opened her beautiful eyes and fixed them on the four non-observant religious who were there in the room. But these sisters could not bear her gaze, and they slowly eased themselves out of the room. The sisters who shared their spirit of non-observance followed them.

When Mother Mariana was finally alone with Mother Francisca, she reprimanded the nurse sweetly, "Why did you try to cure me with these things, my daughter? You may offend against the spirit of poverty so beloved by our Father, Saint Francis!"

Mother Francisca responded, "I was compelled to do so by the other sisters. For how can they know what happens to you? I beg you now to tell me what has taken place, for your countenance was as pale as death."

"My child," replied Mother Mariana. "our Father Saint Francis is indignant and has a complaint with the Convent, for some ungrateful daughters will soon throw off the yoke of obedience to the Seraphic Family, laid out by Our Holy Father Julian II in the Rule for the Religious of the Immaculate Conception."

Hearing this, Mother Francisca, in union with Mother Mariana, began to weep. These two seraphic souls went to unburden their hearts before the Blessed Sacrament, Mother Francisca supporting Mother Mariana, who was still too weak to walk alone. At the hour of choir, Mother Mariana took her place to preside over it.

\* \* \*

## Chapter 18

The day to choose a new Abbess arrived. While the religious were well aware of the outstanding merits of Mother Mariana – who should have been re-elected in order to maintain the splendor of observance to the Rule – some of the sisters allowed themselves to be deceived by the Devil, who wanted to extinguish this shining light.

Under the influence of the non-observant sisters, who wanted a greater relaxation in conventual life and to enjoy the favors of the family of Mother Magdalena de Valenzuela, who held high positions in the ecclesiastical government of Quito, the vote took place with only two candidates: Mother Mariana de Jesus and Mother Valenzuela. With great grief, the Franciscan friars received word that Mother Valenzuela had been chosen Abbess, for they highly esteemed Mother Mariana and the Convent of the Immaculate Conception.

With profound humility, Mother Mariana rendered obedience and handed over the office to Mother Valenzuela.[37] Thenceforth, she became the object of scorn, mockery, persecution, and calumny in the Convent that she had founded. She was falsely accused of serious neglects during her Abbacy, but this prudent virgin sealed her lips and did not defend herself.

### The Friars Minor Are Dismissed from the Convent of the Immaculate Conception

Like a flash of lightning, Mother Valenzuela set to work to free the Convent from its obedience to the Franciscan friars and subject it to the Ordinary. In a short time, she managed to succeed in this. The dire day finally arrived when the Friars Minor were sent away. Before they took their leave, the Father Provincial and other friars met together with the sisters. They gave a moving talk to the Community in the lower choir, showing how holy observance had progressed under their direction since the first day of the founda-

---

37. She exercised the office of Abbess for the first time from 1601 to 1603.

tion. They explained that they were leaving now not by order of the ecclesiastic authority, but of their own will in order to avoid greater spiritual damage to the non-observant sisters.

The Provincial then knelt down and, with his arms in a cross, thanked Mother Mariana and all the observant sisters. He gave them a special blessing and told them, "Our separation will not last forever. We will not see the days of our return, but our successors will again come to govern our beloved Convent of the Immaculate Conception in better days than these. The Rule from our Holy Father Pope Julian II will be observed and there will be many holy religious."

Mother Mariana and the observant sisters, especially the Spanish Founding Mothers, were engulfed in tears. The Provincial told them, "We will record and preserve for posterity these tears, this date, and this event in the archives of our Seraphic Order."

After tenderly blessing the religious faithful to the Rule, especially Mother Mariana, he turned to the non-observant sisters, directing to them words of malediction that would be fulfilled for some even in life, and for others at the hour of death.

The non-observant sisters asked to speak alone with the Father Provincial, but he refused, turning his back to them and leaving them with these last words, "No one is a prophet in his own country." With this, he took his leave, leaving Mother Mariana and the rest of the Founding Mothers in cruel agony. Even the elements of nature joined in the lamentations of the innocent doves who cried at being set adrift from the Franciscan Order. The weather was dreary and the sun refused to illuminate that ill-fated day.

After the separation from the Friars Minor, the direction of the Convent was handed over to the Bishop,[38] and Mother Mariana and her companions submitted docilely to this hard trial. The non-observant sisters now saw themselves free from the yoke of the Friars Minor, who had watched over them with charity. The observance of the Rule began to decay, strict silence disappeared, and lapses occurred in the matter of enclosure. In short, the relaxation of monastic perfection had begun.

---

38. He is referring to His Excellency Bishop Luis López de Solís, who governed the Diocese of Quito from 1594 to 1606.

### THE IMPRISONMENT OF MOTHER MARIANA

Seeing this, Mother Mariana's heart was torn. Feeling obliged to address this situation as a Founder and ex-Abbess, she went to Mother Valenzuela, her Abbess. With profound humility she made her see how the non-observant sisters should be curbed. The result of her efforts was more humiliation.[39] When the Prelate heard this, he ordered that Mother Mariana should be imprisoned for three days: Her veil was to be taken from her, and she should receive the public discipline and eat on the floor in the refectory on each of these days.

The innocent dove was locked in the lower floor prison, near the lower choir. Each day Mother Mariana was taken to the refectory without her veil and the discipline was applied to her before the eyes of the Community. Then she was made to take her meal on the floor, as the non-observant sisters mocked and derided her. The innocent virgin did not raise her eyes. Fixing them on the ground, she humbled herself in order to imitate her Divine Spouse. For these three days, she was also deprived of attending Mass and receiving Holy Communion.

At the end of the three days, they took her from the prison, assigned her a despicable cell, and forbade her to speak with her sisters, watching to see that no one spoke to her. But the Spanish Founding Mothers could not endure this suffering and gave vent to their grief with Mother Mariana. A new order soon came from the Prelate commanding that they should all be imprisoned together for one month.

Thus the innocent doves were imprisoned in that dark, basement prison, deprived of the Sacraments, Holy Mass, and the

---

39. The leader of the non-observant faction, whom the Convent charitably records as simple "the captain," sent a message to the Bishop saying that Mother Mariana was interfering with the government of the Convent and making other false accusations The chief accusation that led the ecclesiastical authority to order the incarceration of Mother Mariana was that she was stirring up resistance to the new spiritual government that had passed to the hands of the Bishop. The letter containing this calumny and others was delivered to the office of the Bishop, who was making an apostolic visit to his Diocese at that time. The reply and order came from the hand of his representative, Don Cristóbal Loarte, the Vicar General of the Diocese, who was related to the sister called the captain. (Cadena y Almeida, *Mensaje Profetico*, pp. 32-4).

Divine Office. The non-observant sisters had also wanted to deprive them of their habits and veils, but the Prelate would not permit this, saying that their habits could not be taken since they were the Founding Mothers. Therefore, only their veils were confiscated.

The captive heroines passed their time in prayer and recollection, making the prison an antechamber of Heaven. The victims could leave only to go to the refectory. They were allowed to wear only the novice veils and made to eat what little was given to them on the floor amid derision and disdain. They would then return to the prison to continue their way of the cross.

Although Mother Mariana was the consolation of her daughters, she could not bear to see them deprived of Holy Mass and the praying of the Divine Office. She wrote a note to the Bishop asking him to allow them to assist at Holy Mass and to pray the Divine Office.

"If it were only I alone," she wrote, "I would endure this silently, as I did before. But I cannot see my daughters and sisters suffer this injustice being dealt to the Spanish Founding Mothers in this Colony." Mother Mariana also asked for the passports for her and all the Founding Mothers to return to Spain, taking with them the remains of Mother Maria Taboada, her aunt.

The non-observant sisters did not want to deliver this note to the Bishop. Mother Mariana left the prison and humbly presented herself before the Abbess, telling her that she could not be prevented from directing herself to the Superior and that she, as Founder, could close down the Convent. Hearing this, the non-observant faction became fearful and granted her request, that is, that she might go personally to the turn-box to send her note to the Bishop and receive his response in her own hands.

This was done, and in his reply the Prelate told her that the complaints against the Spanish Mothers had been so many and were so serious that they must remain imprisoned for the prescribed month, but that he would permit them to assist at Mass and pray the Divine Office. The innocent captives rejoiced to hear this. Their number was fifteen, seven Spanish Founding Mothers and another eight sisters formed by Mother Mariana.

The other observant sisters in the Convent suffered immensely at seeing the injustices and torments inflicted on Mother

Mariana and her companions. When they walked through the lower choir, they would make sounds as they neared the prison so that those inside could hear them. Distressed, they went to the Abbess and asked her to be less severe on their imprisoned sisters. Seeing such humility, modesty, and holiness in these religious who had been accused of serious crimes, even the sisters who were opposed to the prisoners felt inclined to support their position, but they did not do so out of human respect.

In fact, the sisters who supported the holy virgins were themselves taken to prison, so that the number of religious imprisoned for love of the holy observance of the Rule rose to 25.

These imprisoned sisters participated in the Community prayers and assisted at Holy Mass in the lower choir. In the refectory they received penances as if they were novices and were made to eat on the floor, receiving offenses and scorn. In response to such bad treatment, they kissed the feet of the sisters of the Community with such humility and fraternal love that the persecutors themselves were impressed to see their serene and peaceful faces, joyfully suffering persecution, scorn, and calumny from their own sisters.

After the hour of refectory, they would return to the prison and be consoled by their holy Mother Mariana, who would address celestial words to them. Within the blessed walls of that prison, they followed the community life prescribed by the Rule. They requested the Abbess to give them work that they might do for the Convent so that they could work during the hours prescribed for labor. This she did, and these abnegated spouses of Christ sewed and mended the clothing of their persecutors.

They prayed the Divine Office together and sang the divine praises, giving joy to the Heart of their Beloved Spouse. Deprived of Holy Communion, they suffered this indescribable loss without making the least complaint. Their consolation lay in prayer and sacrifice. Nourished by the sweet liqueur of seraphic love, they displayed a disarming serenity and kindness of spirit amid these terrible sufferings. By their resignation and practice of all the virtues, they converted the prison into a Heaven, inhabited by angels.

The Abbess, Mother Magdalena de Jesus Valenzuela, by nature had a tender heart, and she should have taken pity on the sufferings of her daughters. But she lacked strength of character and was quite soft. Thus, she did nothing to stop the non-observant sisters from tormenting these innocent victims.

At times, however, she would go to visit them in the prison and console them. She was always received with great love. The prisoners would prostrate themselves at her feet and bathe them in tears. With compassion, the Abbess would also weep, but she did not have the courage to face the non-observant faction and alleviate their torments. For God so desired to sanctify His spouses with this most difficult trial.

When the day finally arrived for them to leave the prison, the Abbess presented them with fruit as a kind of amends for the suffering of these victims of observance and seraphic love.

When a certain Canon heard about the persecution of the Conceptionist virgins, he went to the Convent to remove them from prison and take them to the northern part of the Colony where he lived. He was quite wealthy and wanted to build a magnificent convent on his best lands and provide it with all that was necessary, on the condition that Mother Mariana and her 25 companions would go there to found a Convent of the Immaculate Conception, for such was the fame of the great holiness of Mother Mariana and her daughters. He told the sisters that he would write to the King of Spain to receive permission to carry out this plan.

"I know that Mother Mariana de Jesus is imprisoned here with her companions," he told the sisters. "How could you do this?"

But the sisters denied it, saying that this was a false rumor.

He replied, "Then let Mother Mariana come to speak with me."

But the sisters made an excuse, saying that Mother Mariana could not come at that moment because of some work that she was doing...

The Canon left, but he returned again and insisted on speaking with Mother Mariana. The sisters, however, told him that he had to have permission from the ecclesiastic authority.

* * *

## Chapter 19

While these unworthy sisters conspired to torment the daughters of the Immaculate Conception with scorn, calumnies, and others sufferings, the imprisoned spouses of the Lamb imitated their Divine Model with sacrifices, penances, prayers, and a life of continual immolation. Thus they placated Divine Justice angered by so many crimes committed in the Colony and by the relaxations being allowed in the Convent. The victims pleaded for pardon and mercy for their sisters. By their prayers and sacrifices, these sacred cloisters of the Immaculate Conception were preserved.

During this difficult trial, the dark prison was visited and sanctified by the presence of God Himself, His Blessed Mother, our Seraphic Father Saint Francis, the apostle of love Saint John the Evangelist, and the Angels, as we shall see below.

### The Miraculous Cross of Heavenly Brilliance

One night while Mother Mariana was praying in her prison bed, the cross painted in the cavity of the wall above her bed became illuminated with heavenly brilliance, making the prison more luminous than the sun. [40]

It wakened all the captive sisters, who asked Mother Mariana, "My Mother, what is happening?"

"My daughters," she responded, "we must thank God Our Lord for consoling those who suffer persecution for justice's sake."

As she spoke, the cross began to grow until it had reached the actual size of the one upon which the God-Man was crucified. At that moment all the Spanish Founding Mothers went into ecstasy, each one being favored with a different vision.

### Words of Our Lord to Mother Mariana

Mother Mariana saw Our Lord Crucified as He was on Golgotha, agonizing and with blood pouring from His wounds. She heard the insults and blasphemies of the Jews.

---

40. This vision took place one night in early May of the year 1601.

Seeing the immense pain His tears caused Mother Mariana, Our Lord told her: "These wounds were opened in Me by the non-observant religious who revolted against obedience to the Franciscan friars, and I will feel this pain in all the future centuries so long as the Convent remains separated from the jurisdiction of the Friars Minor. For throughout time, there will be unworthy daughters who will revolt against the Seraphic Order. But there will also be souls intensely devoted to the Seraphic family who will take great care to carry out the holy Rule."

### SAINT FRANCIS PUNISHES THE NON-OBSERVANT NUNS

Mother Francisca of the Angels saw our Seraphic Father Saint Francis angry with the Convent. Carrying a bow in his hand, he was walking through the cloisters, shooting arrows left and right. One of the arrows pierced the heart of a sister, who died instantly, without anyone knowing the cause.

Then Saint Francis told Mother Francisca, "This sister was the primary cause for the separation of the Friars Minor and the relaxation in the Convent. Upon her weighs all the sufferings and lack of observance of future centuries until that time when the Convent returns to the jurisdiction of the Seraphic family with the exact observance of the Rule given by Pope Julian II. Nonetheless, I will watch that, throughout time, there will always be souls here devoted to the Seraphic Order. By their penitent and abnegated lives, these souls will sustain the regular observance of the Convent."

That morning when the happy prisoners went to Holy Mass, they heard a great commotion in the Community and saw doctors entering to examine a sister who had died during the night. She was believed to have suffered an apoplexy attack, for her face was black and purple of hue.

After the doctors declared that she was dead, the innocent prisoners were released to carry out the body and prepare it for burial. How great was the sorrow of Mother Francisca to bear on her shoulders the body of her persecutor, whom she loved with an angelic love and whose fate she had foreseen in the vision she had been given on that blessed night in prison.

## Our Lady Extinguishes the Light of the Most Blessed Sacrament

Mother Anna of the Conception saw our Immaculate Mother extinguish the sanctuary light of the Blessed Sacrament. As she did so, she told Mother Anna: "My daughter, thus will the spirit of my daughters be extinguished until the Friars Minor return to govern this Convent. For I will always have ungrateful daughters who will violate the spirit of the Seraphic Family – some, through ignorance; others, through weakness; and yet others, through malice.

"But I will also have holy daughters who, loving my Immaculate Conception and my servant Francis, will be firm columns that will preserve the Convent here in the heart of the city where it was founded in order to appease Divine Justice for the crimes committed in it. The infernal serpent will try to destroy this Convent, making use of persons distinguished in learning and virtue, but I will not permit this. For, throughout time, I will have innocent, penitent, abnegated, and faithful daughters who will attract the gaze of God and of His Immaculate Mother and who will be known only by God."

That morning, at Holy Mass, the lamp of the Blessed Sacrament was found extinguished. Despite the efforts of many persons both inside and outside the Convent to light it, for one day and one night it remained dark, even when the non-observant sisters changed the container, wick, and oil.

On the second day, the lamp lighted by itself, undoubtedly because of the early morning sacrifices of the captive victims who had attracted the mercy of Our Lord for this Convent.

## Our Lord Appears to Mother Lucia of the Cross

Mother Lucia of the Cross saw the Most Holy Humanity of Our Lord Jesus Christ. In her vision of the God-Man, she saw His Divine Heart surrounded by thorns and beating violently with love for mankind. His Blood ran in torrents until it flooded the courtyards and cloisters of the Convent, converting it into an ocean of blood.

Our Lord told her, "In this ocean of Blood, My Heart wants to wash the guilty sisters who will return to Me with contrite hearts."

The servant of God then saw all the religious, both faithful and unfaithful, who would ever inhabit these cloisters until the end of time. She saw that through the course of the centuries, some of the guilty sisters would be washed in the Blood of the Divine Heart of Jesus.

### Apparition of Saint John the Apostle

Mother Magdalena of Saint John saw the Apostle of Love, Saint John the Evangelist, who smiled lovingly at her. He revealed to her that on the night of the Last Supper, when he was reclining on the breast of his Master, one of the secrets he was given to know was that of the foundation of this Convent so beloved by Christ, and that in it there would be Eucharistic souls who would make expiation for the sacrileges committed against the Divine Victim.

Mother Magdalena then saw a terrible sacrilege that would be committed in the city of Riobamba. The country, which would then be called the Republic of Ecuador, appeared as a Calvary, and the city of Riobamba, a Golgotha. In this city, she saw a Eucharistic victim making expiation through the violence of his sorrowful love. The Sacred Hosts were being trampled upon by the filthy feet of criminal sons, who would cause the cruel and ignominious death of a Jesuit priest, whose just soul would ascend immediately to Heaven without passing through Purgatory even before the Eucharistic profanations that caused his martyrdom would end on earth

She then saw a person going up and down the streets of the city of Riobamba. When his friends inquired how he was, he replied merrily, "Very well, for I have spent the most enjoyable evening of my life catching friars!" And he continued his jaunt through the outskirts of the city until a beam from a construction site fell on his head, killing him instantly, and his miserable soul descended to Hell.

Mother Magdalena then saw the reparations that the simple people of the country would make. She also saw their Convent of Conceptionists in Riobamba with all the persons who would inhabit it during that time. She saw the tears, prayers, and expiations that the unblemished spouses of the Lamb would make inside the cloister's silent walls rising like the smoke of incense in the solitude of a temple, placating God Our Lord. The day was bleak and rainy, the elements of nature manifested the sadness of the day, weeping for this nameless sacrilege made against their Creator.

Saint John then told her that atonement would be made for this public sacrilege and for the many hidden profanations to which the Sacred Eucharist was victim. And she understood that a Convent of the Immaculate Conception had been chosen by God to make amends for that crime of May 4.[41]

She also saw all the penances and public acts of humility of the religious who would make reparation for this and many sins of the times. She saw a penitential procession taking place with the sisters carrying the insignias of the Passion. In a transport of joy, Mother Magdalena exclaimed, "How I would like to live in those happy times in order to join my sisters and be with them in this act of reparation!"

She further saw that unless such amends had been made, the guilty Republic of Ecuador would have suffered a great chastisement of a total deluge. But she also saw that the sacrifices of the Conceptionist virgins of this Convent would appease the divine anger and that God Our Lord would be pleased with these annual acts of reparation.

She moreover understood that, with the passage of time, a religious soul would become bad. With steadfast cunning, she would try to end the reparation and public penances in the refectory, as well as the penitential procession, the practices that sustained the Convent. I pray that she return to her senses and beg mercy from God!

The Holy Apostle told her that God would be pleased with this procession and pledged to never deny anything so long as it was made with the true and proper spirit, and that the names

---

41. The horrendous crime that Saint John foretold took place 300 years later in Riobamba on May 4, 1897. A soldier broke into the Chapel of the College of Saint Philip, and attacked and wounded Fr. Emilio Moscoso, S.J., who died trying to defend the Most Holy Sacrament. The wretched criminal entered the Sacristy, emptied the chalices, stamped on the Sacred Hosts, and then drank spirits from the chalices. In 1900, Sister Francisca of the Wounds founded the Congregation of Franciscan Mothers of the Immaculata as national reparation for this unpardonable sacrilege (Cadena y Almeida, *Mensaje Profetico*, pp. 87-8).

Mother Mariana and the Founding Mothers grieved to realize this horrendous crime, and also the countless sacrileges that would be committed against Our Lord in the Blessed Sacrament in the 20th century.

of those who took part in it carrying the cross and insignia of the Passion would be recorded for all eternity. With the symbols of the Passion, those souls would be presented before God at the hour of their deaths in order to receive great rewards. Their recompense on earth, however, would be suffering and pain.

Finally, the Holy Apostle told her that the world would not end until the friars of the Seraphic Family returned to govern the Convent of the Immaculate Conception. Then, the religious spirit would shine resplendently, and there would be many very holy religious. With this, the vision came to an end.

### APPARITION OF THE ANGELS AND THE TORTURE WHEELS

Mother Catherine of the Conception saw that the Angels of Heaven had placed torture wheels in diverse parts of the cloisters and patios of the Convent. As religious approached these wheels, the Angels themselves turned them, torturing the sisters until their bodies were lacerated. The Angels then presented these souls with palms and crowns, and with these symbols their souls soared to Heaven.

Then other Angels placed new wheels in the Convent and, as she saw religious approaching them, she heard a voice saying, "These are the heroic penitential souls who, by their voluntary martyrdoms, will make reparation for their sins and those of their brothers, poor sinners. Thus will they hasten the hour of good fortune for this Community."

### MYSTIC VISION AND MYSTERY OF THE INCARNATION

Mother Maria of the Incarnation contemplated the council of the Holy Trinity in its deliberations on how to ransom fallen mankind. The Person of the Divine Word offered Himself to redeem it, making at that moment an act of humiliation so profound that it could never be repeated by any creature. This act alone would have sufficed to redeem a thousand worlds. Notwithstanding, God desired to become Man.

At that very instant, the Blessed Trinity sent from Heaven the Archangel Saint Gabriel to announce the Mystery of the Incarnation to the humble Virgin Mary who was praying in the retirement of her home in Nazareth. The Most Holy Trinity quietly awaited the *fiat* of the humble Virgin. After She pronounced it, the Eternal Father and the Holy Ghost worked that ineffable Mystery. The Holy Ghost compressed the Heart of the Blessed Virgin so tightly with divine love that, from the impulse of this love, three drops of blood fell from it. From them, the Holy Ghost formed a most perfect Body the size of a bean pod, and this Body united itself with the Second Person of the Holy Trinity. Thus did the Mystery of the Incarnation take place.

In this tiny Body, Mother Maria of the Incarnation saw the Heart of the Child God pulsating with love for men and the Divine Word united to Humanity growing in the womb of Mary Most Holy, where He prostrated Himself in the form of the cross. The religious gazed at the tiny hands of the Divine Infant and perceived that they would be pierced with hard nails.

This was followed by the vision of His birth and of how He miraculously lay in the crib. The humble religious later saw his hidden life in Nazareth, and was given to know that throughout the centuries there would be daughters of the Immaculate Conception who, imitating the retired and hidden life of Christ at Nazareth, would sustain the Convent. It was also revealed to her that the common life would reach a greater perfection when the sons of the Seraphim of Assisi will return to govern the Convent. Seeing these marvelous things, the holy religious would have died from the violence of her love if God had not sustained her life.

All the Founding Mothers communicated to Mother Mariana the visions, each one different from the other, that they had simultaneously received on that blessed night. They also attested under oath to the truth of these things in written accounts that are conserved in the archives of the Convent.

### OTHER LESSER VISIONS: PUNISHMENT OF THE NON-OBSERVANT SISTERS

Even the non-observant sisters were given to know that something extraordinary had happened that night. For in the early morning when they were praying the Little Office of the Blessed Virgin Mary (for, despite everything, they had not ceased this practice), they heard celestial music coming from the prison, and saw a refulgent light issuing from it.

Further, at the same time that the Founding Mothers were being favored with the above-mentioned visions, Mother Mariana and the other imprisoned sisters saw the chastisement of their persecutors. It was revealed to Mother Mariana that the present Abbess, Mother Magdalena de Jesus Valenzuela, would die in a few years from a weakened heart and that she would remain in Purgatory until the Final Judgment Day.

All the other sisters saw that the most guilty non-observant sisters, those who had caused the relaxations that would last for centuries, would be lost. Others would suffer their purgatory in that very Convent. In the gardens of the choir courtyard, they would be covered with filthy things. This would be their chastisement. The less guilty religious would leave Purgatory when the Friars Minor will return to govern the Convent of the Immaculate Conception and with the reestablishment of the full observance of the Rule of Pope Saint Julian II.

One can only imagine the suffering that this vision caused to those heroines of seraphic love in their prison, and how they strove to placate Divine Justice in order to save the souls of their beloved sisters. How many humiliations, penances, and sacrifices were made by these innocent virgins! With fear and trembling, they labored for the sanctification of their sisters, begging God Our Lord to hasten the day when the Franciscan Friars would return to govern their Community!

Alas! Since that day, the lack of observance, the relaxations, and so many other evils have increased, being the motive for the tears and sufferings of all the religious victims of angelic love. But it was the evils of these days that caused those future relaxations. For, as the Blessed Virgin told Sister Anna of the Conception, the relaxations of the future centuries would result from sisters entering the Convent who would have never been accepted into the Community of the Immaculate Conception had the Friars Minor been governing the Convent.

Oh! How our holy Religion suffers to see these daughters who stray from the Heart of their God, causing such sufferings to His faithful spouses!

\* \* \*

## Chapter 20

The sufferings of the Conceptionist victims continued. Deprived of their veils and mantles, they suffered the humiliation and despisal of the Community.

During the whole time of their unjust imprisonment, however, the non-observant sisters also suffered, for there was so much sickness that the Convent took on the atmosphere of a hospital. And while many of the non-observant sisters became ill, the fortunate captives enjoyed good health, their cheeks like roses. One could say that God Our Lord had given the health of the persecutors to his innocent and beloved spouses.

### Mother Valenzuela Takes Steps to Free the Prisoners

Finally, the Mother Abbess could no longer bear to see the sufferings of the saintly prisoners. During a chapter, she spoke to the Community, "My sisters, it is impossible to continue to imprison our innocent sisters. We must ask the Bishop to free them. They are needed in the choir for the recitation of the Divine Office, and I miss their presence."

She could not finish, for she broke into tears, joined by some of the religious. Others, however, remained hard as rocks.

After the meeting, the Abbess went to visit the prisoners, who, falling to their knees, received her with filial love. She told them, "My daughters, your trial will soon come to an end. They will set you all at liberty."

Mother Mariana sealed her lips and the others, with their gazes fixed on the ground, followed her example and said nothing.

The Abbess sent a note to the office of the Bishop, asking, among other things, "that liberty be given to the holy prisoners, for they innocently suffer many injustices. No one except Mother Mariana de Jesus should govern the Convent, for she has been the model of sanctity and observance. I, because of lack of character and softness, allowed myself to be led by the other sisters in this wicked treatment of Mother Mariana. For that, I beg a thousand pardons. I know that I do not have the aptitude to govern, and I present my resignation as Abbess. My health also no longer permits me to govern, for it has weakened considerably in this period."

She received the following reply: "Mother, the words you have written me in your letter have pierced my heart. You should have realized your incapacity to govern sooner than this and should never have tormented those who are innocent. This could have caused the closure of your Convent, for the Spanish Mothers are much loved for their sanctity and nobility. You should have realized that they are the ones who should hold the highet posts of importance in the Community. You should know that among the ladies-in-waiting of the Queen of Spain, there is a close relative of Mother Mariana. Some of these ladies have already inquired about her and the other Spaniards.

"Henceforth, you will not permit any of the *criollas*[42] to hold any position of power or office, for the preeminent posts belong to the Spaniards. Free them immediately and restore to them all their privileges. As for your resignation, complete your three years and your time will end."

It would be difficult to imagine the suffering of Mother Valenzuela upon receiving this note from the Prelate. She called the Community together and read it publicly, saying, "Sisters, we deserve no more than this. Let us now go in community to release our sisters from prison."

Seeing that some of the sisters resisted, she cried out, "Under the command of holy obedience, I order that we all go in community to free our saintly sisters."

They entered into formation and moved toward the prison, with those who had resisted following the procession from afar.

When the group reached the prison, they knocked, opened the door, and entered. The prisoners, seeing the Abbess with the whole Community, began to tremble in fear, dreading yet greater sufferings and fearful that they had come to take Mother Mariana. They surrounded their treasure, fixing their eyes on her.

The Abbess then told them that the Bishop had already restored them to freedom, and, in a short speech, she asked pardon for all that they had suffered.

---

42. *Criollas* was the name given to the children of Spaniards who had married the natives of Ecuador.

### The Holy Prisoners Leave the Prison

The innocent victims humbled themselves, kissing the ground and the feet of the Abbess. They also kissed the feet of all the religious present and embraced them. When the Abbess gave the command for them to leave, they went in procession to the lower choir where the innocent victims prostrated themselves on the ground in the form of a cross without saying a word. When they rose, the floor was wet with the tears that they had shed at the feet of their Sacramental Spouse.

This was a day of rejoicing for the Community. The freed sisters were given a time to rest, and then the Confessor was called. He heard their confessions and the next morning, they received Communion with great fervor and took up their duties, reassuming their lives of fervor and observance. Still, there was no shortage of sufferings that their persecutors continued to cause them.

These heroines were the first fruits of the Order, and the glory and honor of the Convent of the Immaculate Conception of Mary Most Holy. The Prelate was right to have ordered their liberation.

If the Spanish Founding Mothers had not suffered this trial, there would not have been saints in the Convent of the Immaculate Conception. For this dark, underground prison was the wine press where the precious wine of divine love was made! Mixing it with the myrrh of sorrow, it was then offered to the Divine Spouse and refreshed His mysterious thirst through the course of the centuries. Added to it is the suffering of many religious souls who will imitate the heroic suffering of their Founding Mothers and will also be victims of angelic love.

\* \* \*

# Chapter 21

During the year 1598, Mother Mariana de Jesus continued to suffer terrible torments, persecutions, and calumnies from the hands of the non-observant sisters. She bore their affronts without making the least complaint, thus imitating her Divine Spouse Who, on the Cross, pardoned and prayed for His enemies.

### The Re-Election of Mother Mariana and a Reproach from Our Lord

Finally Mother Valenzuela's Abbacy reached its end, a most ominous time for the Founding Mothers, and a new election took place. The non-observant sisters did all that they could to have their companion elected, who would permit them even greater freedom in the relaxation of the monastic life. They worked so hard for this that they felt assured of achieving their goal.

For this reason, they were stunned to find that the vote had fallen in favor of Mother Mariana de Jesus, who lacked only the votes of the non-observant sisters .... In face of the victory of their adversary, some of their number became so fearful they suffered attacks; others could not speak in their anger and confusion.

Immediately following the election of Mother Mariana de Jesus and before the ceremonies could begin, Mother Valenzuela rushed forward and rendered her obedience. She could not wait another minute to deliver the office into the hands of the one whom she now desired to be her Superior. As she rendered her obedience, she said, "Reverend Mother, now you will be my mother."

Bewildered and disoriented, Mother Mariana wanted to ask to resign the office. But as she started to speak, God Our Lord took away her voice and she was unable to speak or even move. At that moment, she saw a light that left the Tabernacle, inundating and illuminating the whole altar and lower choir. She was then given to understand all the sufferings, calumnies, and imprisonments that awaited her in her Abbacy. Notwithstanding her desire to suffer, she still interiorly continued to renounce this burden.

Thinking these things, she saw Our Lord leave the Sacrarium carrying an enormous Cross and wearing a crown of thorns.

His eyes filled with tears, Our Lord approached her and said: "I did not falter on the road to Calvary with this large and heavy Cross, which I carried for love of you and all sinners. And yet you would leave Me alone? Woe to you should this Convent close and you return to Spain!"

Our Lord was also bound with cords and carrying the Cross. He seated Himself next to her with a rope around His neck. This gave strength to Mother Mariana. Meanwhile, the religious were rendering her their obedience, kissing her scapular. But, in fact, without realizing it, they were kissing the rope of Our Lord.

"It is My cord that they kiss," Our Lord told her.

How, indeed, could her heart not be moved upon seeing the tears of her Divine Spouse Who begged her to accept the cross of the Abbacy!

After being invested with the insignias of the Abbess, Mother Mariana felt in her soul such a profound humility that she believed herself to be the most abject creature on the face of the world. "It is just that I suffered," she told herself, "and my sisters were right to treat me as they did."

### OUR LORD PUNISHES AN ATTEMPT OF SCHISM BY THE NON-OBSERVANT RELIGIOUS

The procession with the new Abbess took place immediately, followed by the commemorations. Everyone was joyful with the exception of the non-observant sisters, and especially that one who had conspired to be elected Abbess. This unhappy sister, who had been waiting eagerly to assume this office, manifested a death-like sadness.

Mother Mariana, who knew what was taking place in the heart of this sister, approached her persecutor amid the rejoicing of her daughters. With a maternal expression and kindly tone, she said to her, "My dear sister, why are you looking like this? What interior suffering or sadness do you bear?"

The sister, however, responded with arrogance and insolence, "Nothing is wrong. Go and enjoy what you have coveted so greatly."

Mother Mariana left her without saying a word. But Mother Valenzuela reprimanded her impertinence, saying, "What is this, sister? Why are you behaving like this during our festivities? If you would feel better apart from us, then retire to your cell."

"Yes, Mother," replied the sister bitterly. "Many thanks for that."

And she left, taking with her all the non-observant sisters, who gathered together to intone sad songs expressing their grief.

Distraught by such a display of insolence, Mother Valenzuela fell into a faint. Mother Mariana went to her, and, supporting her in her arms, she commanded Mother Francisca to bring water. The latter flew to comply with this order, returning with this and other remedies. Together, they worked to bring Mother Valenzuela back to consciousness. Her first words upon coming to herself were, "Oh, my poor sisters!"

The religious continued the festivities celebrating the election of their new Abbess. But, as night approached, the insolent sister who had wanted to be Abbess died suddenly from no apparent cause. For this rebellious sister had been the ringleader of a small group that was conspiring to split the Convent and form another community. But God Our Lord did not permit this split, for "the kingdom divided will be destroyed," and He took the life of the unfaithful instigator.

When her companions saw that their leader had died, they blamed Mother Mariana, saying that she had done something to kill her. The innocent Abbess was silent, saying nothing in her defense. How terrible, indeed, are the unbridled passions in religious persons! And how cruelly they can persecute and torment the innocent victims of their jealousy!

The Divine Spouse, however, had clearly shown the hand of His justice. For since the non-observant sisters had separated themselves to sing canticles of grief, God gave them a true cause for such mourning by taking the life of their leader who had wanted to be Abbess.

But even this did not open their eyes, which were blinded by the infernal serpent. At their iniquitous meetings, they continued to calumniate and persecute their holy Abbess, Mother Mariana, who suffered a double agony, first, to see the scheming of the non-observant sisters; and second, from the continuous sufferings they caused her, as we shall see.

With the death of this poor revolted sister, the Community festivities ended, and funeral preparations began.

### THE NON-OBSERVANT SISTERS SCHEME AGAINST MOTHER MARIANA

Mother Mariana realized all that was taking place in the hearts of the non-observant sisters. To placate their ire, she tried to satisfy their desires even before they expressed them. She personally attended to their needs with a celestial sweetness and humility. In their arrogance and pride, these rebellious sisters would at times disdainfully accept what she brought them; at other times they would haughtily respond, "Put it down there."

Mother Mariana continued, then, to be the object of their anger and contempt. At the end of the first month of her Abbacy, the non-observant sisters went to Mother Valenzuela with their complaints and asked her to write the Bishop so that he might give an order to imprison her. They wanted her to accuse Mother Mariana of causing unrest in the Convent and to say that they could no longer tolerate her stern treatment. She should tell him that after only a month under her government, life had become intolerable, and beg him to put an end to such a harsh government.

Mother Valenzuela replied that she would indeed write the Bishop a letter, and told them to come back later so that they could sign it. She then composed a letter that exposed the non-observant sisters as the source of agitation inside the Convent. She asked that they be imprisoned, listing all of their names.

When the non-observant sisters read what Mother Valenzuela had written, they became furious. They resolved to write the letter to the Prelate themselves, without her assistance.

In fact, Mother Mariana would not tolerate inobservance of the Rule, but she employed the most gentle and tactful means she could to correct the sisters in their transgressions against it. She would sweetly admonish her, "My dear sister, let us not forget that in this house we are obliged to keep silence. Let us, then, be more careful." But her attempts were futile, and for her efforts, she suffered unspeakable torments.

The situation was further confused by certain orders of the Bishop who had jurisdiction over the Convent, for they were of a tenor that to obey them would compromise the conscience. Thus observance to the Rule diminished, and the life of the Convent wavered precariously and threatened to die from the loss of the government of the Friars Minor, who had sweetly instructed their daughters in strict observance of the Rule. The secular Prelate, on the contrary, neither understood the Rule nor could he hold in check the non-observant faction of sisters.

Mother Valenzuela was a good religious, but she did not have the gift for governing. Lacking character and firm resolution, she had allowed herself to be swayed by the non-observant sisters. Now she was suffering profoundly for having been the one to request that the Franciscan friars leave in order to please the rebellious sisters. Upon her conscience fell all the weight of non-observance of the Rule.

Seeing that the humility and sweetness of Mother Mariana could not subdue these rebellious sisters, Mother Valenzuela fell ill in her grief. During the sickness, her only consolation was Mother Mariana.

### Mother Mariana Is Imprisoned

Meanwhile, the conclave of non-observant sisters wrote the Bishop a note along these lines: "Mother Mariana de Jesus breaks the silence whenever she desires. She does not assist at Community prayers. She privately indulges herself and her friends with extra food. The Convent is conspiring with the Franciscan friars, with whom she converses into the late hours of the night. Furthermore, Mother Mariana is striving to overthrow the jurisdiction of Your Illustrious Lordship. We beg you to imprison her."

They also included other such accusations. The note was sealed and sent, although God Our Lord revealed to Mother Mariana what it contained.

Two notes from the Prelate were not long in returning: a private one to the non-observant sisters, whose contents God Our Lord revealed to Mother Mariana. The other was addressed to her.

It said the following: "Mother, for having so gravely transgressed your Rule and for communicating with the Friars Minor until late into the night, I order your temporary dismissal from the office of Abbess, this seat remaining vacant until further notice, and your immediate imprisonment."

Reading this note, Mother Mariana wept. Mother Francisca, seeing her grief, inquired, "What has happened, my Mother?"

But Mother Mariana did not reply. Instead, she went to the lower choir to pray.

Meanwhile her persecutors were looking for her. Finding her in the choir, they triumphantly commanded, "Leave the choir, Mother, and go to the prison in obedience to the Bishop's order commanding us to put you there."

The innocent victim complied, telling them, "I would like to get the Breviary from my cell."

"No," her persecutors responded, "the Divine Office is for the observant sisters, not for you." And they took her to the Convent prison.

The other religious, who knew nothing of the Bishop's letter and command, were searching for their Abbess but could not find her anywhere. One of the persecutors finally told them, "We no longer have an Abbess. We will have a new election, for Mother Mariana is in prison."

How this sword of sorrow pierced the hearts of the Spanish sisters! They immediately went to her. "Our Mother," they said to her from outside its walls, "what shall we do?"

"My daughters," she replied, "leave me here, and pray for me."

\* \* \*

## Chapter 22

While the Community of faithful sisters mourned the imprisonment of their Abbess, the persecutors put on triumphant airs and tried to restore the health of Mother Valenzuela so that they could make her Abbess. They had an interest in seeing her well because in the note that they had written to the Prelate requesting the imprisonment of Mother Mariana, one of the calumnies was that Mother Valenzuela had fallen ill because of the rigorous treatment she had received from the Abbess.

The non-observant sisters, therefore, were constantly at her bedside, which caused Mother Valenzuela great disgust. For Mother Valenzuela, who had recognized her error and no longer supported the non-observant sisters, was now firmly united to Mother Mariana and the other Founding Mothers.

Sick in bed, Mother Valenzuela remained ignorant of the imprisonment of Mother Mariana. All her consolation had been in her Abbess, who had tried to help her regain her health by every means possible, treating her with sweetness, charity, and a maternal love.

Now, seeing that Mother Mariana was no longer there to assist her, she called out for her, requesting her presence. The persecutors responded that she was busy, but the ill woman continued to call out for her. When Mother Mariana did not come, she began to weep, saying that Mother Mariana had died.

A non-observant sister then told her, "No, she is not dead, but imprisoned."

Hearing this, Mother Valenzuela fainted. Two days passed with her lying in a deathlike state from the terrible heart attack she had suffered. The religious were worried that she had, in fact, really died.

When, deathly pale, she returned to consciousness, the doctors said that it was a miracle, for the attack had touched not only her brain, but also her heart, and they had warned that if this would happen often, she would die from it.

The Community became greatly alarmed when Mother Valenzuela, weeping, begged them to dress her and carry her to the prison. "I want to be in prison with my Abbess," she said. "I should be there with her." The non-observant sisters did not know what to do. However, after conversing among themselves, they decided they could not do what she requested.

### THE OTHER SPANISH FOUNDING MOTHERS ARE ALSO IMPRISONED

Under the solicitous care of Mother Francisca, Mother Valenzuela's health improved as the days passed. Noting her improvement, the rebellious sisters pretended that this had happened by a miracle of Mother Mariana and the nurse, whom they also subjected to insults. Finally, they put her in the prison with Mother Mariana.

Mother Valenzuela then asked for Mother Maria of the Incarnation, the Convent secretary. In response, the non-observant sisters arrested her as well. As they led her to the prison, this holy religious questioned them, "Upon whose orders do you take me to the prison?"

They replied, "On orders from our superiors."

The religious tried to resist, for she realized that no order from the Bishop existed. However, to avoid causing greater scandal, she entered the prison. And with each day that passed, they continued to imprison another of the Founding Mothers.

When Mother Valenzuela learned that Mother Maria of the Incarnation and all the other Founding Mothers had been imprisoned, she became furious. Exerting great effort, she rose from her bed and strongly reprimanded them, crying out: "How can you commit such injustices against our holy Founding Mothers? Because of you, the Convent will be destroyed, and your names will be written for posterity in ignominy!"

She directed yet more serious words to them, but the non-observant sisters would not relent. This was the first time that Mother Valenzuela broke the silence.

"Mother," they told her, "do not defend the Spanish sisters, for they are guilty." As proof, they presented outrageous falsehoods about the innocent victims. When she vehemently protested and accused them of lying, they would smile, shake their heads, and say, "Poor Mother Valenzuela is delirious."

## Chapter 22

When, trembling and weak, Mother Valenzuela could finally walk a bit, the first place she went was the prison. Knocking on the door, which she wished she had the strength to break, she said, "Who has the key to this door so that I might enter this Heaven?" She then called out for the Mother Abbess.

Mother Mariana respectfully went to the door, and Mother Valenzuela asked her: "What is going on here, my Mother?"

Mother Mariana told her about the note that the non-observant sisters had written to the Bishop, as well as his reply with the order to imprison her. Hearing this, Mother Valenzuela became profoundly distressed and agitated. When the non-observant sisters found her there outside the prison door, they thought that she truly was in a state of delirium.

Right there in the prison cloister, the non-observant sisters began to argue among themselves.

"It is your fault this is happening because you wrote the note," accused one.

"But it was you who told me what to write," answered the other.

"But it was you who added this point," added another.

And so they bickered among themselves, and became divided. Since Mother Valenzuela was well enough to write, she immediately directed another message to the Prelate, professing the innocence of the Abbess and the other Spanish Mothers, and asking him to free them.

But since the government of the Convent was in the hands of the non-observant faction, the note was not sent. Instead, the sisters tore it up and lied to Mother Valenzuela, telling her they had sent it.

When she would ask if a response had arrived, they would reply, "It will come soon, Mother."

Confused at the delay, she called for her confessor to inform him of the injustices being committed against the innocent prisoners. Since the non-observant sisters had spoken to him first and insisted on the guilt of the Spanish Mothers, the confessor pretended the matter was out of his hands.

He told her, "I can do nothing, for the Bishop is angry with the Spanish sisters."

## The Edifying Behavior of Mother Mariana and the Founding Mothers in Prison

This situation caused Mother Valenzuela indescribable torment for she realized that she was the cause of these injustices committed against the innocent Mothers. Her only consolation was to go to the prison of the innocent victims, finding refuge in the prison cloisters. There she would sit on the stone benches outside the prison and the good obsrvant sisters would join her there, disputing for the honor to keep company with the holy prisoners.

"This evening you are going to go to prison," they would say. Or, "Mother, tomorrow you and the other observant sisters will join your friends."

Even facing this group and Mother Valenzuela, who was frustrated beyond words because she could stop neither this torrent of fury, envy, and lies, nor the growing relaxation of the Rule inside the Convent, the non-observant sisters continued to torment the captives. These revolted sisters did whatever they wanted, and during this ill-fated month, life in the holy cloisters was very bitter indeed, for the infernal serpent was in power.

It is worth noting that these poor non-observant sisters, who met often with their confessors, nonetheless did not receive Communion even once during this month, most probably because their consciences tormented them about the terrible way they were treating the saintly and illustrious Abbess, Mother Mariana de Jesus, and the rest of the Founding Mothers and other observant religious.

What a sad and lamentable epoch in the Convent of the Immaculate Conception when the infernal serpent had seized control of the native sisters in order to destroy, by means of division and non-observance of the Rule, the motherhouse of the Order of the Immaculate Conception in Ecuador. These chronicles should be blotted with tears of blood. Let it be known that these shameful times are recorded here only so that they might resplendently reflect the mercy of God and the Blessed Virgin in preserving this Convent, which was not destroyed during this ill-fated epoch undoubtedly in part because of the penances, prayers, and continual immolation of the saintly Abbess and the Spanish Mothers, who placated the divine ire.

During this time, strict observance of the Rule shone resplendently only in the prison. When Mother Francisca was imprisoned, she brought with her the Breviary of Mother Mariana. With the rest of the imprisoned sisters, they prayed and sang the divine psalmody, these melodious verses consoling the Heart of their Divine Spouse, so sorely wounded by the non-observant sisters.

This prison, then, deflected the hand of Divine Justice and become an altar that exhaled the sweetly scented incense of its sacrificial victims. Happy the Convent that housed those sweet doves, whose tender cooing consoled the Divine Lover. Blessed are the Spanish Mothers who founded this nest of the Immaculate Conception and who, sighing plaintively like mourning doves, placated the Divine Spouse, preserving the Convent by the violence of their sacrifices and their love.

### Lights and Sweet Voices from Heaven Inundate the Prison

But the Queen of Heaven and Earth did not forget her faithful daughters. With unmatched fervor, they paid homage to her each day with the recitation of the early morning Little Office. Worthy Spouses of their Crucified Lord, they bore the cross with dignity and valor.

One night at midnight, the holy Abbess, as was her custom, prepared to pray while her sisters slept the tranquil sleep of the just. Prostrate with her forehead on the ground, she humbled herself in the presence of her Lord and God. Believing that her many faults were the cause for divine anger against her beloved Convent and judging herself to be the most culpable creature on earth, she begged His mercy and pardon.

At the height of her prayer at 1 a.m. on January 16, she heard the strains of a melodious voice, accompanied by a zither of heavenly tone. As she listened in marvel, the prison became illuminated with a celestial light. Quickly she rose to her knees, calling out several times to her sleeping sisters so that they might also be consoled by the celestial music. They did not awaken, however.

Mother Mariana remained kneeling before the cross that had been painted on the prison wall. Suddenly she saw before her the Seraphic Saint Francis, playing the zither, and Mother Maria de Jesus Taboada, her Mother and Founder, who was intoning couplets of mournful love.

Inebriated with joy, Mother Mariana could not say a word. Her heart longed to partake of the celestial happiness of her Mother and Founder.

Then Mother Maria spoke to her, "My daughter and niece, you have never been so pleasing to Our Lord as during this present time, when sorrow engulfs you. Ah! If you only knew the value of suffering unjustly for love of conventual observance! To recompense your constancy and your humble suffering, my Seraphic Father and I have come to delight your ears and fill your heart with celestial consolation."

Saint Francis spoke: "My daughter and beloved bride of the Spouse of virgins, your sufferings and those of your daughters and mine, as well as the tears and prayers that rise to Heaven from this prison, have touched the magnanimous Heart of God and his Blessed Mother. In His infinite love for you, He sent us to comfort your downcast spirit.

"Hear this zither: it is the same one that a winged spirit played for me during an ecstasy of love and joy I experienced in times long past when I lived on earth. Now, in Heaven, I play it for my sons and daughters on earth to console them during the unjust persecutions they suffer. Some hear this celestial music with their bodily senses, as you do. Others can hear it only in the depths of their souls.

"Take courage and remain steadfast in your suffering for conventual observance, for the rewards in Heaven that await the observant religious are great. Whoever loves me will be loved and blessed by God, but whoever swerves from my spirit, I will neither recognize nor defend before the Supreme Tribunal. This Convent, so beloved by me, will always be privileged. I will unceasingly watch over it until the end of time, for in all centuries it will have faithful and loving daughters.

"Now expand your heart and prepare yourself, for Our Sovereign and Queen is coming to visit your prison. We are only her messengers."

Saying this, Saint Francis and Mother Maria de Jesus Taboada disappeared.

### THIRD APPARITION OF THE BLESSED VIRGIN ON JANUARY 16, 1599

In a light more brilliant than the one that was fading away, a most beautiful Lady appeared. She carried her most precious Son in her left arm and a crosier in her right. On the crosier was a cross of diamonds, each one shining like the sun. In the middle of the cross was a ruby star engraved with the name Mary, which radiated lights, one more brilliant than the next.

The humble Mother Mariana did not believe herself worthy of such a favor. She feared that this might be some imaginary illusion brought on by her great sufferings.

Summoning all her strength, she raised her armsand said: "Beautiful Lady, Who art thou and what dost thou desire of me in this obscure place where thou dost find me with my suffering daughters? Perhaps some sin, hidden from my sight, has roused divine ire against this amenable garden? If such be the case, let me, the guilty one, die, but save the innocent ones and this beloved Convent.

"If I stand before a figure of my imagination, then I beg thee, by the mysteries of the Most Holy Trinity, the real presence of Jesus Christ in the Eucharist, and the Divine Maternity, to depart from me, leaving me in the obscurity of the Faith, so sweet and enchanting for me!

"I do not refuse suffering, nor have I ever refused it, because I love Jesus, and this love makes me want to make myself like unto Him. I only implore strength and valor, for, distanced from the Seraphic Family, religious life is difficult and obscure."

### OUR LADY REVEALS WHO SHE IS AND THE DESIGNS OF GOD FOR THIS CONVENT

Then the divine apparition spoke these words: "My most beloved daughter, why are you so slow and heavy of heart? This is no figure of your imagination who stands before your eyes. I am Mary of Good Success, your Mother from Heaven, an invocation well known in Spain,[43] and one to whom you have often resorted. There is no hidden sin in you nor any of the observant sisters who love my servant Francis and his Seraphicfamily. The tribulation that my Most Holy Son has given you is a celestial gift to embellish your own souls and to hold back the divine ire, so ready to unleash a terrible chastisement upon this ungrateful Colony. How many hidden crimes are committed in it and the surrounding area! For precisely this reason, this Convent was founded here so that the God of Heaven and Earth would receive reparation in the very place where He is offended and unrecognized. For this reason also, the Devil, enemy of God and of the just, both now and in future centuries will use all his malicious cunning to try to destroy this Convent, my foundation and legacy. Toward this end, he will avail himself of persons of authority and dignity, often under the pretext of improving the situation and bringing greater peace!

"Oh! The ignorance of the learned and the folly of mortals who do not recognize the secret designs of God in His works! Remember the words of the Royal Prophet: 'How marvelous are the works of the Lord!' Be convinced of this truth; teach and impress upon your daughters – both those who live now and those to come – that they should love their divine vocation. Let them also love the glorious place that God and I chose for our property and inheritance. God, absolute Master of all that exists, chooses where He will accomplish His secret designs, and no creature can thwart Him without incurring divine malediction.

"Throughout the centuries, I will live here in the person of some of my daughters. For here, amid the tumult of the ungrateful world, God will have some contemplative spouses worthy of His Majesty. Those souls, who will suffer obscurity, silence, humiliation, and scorn even from within the bosom of their Community, will placate Divine Justice and gain great benefits for the Church, their country, and their fellow man. Without them, Quito would not continue to exist."

---

43. The devotion to Our Lady of Good Success was approved by Pope Saint Pius V in 1571 to honor a statue found miraculously in a cave in Catalonia by the founder of the Order of Saint Francis of Paola. See *Our Lady of Good Success Novena and Prayer Booklet*, (Oconomowoc, WI: The Apostolate of Our Lady of Good Success, 2003).

## Prophecies Regarding the Future of the Colony and the Convent

"In a short time, the country in which you live will cease to be a Colony and will become a free Republic. Then, known by the name of Ecuador, it will need heroic souls to sustain it in face of so many public and private calamities.[44]

"Here [in this Convent] God will always find these souls, like hidden violets. Accursed would be Quito without this Convent. The most powerful king on earth with all his riches could not erect new buildings on this site, for this place belongs to God. Just as Julian the Apostate with all his mendacious powers could not rebuild the Temple of Solomon, the power of men against the Lamb of God is futile!

"With maternal solicitude, I will watch over this Convent and its properties. If it is necessary to uphold these walls that guard the cloisters with miracles, I will make them. All those who strive to sustain and preserve this beloved place will be blessed by God and His Mother, to whom you speak. Their names will be written on the shining star of rubies that you see in the middle of this crosier, the symbol of my power and authority in this house. As for those who work to destroy this Convent, I will take the lives of some when they least expect it; to others will befall great difficulties, and all will receive in eternity what they deserve in justice.

"In the 19th century a truly Christian president will come, a man of character whom God Our Lord will give the palm of martyrdom on the square adjoining this Convent of mine. He will consecrate the Republic to the Sacred Heart of my Most Holy Son,

---

44. It is interesting to see that Our Lady specified that the new country would take the name of the Republic of Ecuador. This apparition took place on January 16, 1599. In an autobiography of Mother Mariana written in 1735 by Fr. Bartolomé Ochoa de Alácano y Gamboa, O.F.M., he records these prophetic words precisely (Cadena y Almeida, *Apariciones*, pp. 120-1).

In fact, the Republic of Ecuador was declared on August 19, 1809. The following year witnessed a terrible massacre of the nobility, even women and children being put to the sword. Independence was definitively secured on May 22, 1820 after the Battle of Pinchincha. Since that time, Ecuador has been torn by internal dissensions. Backed by the powers of Freemasonry, the Liberals took power in the 19th century. In the early 20th century the government instituted a policy of strident anticlericalism and introduced laws to deprive the Church of her power and possessions.

and this consecration will sustain the Catholic Religion in the years that will follow, which will be ill-fated ones for the Church.[45] These years, during which the accursed sect of Masonry will take control of the civil government, will see a cruel persecution of all religious communities, and it will also strike out violently against this one of mine. These unfortunate men will think the Convent destroyed, but God lives and I live, and we will raise up powerful defenders and set before these enemies difficulties impossible to conquer, and the triumph will be ours.[46]

"During this time there will be beautiful souls in this Convent, who, like solitary doves cooing plaintive notes of mournful love, will attract the mercy of God upon His Convent, His unworthy country and the attacked Church, souls so obscure and unknown to all that they themselves will not know how their Lord and God is forming them."

### OUR LADY OF GOOD SUCCESS COMMANDS A STATUE OF HERSELF TO BE MADE

"Thus it is the wish of my Most Holy Son that you command a statue of me to be made, just as you see me now, and that you place it upon the Abbess' chair so that I may govern my Convent.

---

45. A century and a half later, in 1873, the truly Catholic president Gabriel Garcia Moreno made a public consecration of the Republic of Ecuador to the Sacred Heart of Jesus. This act infuriated the Freemasons, and the German Grand Lodge gave an order for his death. On August 6, 1874, on his way out of the Cathedral in the square of Quito adjoining the Convent, as Our Lady had forewarned, he was struck down and killed by assassins. Under his presidency (1861-1865 and 1869-1875) civil and religious affairs were reorganized favoring the Catholic Church. The Jesuits were recalled and charged with the education of youth, a concordat with Rome established, and new Dioceses erected. After his death, persecution of the Church recommenced under the influence of Freemasonry.

46. The year saw the installation of a secular liberal government that effectively established the laicism of the State, with laws of civil matrimony, divorce, and equal rights for all religions. The Law of *Manos Muertas* of 1902, which despoiled the goods of religious communities and deprived the religious of their monthly stipends, led to the gradual disappearance of many religious institutions. In 1909, to complete the attack, Miguel Valverde introduced a decree in Congress that would abolish all monastic establishments of contemplative women and sell their properties. There was a vicious fight, and in the end, the decree was not approved. During this turbulent period, the sisters of the Immaculate Conception Convent suffered greatly and had recourse to *"la Mamita Virgen del Buen Sucesso,"* as the sisters affectionately called her, asking her assistance in this great trial (Cadena y Almeida, *Mensaje Profetico*, pp. 46-61).

In my right hand, place the crosier and the keys to the cloister as a sign of my proprietorship and authority.

"In my left arm, place my Divine Child: first, so that men understand how powerful I am in placating the Divine Justice and obtaining mercy and pardon for every sinner who comes to me with a contrite heart, for I am the Mother of Mercy and in me there is only goodness and love; and second, so that throughout time my daughters will understand that I am showing and giving them my most Holy Son and their God as a model of religious perfection. They should come to me, for I will lead them to Him.

"When tribulations of spirit and sufferings of body oppress them and they seem to be drowning in a bottomless sea, let them gaze at my holy Image, which will be for them a star for the shipwrecked. I will always be there, ready to listen to their lamentations and calm their weeping. Tell them that they should always have recourse to their Mother with faith and love, for it is my desire to live with them and in them. The sufferings of your daughters will conserve their Convent for all times. Tell them that they should imitate my humility, my obedience, my spirit of sacrifice, and my absolute dependence on the divine will. These are the wings on which my daughters through the ages who venerate the mystery of my Immaculate Conception will soar with mysterious agility to the highest summits of sanctity in the quiet retirement of their cloisters under the pure gaze of God."

### THE PRELATE WHO WILL COME TO RESTORE THE AGONIZING COMMUNITY

"The separation of the Friars Minor has taken place by divine permission. Woe to those who openly worked to obscure the light of my Convent! But after some centuries, they will return to govern this beloved flock, which will always lament their absence and feel their loss. [47] Then, this beloved garden of mine will be a fecund garden where the Celestial Spouse will find His rest amid its sweet fragrances, rare flowers, and exquisite fruits.

---

47. When will the Franciscan friars return to the spiritual direction of the Convent? This will depend on the will of God and the intervention of Our Lady. It will be during a time – we hope not too distant – of great fervor and holiness in the Convent, when the Rule is faithfully observed in all its details, a "golden era," as Our Lady called it.

"Neither you nor your present-day daughters and sisters will see the happiness that will dawn for this blessed Convent. However, you and your faithful and obedient daughters should make sacrifices and implore God to hasten that time to come on this earth, for today marks the beginning of a dark night. But a golden era will come for this my Convent. Then a *Prelado* [prelate], my most beloved son, blessed and prized before God, will understand by divine light the necessity for the daughters of my Immaculate Conception to subject themselves in exact obedience to the Friars Minor for their sanctification and perfection. This Prelate will ask the Vicar of my most Holy Son here on Earth to restore the jurisdiction over this Convent to the Friars Minor.

"The day will come when the corruption of customs in the world will have seemed to have reached its apogee, and when my agonizing Community will find itself deprived of earthly goods and overflowing in bitterness and sorrow. The Friars Minor will raise up their downcast spirits, attract true and saintly vocations, and form religious worthy of the name.

"During this time, the Community of Franciscans, dearly beloved sons of My Immaculate Heart, will be observant in every detail. None among them will be unfaithful to their Seraphic Father, whose virtue will be recognized and loved by all. They will attract the hearts of the good and the evil, and all will respect them. For God Three Times Holy and the Seraphic Stigmatic [Saint Francis] will have separated the wheat from the chaff, leaving only the pure wheat and the most perfect grapes in order to nourish, with the health-giving bread of practical teaching, the delicate souls of their sisters, the observant religious, so needed in that time. Founded on on solid virtue and from the heights of their seraphic and humble contemplation, the observant sisters will be inebriated with the plentiful wine of Divine Love and close union with God.

"Happy, blessed, and beloved by God will be my daughters of this time who, with humility and simplicity, will manifest their desire to subject themselves to my Franciscan friars, following the Rule and obeying that Prelate, my much beloved son. Their names will be written in the Sacred Heart of Jesus, their Divine Spouse, and in my own. They will merit special honor among the daughters of my seraphic servant Francis. Those who will oppose them will be counted as worthless straw, worthy only of the punishing fire."

### How the Height of the Mother of God Was Measured

The humble religious opened her spirit to the Blessed Virgin Mary, her Celestial Mother and Abbess. Then she timidly addressed her about the statue she wanted her to have made: "Most beautiful Lady, Thy beauty enchants me. Oh! If thou would only allow me to leave this ungrateful earth and take me with thee to Heaven! But permit me to say, that no human person, even the greatest expert in the art of sculpture, could make a wood statue in thy enchanting likeness and details as you ask. For this mission, I request my Seraphic Father to carve thy holy statue in the finest wood, aided by the Angels of Heaven, for I could never explain, nor much less give the measurement of your height."

To this, the vision responded, "Remain undaunted, my daughter, I will agree to what you ask of me. My servant Francis with his own wounded hands will carve my statue and the angelic spirits will assist him. He himself will place on me his cord, the symbol of all his sons and daughters who belong so closely to me. As for the height of my form, you yourself will measure me with the seraphic cord that you wear around your waist."

The religious replied, "Beautiful Lady, my dearest Mother, how can I, still a wayfarer on this earth, dare to touch thy divine forehead, which even the angelic spirits dare not do? Thou art the living Ark of the Covenant between poor mortals and God. And if Oza fell dead only for his fault in touching the Holy Ark to keep it from falling to the ground, how much more do I, a poor and weak woman, have to fear?"[48]

---

48. The Israelites had a great reverential fear of the Ark of the Covenant in the Old Testament. Only the priests were allowed to touch it. The Lord struck down Oza for touching the Ark to steady it when the Israelites were moving it to Jerusalem (2 Kings 6:6-7). In the Apostolic Constitution *Munificentissimus Deus* (1950), Pope Pius XII explained how the new Ark of the Covenant is Our Lady and superior to the old, since the most pure body of the Virgin Mary is an Ark "built of incorruptible wood ... preserved and exempt from all the corruption of the tomb and raised up to such glory in Heaven" (n. 26).

The Blessed Virgin responded: "Your humble restraint pleases me, and I see your ardent love for the Mother of God to whom you speak. Bring your cord to me and place one end of it in my hand. Then you should touch the other end of it to my foot."

The exultant religious did what Mary Most Holy ordered, trembling with joy, love, and reverence. [49]

The Holy Virgin continued: "Here, my daughter, you have the measurement of the height of your Heavenly Mother. Tell this to my servant, Francisco del Castillo,[50] and describe to him my features and bearing. He will do the exterior work on my statue, for he has a delicate conscience and scrupulously observes the Commandments of God and the Church. He is the only one worthy of this grace. You, on your part, must aid him with your prayers and with your humble suffering."

### LAST WORDS AND BLESSING OF OUR LADY OF GOOD SUCCESS

"Soon you will leave this prison, which will remain a privileged place in this Convent of yours and mine, because the innocent have suffered here. Blessed are they who suffer persecution for justice's sake, for the Kingdom of Heaven belongs to them. I say this to you, your daughters and companions in prison, and also to all my daughters who will suffer through the centuries for the Seraphic Family to preserve regular observance of the Rule.

"With my own hands, I receive your tears and secret sufferings and convert them into beautiful pearls to present to my Most Holy Son, so that He might hasten the day of your seraphic freedom. For since today, their captivity begins. Encourage your suffering daughters. Now, I give my maternal blessing to you and all of my daughters.

"Awaken your sisters from their sleep so that, with you, they might raise their voices in reciting the Matins of the Little Office, which gives me such great pleasure, for it is the mainstay of

---

49. The majestic statue of Our Lady of Good Success, made according to these specifications, stands 5 feet 9 inches tall.

50. For more on the role of the artist Francisco del Castillo in the making of the miraculous statue, see Marian T. Horvat, *Stories and Miracles of Our Lady of Good Success*, pp. 42-4.

this, my Community. Without it, its members would lack the true religious spirit, and they would see themselves wither like plants exposed to the harsh winter air."

After saying these words imbued with divine mystery, the divine apparition disappeared, and the happy Abbess lit her lamp to awaken her daughters, who were peacefully sleeping.

The voice of their Abbess awakened the imprisoned sisters at 4 a.m. Kneeling, they said the first prayers of the day and each one received the blessing of their Abbess. In it, she included the blessing of their Heavenly Mother. Then, with extraordinary fervor, they began to pray the Little Office. The Angels took new delight in carrying these ardent prayers to the heavenly kingdom, prayers that emanated from hearts purified by suffering, making them powerful in placating the divine ire and obtaining pardon and mercy for the culpable Spanish Colony.

### VISION OF THE INFERNAL DRAGON

After the praying of the Matins and Lauds, Mother Mariana remained in prayer. As she prayed, she saw in the Convent an immense and monstrous dragon, whose large, round eyes spit fire in every direction. This fire consumed the unfaithful sisters who had plotted so unceasingly how to banish the Franciscan friars forever and oppress the holy and innocent Founding Mothers. The dragon prowled throughout the Convent and its courtyards, but it could not enter either the choir or the prison. When it approached these places, the monster trembled in confusion and fled in terror.

Having finished the hour of Tierce and before beginning the recitation of the Sext, she told her sisters: "My daughters, let us offer the remaining hours of the Office for our poor sisters who walk in darkness and persecute us unjustly. I see how the infernal dragon is instigating them. It saddens me that these sisters, spouses of my Lord and God, are losing their souls. The tears, sorrows, and loss of the spirit of the Order that our sisters in the coming centuries will suffer weighs heavily upon these guilty sisters. Oh! If they could only realize this now, as we do!"

When they recommenced the praying of the Little Office, all the Founders, along with Mother Mariana, saw the terrible dragon prowling through the Convent. At the end of the morning prayer, the religious and their holy Abbess all took the discipline. After this, they began the mental prayer prescribed by the Rule.

During it, they all saw their seraphic Father Saint Francis with a bow in his hand, shooting flaming arrows at the dragon, who tried to flee but did not know where to go. Badly wounded and covered with arrows, it gave a horrible cry. Exerting all its strength, it caused the earth to open and withdrew into this abyss. At that very moment, 5:15 a.m., a long, strong tremor of the earth took place. This tremor caused fear and commotion among the inhabitants of the city, and the sisters could hear the cries and shouts of persons begging to God for mercy.

Inside the Convent, Mother Valenzuela attributed the earthquake to Divine Justice meting out a chastisement for the injustices being done against the holy Founding Mothers. The non-observant sisters awoke sick with strong pains in their bodies. They cried out, saying that the walls were falling down on them, but they were unable to move. Only one sister, the worst tormenter of the innocent Founders, managed to rise with great effort to try to prevent Mother Valenzuela from going to help her innocent sisters in the prison.

Be it understood that during this ill-fated time in the Convent, Mother Valenzuela did not command. Rather, a resentful non-observant sister had unjustly assumed the direction of the Convent, and neither the insinuations nor reproofs of Mother Valenzuela could do anything to bring her to her senses.

Sorely afflicted and suffering enormously, Mother Valenzuela, along with the rest of the observant sisters in the Convent, fled to the door of the prison. There they were consoled by their holy Abbess, for, in her, they found all the virtues that the non-observant sisters lacked.

### LIFE IN PRISON

Mother Valenzuela had employed every means in her power to free the innocent sisters from prison. She could neither eat nor sleep in peace. As for the captives, they had converted the prison into a true Heaven, so much so that the Queen of Heaven visited them there. In union with their Abbess, the innocent victims implored light and mercy for their poor sisters, whom they loved with all their hearts.

As generous and faithful daughters of their Crucified Lord, Mary Immaculate, and the Seraphim of Assisi, they bore no resentment in their hearts. Deprived of every human good, for even their food was frugal and sparse, they suffered a thousand hardships. Less virtuous souls, wearied by such suffering, would have given in and ceded to the demands of their negligent sisters, who wanted to abandon observance of the Rule. But they maintained their happiness, peace, confidence, and holy tranquility in prison.

Their holy Abbess, with her generous and magnanimous heart, or better said, her truly virile heart, tried to divert and cheer her sisters, fostering their love for Mary Most Holy and animating them with the hope of Heaven. Would that we could hear the words that this blessed soul spoke about the beauties of Heaven to her sisters and daughters!

As the Author of every perfect gift had endowed Mother Mariana with beauty of both soul and body, her very presence attracted all to her. Further, she was gifted with a beautiful voice, sweet and melodious in song, and she had learned to play several instruments.

The Marquesa, a lady of Quito who knew and admired Mother Mariana greatly, had ordered a beautiful harp made in Valladolid and presented it to her at the time of the foundation of the Convent.[51] In the prison, Mother Mariana would play on this harp with the greatest of unction, heartening herself and her daughters.

Curiously enough, when the non-observant sisters would imprison Mother Mariana, they themselves would bring her the harp. Then, when she played and sang, they would go to listen to her beautiful voice whose sweetness they could not resist.

And just as in times past the bad temper of Saul would lift when he heard the harp of the young David, they found comfort in hearing her singing and playing. The observant sisters who were

---

51. More stories of the holy widow, the Marquesa Maria de Yolanda, and her role in the making of the miraculous statue of Our Lady of Good Success are told in Volume II of this biography by Fr. Manuel Pereira. See also, M. T. Horvat, *Stories and Miracles of Our Lady of Good Success,* pp. 45-50.

not imprisoned would also go to hear her play and were consoled to hear the melodious voice of their Mother. As they listened, they would shed tears of compassion and yearn for the hour when they would again be united with their holy Mother and Abbess.

During this imprisonment, Mother Mariana de Jesus composed the moving verses filled with divine unction transcribed below. Accompanied by her harp, she sang and taught her daughters these verses dedicated to her Heavenly Mother.

They accompanied her in song, each voice harmonizing with the other, making a lovely concert of angelic voices. For Mothers Francisca of the Angels, Lucia of the Cross, and Maria of the Incarnation were also gifted with beautiful voices, inferior only to that of Mother Mariana. The sad melody that raises heart and soul to Heaven was composed by Mother Mariana while she was in prison.

### Verses that Mother Mariana Composed in Prison in the Year 1599 [52]

Beautiful Maiden,
Delight of God,
Come visit my soul,
Quickly I implore.

In cruel bitterness
Amidst pain and grief.
Thou art my consolation,
And thou givest me strength.

Like a withered leaf
That falls from the tree of God,
I feel far removed from the tree
of the Franciscan Order

Oh! most blessed tree!
Beloved of God.
Lacking your shade,
I lack love.

Such a small weak vessel
On the tempestuous sea,
My soul drifts aimlessly
Without oars and light.

I implore thee, my Mother,
Sustain me in my strife.
Console me in my sorrow
And relieve me in my pain.

Save, then, thy house,
Which was founded by thee.
Where peace and love
Reside hidden in it.

Oh! Stigmatic Father,
Francis of Assisi!
Be thou my advocate
In this fateful battle.

Watch over your children,
Who amid their sad tears,
Implore thee lovingly
For strength and fervor.

A thousand times cursed
Be those who love not Francis,
Soldier of Christ
My Father and my beloved!

When Mother Valenzuela heard these sad strains, she was moved to extraordinary action. She went to the non-observant nuns and, with unusual vigor, told them that she, more than they, had the right to govern the Convent since she had been the Abbess. Almost violently, she snatched the keys from the impudent one who had assumed for herself the government of the Convent. Forthwith she wrote a very formal note to the Bishop vindicating her innocent Abbess and all the Founding Mothers.

\* \* \*

---

52.
    Hermosa doncella,
    Delicia de Dios,
    Camina hacia mi alma
    Con paso veloz.

    En mi cruel amargura,
    En pena y dolor,
    Sois Vos mi consuelo,
    Y dadme valor.

    Cual hoja marchita,
    Del árbol de Dios,
    Me arrastro muy lejos
    Del árbol Menor;

    Oh! árbol bendito!
    Querido de Dios,
    Faltando tu sombra,
    Me falta el amor;

    Cual débil barquilla,
    En mar tempestuoso,
    Fluctúa mi alma,
    Sin remo y sin luz.

Pidiéndote Madre,
Sostén en mi lucha,
Consuelo en mi pena,
Alivio en mi mal.

Que salves tu Casa,
Fundada for Tí,
Do ocultos residen,
La paz y el amor.

Oh Padre Llagado!
Francisco de Asís,
Sed Vos mi abogado,
En lance fatal.

Cuidad de tus hijas,
Que tristes, llorosas,
Te piden, ansiosas,
Valor y fervor.

Maldito mil veces,
Quien no ame a Francisco,
Alférez de Cristo,
Mi Padre y mi amor!

## Chapter 23

In her note to the Bishop, Mother Valenzuela told him that God was angry that such a great injustice was being committed in the Convent, and that she feared the city would be destroyed by an earthquake coming from Pichincha Mountain, whose fierce volcano at that time was threatening the countryside.[53] She explained that she had wanted to tell him before now what was happening, but the non-observant religious had not allowed her to do so. Finally, she explained, she had overcome her weakness, made herself heard, and taken the keys by force from them so that she could recount the true state of affairs inside the Convent to him.

She asked that he respond immediately to her note, and that he give a signed written order for the release for the holy and innocent prisoners. He should also command that Mother Mariana de Jesus Torres, so worthy because of her virtue, strength of will, and strong guidance, should continue governing the Convent until the conclusion of her term.

### The Order to Release the Prisoners Arrives

The petition of Mother Valenzuela, to whose name posterity will be grateful – for she sinned because of a lack of character rather than from malice – was heard, and everything she asked was done. Under holy obedience, the Bishop ordered that she and the whole community – with no exceptions, not even the sick – should go immediately in triumph and joy to release their innocent sisters from prison. Then all should acknowledge Mother Mariana de Jesus Torres as their legitimate Abbess, rendering her obedience and restoring her to the Abbess' chair in the upper choir of the Convent. All the keys to the cloisters and other buildings should be handed over to her. The Bishop also directed that only the Founding Mothers should occupy the higher posts of command in the Convent, because they were the ones suited for this.

---

53. Pichincha is an active volcano two miles outside the city of Quito. The area surrounding Quito had recorded large eruptions in 1566, 1575, and 1582; therefore, its rumblings set fear in the hearts of the inhabitants of the city. After a 300 year period of dormancy, Pinchincha came alive again in 1981 and covered the city with ash in late summer of 1999.

Further, he ordered that the rebellious *criollas* be given the lowest places, and that the leader be locked in a secluded room with a crucifix and a skull so that she could reflect upon her actions. She should not be placed in the prison, he added, since she was unworthy to stay in the same place where the innocent religious had been unjustly imprisoned.

After she read the note, Mother Valenzuela, quite well satisfied with its contents, rang the community bell. Hearing it, the religious were alarmed. When all were gathered together, including the sick sisters, Mother Valenzuela read the stern note. The observant sisters wept from happiness, and the non-observant sisters, from anger and disgust. The sick sisters, and their number included the leader, wanted to return to their beds, pleading that their illness prevented them from accompanying the group to the prison. Mother Valenzuela, however, vigorously asserted herself and told them that either they would obey the Bishop or they would suffer the consequences. With the sick sisters at the head of the procession, they all prepared to file down to the prison to free the innocent captives.

**ROSES FROM HEAVEN**

As the procession was about to begin, the outside bell rang. Mother Valenzuela went to the turn-box [the opening in the wall where the city residents left packages and messages for the sisters] and found a bouquet of roses and lilies there. She understood that these flowers had come from Heaven, for they were out of season and there was no one outside to say who had sent them, so that they might crown the heads of the innocent Founding Mothers with wreaths. Everyone helped to carry these garlands except for the non-observant nuns, who were not obliged to do this.

Hearing the happy uproar in the Convent, the prisoners became frightened. But their Abbess told them: "My daughters, the hour to leave this holy place has arrived. Let us prepare to rejoin our guilty sisters, whom we will warmly embrace to our hearts. Let us pray a Hail Mary and kiss this blessed floor that has allowed us to acquire so much merit for our souls. From this, let us learn that everything in life passes. The day and hour of deliverance from our prison has arrived for us. But let us not forget to entreat God in His goodness to hasten the day of liberty for our future sisters with the return of obedience to the Franciscan friars."

By the time the Abbess finished speaking these words, Mother Valenzuela had arrived at the doors of the prison. Throwing them open, she and the rest of the religious entered that blessed place. They all vied to be first to embrace their Abbess. But Mother Valenzuela pushed herself forward, and, in a flood of tears, grasped her tightly in her arms. She then embraced each of the Founding Mothers. Mother Mariana, however, extended her arms first to the most guilty sister and then to other non-observant sisters. They would condescend to make only a civil response.

### Imprisonment of the Non-Observant Leader

One by one, the observant sisters lovingly embraced their Abbess and the other Founding Mothers. Showering them with the flowers they carried, they began to process to the choir in accordance with the orders of the Bishop's letter, which Mother Valenzuela read aloud to the whole Community.

When she reached the part that ordered the most guilty sister into solitary confinement in a secluded room, Mother Mariana could not contain her tears. She wanted to prevent this indignity and suffering for her guilty sister. But Mother Valenzuela emphatically insisted that she had to carry out the orders of the Bishop to the letter. So she locked the guilty sister in the room, and handed the key to her Superior.

She then proceeded to assign all the higher posts in the Convent to the Founding Mothers. The atmosphere of joy was similar to that of the first day of the election. The non-observant sisters, unable to conceal their unhappiness, alleged illness in order to separate themselves from the Community.

### How Mother Mariana Treated the Non-Observant Sisters

The saintly Mother Mariana visited the non-observant sisters often, speaking to them of God and the Blessed Virgin and doing all that she could for them. She never mentioned her own recent sufferings or her month in prison.

When they finally left their sickbeds, these sisters rejoined the community life. Mother Valenzuela was careful to see that they occupied the lowest places, in conformance with the Bishop's orders. Anguished and humiliated, they were forced to comply.

The holy Abbess also constantly visited the guilty leader, who had been locked up in a room apart from the others. She ordered that a table, chair, and good bed be placed in the room. She carefully saw to her needs and meals, she herself performing all the humble acts required for a person in prison or seclusion. She brought her fruits, bread, and a sweet milk to try and make her life less miserable. In short, she did everything that a loving mother can do for a cherished daughter.

However, this guilty sister received Mother Mariana with scowls and coldness. At times, she would accuse the Abbess of making intrigues with the Bishop to unjustly procure her seclusion. Therefore, she said, it was only right that Mother Mariana should at least try to afford her some relief for this wrongdoing, but that the day would come when she would see justice done and the Abbess once again imprisoned.

The Abbess would not respond a word to these things. Instead, she would help the sister to pray the Divine Office, speaking to her often of God, the Most Holy Virgin, and the wondrous joys that God Our Lord has reserved in Heaven for His faithful servants.

### Mother Mariana Obtains Freedom for the Captive Sister

After eight days had passed, Mother Mariana wrote to the Bishop, begging liberty for this suffering sister, for she did not have the heart to see her suffer any longer in this seclusion. She reminded him that human weakness is great and capable of many errors. The Prelate responded that this nun should remain in seclusion for one complete month. How long this seemed to the kindly Abbess, whose heart, a volcano of charity, burned with a divine fire that communicated itself to all who came near her or even spoke to her!

At the end of the month, she again sent a note to the Bishop asking authorization to release the non-observant sister from seclusion. The Prelate replied that he would give no order, but leave the matter in her hands. She could release the sister, or she could keep her locked up for as long as she deemed necessary.

After reading his reply, she went to Mother Valenzuela to inform her of what the Bishop had said. Mother Valenzuela argued that the revolted sister should remain imprisoned to prevent her from disturbing the spirit of other non-observant sisters.

"No, Mother," replied the Abbess. "My heart cannot allow this poor sister to be locked up any longer. She suffers without consolation, and I must do everything possible to alleviate her cross so that she does not fall into despair. For I fear that with her little virute, the least weight could make her succumb."

Mother Valenzuela replied, "Your Reverence is very charitable, but you are going beyond the limits of charity. Release her, then, but I would not do so."

Without losing another minute, Mother Mariana went to the room of the recluse. Entering it, she found the defiant sister lying on the bed, moaning in pain from a colic. The holy Superior approached and embraced her, saying, "My dear sister, you need no longer stay here. Today I have obtained permission from the Bishop to release you from this seclusion. Since you are ill, I am going to prepare a bed for you immediately in the infirmary so that you can be better attended."

"Then I allow you to do so," replied the religious coldly.

Leaving the key with the sick sister, Mother Mariana went quickly to the infirmary and called for Mother Francisca of the Angels. She told her, "My daughter, our poor sister in seclusion is sick with colic. Let us prepare a bed and all that is necessary to restore her to health. I have just received permission from the Bishop to release her from seclusion. Let us remember that since it is she who is forming our souls for Heaven, we should love her dearly. For if the beautiful statues had the use of reason, they would cherish the instruments that carved and polished them. We, then, who have the use of reason, should do what the statues cannot do."

### The Ingratitude of the Non-Observant Sister

Together, they quickly prepared a bed and the other necessary things to cure their sick sister. Then they both went to the room of the sick sister to transfer her to the infirmary.

The holy Abbess told the recluse: "My dear sister, everything is ready in the infirmary. Here is the nurse herself to carry you there, for she loves you like a dear sister."

Approaching the sick sister, Mother Francisca of the Angels embraced her, saying, "Poor little sister, you are sweating and cold. I am going to help to make you well."

But the sick sister coldly retorted, "It was you who made me like this."

The two religious placed a cover on the ground and lifted the sick sister onto it since she was too ill to take a step. On their way to the infirmary, they met Mother Anna of the Conception and Mother Magdalena of Saint John. After they heard what was happening, the two approached the sick sister, and, with comforting words, helped to carry her to the infirmary, where they lay her on the bed prepared for her. Immediately they began to attend to her.

Mother Francisca of the Angels prepared an ointment of animal fat, chamomile, and anise, and the charitable Abbess massaged this on the poor sister's stomach, assisted by Mother Anna of the Conception and Mother Magdalena of Saint John. Meanwhile, Mother Francisca of the Angels and Mother Lucia of the Cross prepared an enema. After these remedies had been applied, the sick sister was finally able to move. Relieved from the terrible pain she had been suffering, she thanked them. The Mothers embraced her lovingly. But she returned their solicitude and caresses with coldness.

Thus is the example of Saints. The holy Founders of the Convent of the Immaculate Conception of Mary Most Holy bequeathed a great practical lesson to their future daughters so that they might follow their example when, through the course of time, they would have bad sisters who formed their crowns of thorns. Nor will this Convent every lack such bad sisters, who will make the others exercise the virtues of patience, charity, humility, and tolerance, so necessary for the daughters of the humble Seraphim of Assisi.

After recovering from this sickness, the guilty sister did not amend her life. Restless and agitated, she constantly perturbed the spirit of her sisters and would not leave them in peace. During this term as Abbess, Mother Mariana suffered much and earned great merit, as did the good and observant religious and all the Founders. Thanks be to God, the greater part of the sisters were observant religious, formed by Mother Mariana. This model Abbess suffered everything in silence and with most exemplary humility so that, throughout the centuries, she might be imitated by all the fortunate religious in this Convent, the Abbesses as well as their subjects.

\* \* \*

## Chapter 24

Amid these many interior sorrows, the holy Abbess governed with humility, prudence, and mildness. Yet she never permitted the least deviation from the Holy Rule. Humble of heart, she believed herself to be the one most lacking in virtue and intelligence. Shedding tears over her inadequacies in the presence of the Sacramental Jesus, she would attribute the faults of the non-observant sisters to her own flaws. To atone for these, every evening she would make the Way of the Cross, which she ended in the lower choir.

On Mondays and Fridays, she would kiss the feet of the religious of her Community, thinking herself fortunate to be able to touch with her lips the feet of her holy sisters, as she used to call them. On Wednesdays and Saturdays she would eat on the floor without her veil and with a cord around her neck, considering herself unworthy to eat in the company of her sisters in the refectory. On Thursdays she would lay on the floor so that her growing Community would step over her, judging herself fortunate to be able to live in this holy house where God and her heavenly Mother had dispensed so many favors despite her lowliness and absolute worthlessness. On Tuesdays, she always placed something bitter in her food. Thus did she habitually divide the days of the week.

At times Mother Valenzuela would remark with great concern that she was overexerting herself and that if she did not take care, Mother Mariana would soon leave her alone in the world.

She would exclaim with embarrassment and affection, "Oh no, dear Mother! It is Your Reverence who will leave me alone, and not I, you. It is only that this poor dust of the earth desires to be, at least for some moments, where it belongs. For if the saints considered themselves as nothing, how much more so should I think this of myself, who, in reality, am nothing?"

### How Mother Mariana Corrected Those Who Committed Faults

Her prudence was admirable and worthy of being imitated not only by her present and future sisters, but also even by Bishops.

On the various occasions when, as Abbess, she had to correct abuses, curb the non-observant sisters, make an admonishment, or dispose some matter, she would first consult with Our Lord in the Eucharist. Weeping like a child and applying the discipline to herself, she would implore His counsel. Then, she would do what she should, her heart expanded by her love. With her blushed cheeks making her more beautiful, her very appearance would attract the hearts of her daughters, who loved her so intensely, except for those few imprudent ones.

She never brought up past wrongdoings or received her daughters with a severe or forbidding countenance. Neither would she speak imperiously to them. Instead, she corrected them with winning charm. Going to the cell of some sister who had committed a fault, she would first embrace her and then speak to her of the sublimity of being a religious and of the glory that awaited the observant and mortified religious in Heaven.

After this, she would tell her: "My dear sister, it seems that you did not remember such and such a thing, for these faults have been repeated many times. We have memories so weak that some things escape us. Thus I will give you a small reminder so that you take the highest care to avoid these things, for, living in community, it is most critical that in all things we give each other good example. When we reach Heaven, we will be happy for the good example that we gave to our beloved sisters.

"Let us remember the life of the Child Jesus in the humble little house of Nazareth. How we should imitate Him here in our cloister! The Gospel tells us only a few words about Jesus in Nazareth, '*Et erat subditus illis*' ['And he was submissive to them']. But these few words tell us much.

"How many volumes of books could be written about the daily life of Jesus in Nazareth. However, He did not want anything to be written about this period of His life, because this is the part that should be lived in all the convents of His beloved spouses. Anyone who wants to know how Jesus acted in Nazareth need only look to the cloistered religious, and, therein, he would find his answer. Because of this, I, your poor Mother and sister, beseech you and rightly oblige you to take care that Christ is always living in us. I will help you with my poor prayers and small sacrifices. If something is lacking to you or causing you doubts, do not be afraid to come to me. Perhaps I can help you to resolve your concerns, for, although your Abbess is the least and most ignorant of creatures, the Holy Spirit assists her and lovingly directs the souls of the virgin spouses of the Eucharistic Christ."

The sweetness yet admirable firmness of these admonitions and reprisals were such that not even the non-observant sisters could resist her at these moments. All their wrongdoings were committed out of her presence.

With each day that passed, Mother Valenzuela's admiration for the humble Mother Mariana increased. For, at times, she could reprimand without a word, but only a look – a kind and winning look for the observant religious, but a terrible one for the non-observant sisters.

### A New Order for the Imprisonment of Mother Mariana

The life of Mother Mariana was one of suffering and contradictions, a distinctive mark of the servants of God. For she, so humble, sacrificial, and obedient, was accused and reprimanded repeatedly by the Bishop Ordinary.

This Prelate, who did not understand the internal affairs of the life in the Convent, again allowed himself to be swayed by the lies of the non-observant nuns. Before believing their accusations, he should have first gone to the Convent and carefully examined the situation to arrive at an understanding of the truth. But God, in His secret designs, disposed things otherwise so that the Seraphic family would have a heroine of suffering and humility in this Conceptionist daughter.

At the anxious request of the rebellious religious, the Bishop made a pastoral visit. Once again, the non-observant sisters made so many accusations against the Abbess that we might say the few triumphed over the many. Vacillating, the Bishop was unsure of what to do.

Finally, his secretary said, "Your Excellency should exercise care in deciding this matter because there are many accusations against Mother Mariana de Jesus Torres!"

The designs of God are mysterious indeed! The Prelate ordered that her title should be taken away and she should be placed in seclusion in her cell, giving the government during this interim to the Vicar Abbess of the Convent.

When she received this order, the humble Abbess said: "My dear sisters, I go to my cell in seclusion. For some time God has been calling my heart to yearn for solitude. My position among my sisters is cumbersome to me, for I was born to obey and not to command. I know my insufficiency for the latter. Pray for me that I love you all without exception as the beloved and chosen spouses of Our Lord. Pardon me for all the bad example I have given you. I, on my part, will never forget you in the presence of my Lord.

"However, I must tell you that my conscience does not accuse me of any of the charges raised against me. For these things, I do not deserve punishment. I do not regret my diligence in observing the Rule and the solicitous care I took in rebuking individuals privately and in community. On the contrary, my conscience is at peace that I have carried out my duty. If this has angered one among you, then I mind not, for I would that the whole world were angered rather than my Lord and God.

"The office of Abbess is very critical and most serious. Exercising it, many great souls are lost. And mine, so small, does not want to further endanger itself because of other guilty souls."

When Mother Mariana had finished speaking, Mother Valenzuela cried out in a broken voice, "Your Reverence will not go alone. I will accompany you. Why is innocence persecuted, calumniated, and punished?"

Then, to the Vicar General, she said, "Who are the unwise sisters who act like this?"

The other observant sisters were weeping. But the captain and her followers showed no remorse. They approached Mother Mariana and told her, "Let us go, then, to the prison, as the Bishop ordered. For in reality he ordered you to be placed there, and not in your cell in seclusion."

Mother Valenzuela, who heard some of these words, became indignant. "What are you brazen souls saying now?" she asked angrily.

Then, stepping between them and Mother Mariana, she said, "Isn't her seclusion in the cell sufficient for you? You want even worse for her, the prison! The prison should be for you!"

Joined by the Vicar Abbess and some of the other observant sisters, she was prepared to stop these impudent sisters. But the discerning Abbess said: "Let them be, my Mothers and sisters. They are only instruments of the Divine Will. Nonetheless, read aloud the order of the Bishop."

Mother Valenzuela then made one of the non-observant sisters read it aloud, which caused a great altercation in the Community. Thanks be to God, the majority of the sisters were observant. However, that small faction of non-observant sisters had upturned the Convent.

### AMID THIS ORDEAL, OUR LORD APPEARS

Clearly this innocent lamb would have been freed if she had chosen to defend herself and allowed Mother Valenzuela, the Vicar Abbess, and the others to support her cause. At that very moment, however, God had manifested to her that, if violence was used, the souls of all those non-observant sisters would be lost. She was also given to understand that this humiliation was necessary in order to save the Convent founded by her holy aunt, the other Founding Mothers, and herself, as well as to save the souls of the non-observant sisters.

At this moment, she saw Our Lord Jesus Christ, tied and handcuffed by the barbarous Jews after the betrayal of Judas. She saw Him unjustly accused and calumniated in the tribunals of the iniquitous pontiffs, treated with great cruelty and ignominy. At the same time, she saw what was passing within His Divine Heart: His sentiments of loving magnanimity toward His very persecutors, His heroism in offering His sorrowful Passion for so many ungrateful souls, and His profound sorrow over the perdition of such souls and ingratitude of His ministers and spouses throughout the course of the centuries until the end of the world. She saw how the Divine Master suffered His interior and exterior Passion.

Turning toward her, He said with loving tenderness, "My spouse, do not leave Me alone in such great bitterness and sorrow. If you truly love Me, I ask that you do not leave Me, but accompany

Me during your days on earth. Know that this generous sacrifice will germinate the seed of this Convent so beloved of My Heart, so that it will have victim souls of suffering and sorrow throughout time. These souls, under My gaze, will live in the practice of the most sublime perfection, being the columns of your Community and deflectors to deter My divine anger in the ill-fated times that the Church will see on this soil. Let us go, then, to your seclusion, for there I desire to speak alone with you and make you a participant of My sorrows."

### Mother Mariana Is Unjustly Imprisoned for the Fourth Time

Filled with the love of God, the Abbess rose from her seat. Kneeling, she handed the keys to the Vicar Abbess, kissing her feet and hands. She covered her beautiful face with her veil, and, with grave steps, she walked to her cell, whose window opened to the Church. There she had all her precious jewelry, which were her instruments of penance and the enormous cross upon which she would often lay outstretched in the form of a cross.

She left the key in the lock so that they could lock her in if they so desired. However, Mother Valenzuela and the Vicar Abbess, fearing that the non-observant sisters might do this, left the door unlocked and took the key. Mother Mariana then barred the door from within and began her time of seclusion.

### Verses that Mother Mariana Sang in Seclusion in her Cell

During this time, Mother Mariana composed these expressive, sorrowful verses. In addition to her keen intelligence and extraordinary unction, she was gifted with a profound ascetic and mystical understanding. The Seraphic family could well claim that Mother Mariana de Jesus Torres, Spanish by birth, Abbess and Founder of the Convent of the Immaculate Conception in Quito, could vie with the Spanish Founder of Carmel [Saint Teresa of Avila], with Mother Mariana being a hidden violet in the verdant garden of Mary, Our Immaculate Mother, and the great Saint Teresa a vibrant bugle of Jesus Christ.

By way of note, the confessors and directors of this great soul are certain that Mother Mariana received the gift of infused wisdom, as demonstrated by her celebrated writings on the gifts and fruits of the Holy Ghost, the mystery of the Immaculate Conception, and even on Papal Infallibility. The Seraphic family sent these writings of Mother Mariana to Rome for review and approval. However, a disastrous shipwreck submerged these marvels, as well as other important papers of the Franciscan Order, in the depths of the sea.

According to information from trustworthy sources, Mother Mariana preserved the drafts of these works, which still exist today in the Convent closets, along with the *Cuadernon* [the grand Notebook] recording the events and miracles of her life and the biographies of the rest of the Founding Mothers.

These were the verses[54] Mother Mariana composed in the seclusion of her cell:

In a faraway willow
My lyre in hand,
I see myself captive
And begin to weep.

Far off in the distance
Of the centuries gone by,
I see Francis and his children
Coming to me.

They bring their great happiness,
Their peace and joy,
To soothe so many sorrows
That have become my home.

Oh! Fortunate day
Of blessed joy!
Come quickly, come quickly!
I am eagerly waiting!

But here on this soil
Of so much grief,
Where I taste my tears
Without hope of joy.

When an end will come
To my days here on earth,
My sorrows will end
And I will enjoy happiness.

Then I from Heaven
With holy dedication,
I will guard from here
Holy observance of the Rule.

Throughout the centuries,
Good daughters will I find,
Lovingly and exhaustively
They will serve God.

---

54. En sauce extranjero, colgando mi lira, me miro cautiva, y empiezo a llorar. Más allá, en lontananza, pasados los siglos, a Francisco y sus hijos, los veo venir. Trayendo la dicha, la paz, la ventura, que en tanta tristura, Se encuentra mi hogar.
Mi día dichoso, de santa alegría, venid presuroso, que ansío por tí!
Mas yo, en este suelo, de tanto quebranto, do bebo el llanto, no espero gozar.
Cuando haya acabado, mis dias mortales, terminan mis males, empiezo a gozar.
Y ya desde el Cielo, con santo desvelo, la santa observancia, de aquí celaré.
Y en todos los siglos, tendré buenas hijas, que, amantes, prolijas, a Dios servirán.

It is a great privilege to be in this Convent, for there great marvels took place, and in it saintly religious have lived, who will be followed by other hidden souls, forgotten and despised by their own and the outside world in their quiet retirement. They are souls, nonetheless, who, by their austere and secret penances, deflect the ire of Divine Justice.

Thou art good, my God, that in Thy merciful wisdom, Thou didst create convents with such souls in them! Weak women who become Thy spouses do thus attract and stimulate the admiration of wise and strong men! I confess that my sisters of the Immaculate Conception are walls of fortitude and, for their brothers, the Franciscan friars, a stimulus to progress in religious perfection.

### The Lava of Calumnies

While she remained secluded in her cell by order of the Bishop, this holy Abbess practiced all the virtues to a heroic degree. Her life was that of a cloistered hermit. How rigid were her penances, according to her spiritual director, and how solid her humility, how magnanimous her generosity, how childlike her simplicity, and how ardent her love for Jesus and Mary!

During the next pastoral visit, the Abbess remained in seclusion. They took the seal from her and deposed her ignominiously of her office of Abbess. She was despised by her own daughters and by the Bishop. For, during this time, by divine permission, the infernal demon spewed forth scurrilous calumnies like lava from a burning volcano. He used as his instruments the non-observant sisters, who were instigated by the rebellious captain, for whom regular obedience and the practice of virtue were disagreeable.

This long, painful trial, suffered in silence and with humble resignation, sanctified the soul of Mother Mariana de Jesus Torres, one of the Spanish Founding Mothers of the Convent of the Immaculate Conception in Quito. It prepared her to receive an abundance of special graces in her intimate communication and contact with God and His Blessed Mother. For it was these sufferings that earned her the high throne of glory that today she occupies in the Celestial Jerusalem!

## Prayer

*Oh! unconquerable heroine and my dear sister! From Heaven which you enjoy with Christ, the Pure Spouse of chaste souls, deign to turn toward us your beautiful blue eyes, which symbolize profundity of the love of God. Look down on us and dry the tears of your brothers, the Friars Minor, and of your Conceptionist sisters, who still mourn and weep in this earthly valley of exile. Obtain for us daily fervor in the fulfillment of our holy Rules; animate in us the spirit that our Stigmatic Father, the Seraphim of Assisi, left us for our inheritance.*

*And for this brother of yours, who, in longhand and with this rustic feather pen writes your life, bless him from Heaven and obtain for him humility, strength to sustain the daily trials of spirit, and, in the end, a tranquil and holy death so that from his poor deathbed, he may go to keep you company in Heaven, where, with the Seraphic Father, you reign glorious with Christ and Mary for all eternity. Amen.*

\* \* \*

## Chapter 25

During this sad period, another person representing the Bishop made a secret visit to the Convent. Mother Valenzuela, the Vicar Abbess, and the observant sisters spoke to him about their worthy Abbess and showed him the falseness of the innumerable calumnies that had been spread about her, calumnies all the more surprising because they were made by religious sisters. They made him understand that only jealousy and bad will could induce anyone to obscure the shining light of sanctity of Mother Mariana de Jesus Torres, who, as a simple sister as well as Abbess, was an almost inimitable model of religious perfection. "Who among us," the sisters would often ask, "could have suffered so much and with such sweetness, silence, patience, resignation, and prudence?"

### The Bishop's Representative Wants to Free Mother Mariana

Hearing this, the Bishop's representative felt a great admiration for Mother Mariana and promised to do all in his power to free the holy and virtuous Abbess who suffered so unjustly. In fact, he exposed the whole situation to the Bishop, who sent a formal note to the Vicar Abbess, ordering her to free Mother Mariana and restore her as Abbess and Mother of the Community. The command was carried out immediately amid the general recognition and rejoicing of the religious.

The next morning, the same representative of the Bishop came to the Convent to speak in the confessional with Mother Mariana. This soul, so simple and so holy and, at the same time, so intelligent and dignified, presented herself to the Confessor. With the integrity of an innocent soul, she responded to all that he asked with moderate words, neither loquacious nor condemnatory of any person. She pardoned everyone, attributed what had occurred to divine permission, and affirmed that it would be futile to hope to attain Heaven without suffering during this mortal life.

The Bishop's representative marveled to see the virtue of this religious. Above all, he was impressed by her admirable tranquility and integrity of spirit after the terrible sufferings through which she had passed. He later assured the Bishop that she seemed to him like one of those heroic martyrs from the early days of the Church, and that the Prelate had a duty of conscience to make amends to her for all the unjust punishments that had been inflicted upon her.

#### NOTE FROM THE BISHOP TO MOTHER MARIANA

The Bishop, who had a tender heart, for he was not by nature an unjust man, suffered keenly when he realized that he had oppressed a just soul with unjust slanders.

Taking pen in hand, he wrote the following note:
"Reverend Mother Mariana de Jesus Torres, most worthy Abbess of the Sisters of the Immaculate Conception of this city of Saint Francis of Quito:

"Having been badly informed about Your Reverence by the scurrilous calumnies from the mouths of those poor women who do not deserve the name of religious, I committed an act of great imprudence by ordering your seclusion without prior investigation. Today, the truth having been brought to full light, I order Your Reverence to be now and forever the one who governs and rules this Convent, above even the governing Abbess, who should consult you in everything and seek your counsel in all she does, obeying you as Mother and Founder. All, without exception, should respect and obey you, and Your Reverence will have the authority and right, for all times, to reprimand and chastise the guilty.

"For all that Your Reverence has done in the Convent, I thank you in the name of God, for you have acted well in everything, imitating your Divine Spouse, Who passed His life on this earth doing good, even to those who were His persecutors. A similar thing happened to Your Reverence, and for this reason you should saintly rejoice in Our Lord, Who sends His cross to those whom He most loves because He deems them worthy of such a supreme gift.

"Henceforth, anyone who shall denounce Your Reverence to me will be imprisoned and immediately will receive the greater penances, and these bad-intentioned daughters will be obliged to ask your forgiveness. Since your Abbacy is ending soon, continue until the time of the canonical election to rule your Community with your special gift for governing and the keen discernment that God, prodigious in His graces, has bestowed on you.

"Blessing your Reverence in the Name of the Father and of the Son and of the Holy Ghost, I sign myself as your father and Prelate." It finished with the signature of the Bishop

Her liberty once again restored, the holy Abbess continued to govern the Community with that humility characteristic of her great soul. Never referring to her prior sufferings, she treated her enemies with an affability and sweetness that made her the mistress of the hearts of all her daughters.

These poor non-observant sisters, however, were contradictory. Always agitated, perturbed, irritable with each other, they were continually making complaints against Mother Mariana. As their loving Mother, she would calm, console, and counsel them; nonetheless, as their Abbess, she would demand obedience and give orders without distinction or preference. In this way, she made herself not only loved, but also respected.

### Difficulties in Electing a New Abbess

When the term of Mother Mariana's Abbacy ended, a new canonical election was held, and a representative of the Bishop came to the Convent to preside over the proceedings. The sisters were so divided, however, that after two days they still had not succeeded in electing an Abbess. A most distressing confusion reigned.

Mother Valenzuela went to Mother Mariana and told her, "Reverend Mother, as Founder, you should continue to be Abbess."

Mother Mariana replied, "No, Mother, according to the Rule, an Abbess should govern for no more than three years for the good of herself as well as those governed. Instead, it might be necessary for Your Reverence to take up the office of Abbess in order to put an end to so much dissatisfaction. Under the present circumstances, a person is needed who is worthy and experienced in conventual government, and this person is Your Reverence."

Mother Valenzuela responded, "I have neither the character nor strength for this, my Mother. It would be much wiser to elect one of the other Spanish Founding Mothers. All are capable and virtuous ladies. It seems to me that Mother Francisca of the Angels would have the capacity to govern well. I will give my support to her."

To this, the Abbess responded: "If you want one of the Founding Mothers, choose Mother Lucia of the Cross or Mother Catherine of the Conception or Mother Magdalena of Saint John, but not Mother Francisca of the Angels, for this office would not be right for her at this time. She, along with others, sustains our burgeoning divine worship, and we must do all that we can to preserve this, for upon this our happiness depends.

"The office of Abbess requires great vigilance over the whole Convent, both the buildings and the persons within. Burdened with two enormous weights, Mother Francisca of the Angels could not carry them out properly without saddling her soul with the serious neglect of both. In electing an Abbess, we should always act with great charity toward others. Mother Francisca will be Abbess when others, who have been properly trained, can exercise with perfection the duties of the Divine Office. But now would not be the proper time for her to become Abbess."

"Who, then, does Your Reverence choose," asked Mother Valenzuela, "so that I might choose the same?"

But Mother Mariana replied, "Your Reverence knows better than I that we should not reveal our personal preferences, but that we should let our consciences be led by God so that the election cannot be declared null. All that I can tell Your Reverence is that we should pray much in order to forestall scandal in our Community."

### PROCESSION OF THE NON-OBSERVANT SISTERS

On the third day, the Bishop returned for another vote. He first delivered a short and very serious talk, but to no avail. The non-observant sisters did everything they could to try to elect their captain as Abbess. Some of them even managed to vote more than one time. Confusion and agitation raged rampant. Again no result was reached, and the Bishop retired to return on another day.

The non-observant sisters used the time to stir up more agitation in their efforts to win over more sisters to their cause. Taking into their party the lay sisters and the devotees,[55] they resolved to present themselves in a procession before the Bishop and ask him to confirm the election of the captain as Abbess. For, they said, "Mother X would be a person very capable for this office, far surpassing Mother Mariana in her intelligence and virtue. Since your Excellence neither knows her nor has dealt with her, you do not know her. And while Mother Mariana has a very strong character, she is not intelligent."

This, then, was the plan of these poor shepherd-less sheep who had gone astray because they wanted to be their own shepherd. The non-observant sisters considered themselves strong enought to reach their goal because they had won to their side the lay sisters, who, lacking humility, had become insubordinate and filled with demonic envy. Proud and filled with themselves, they were told that they could change their humble positions of serving the sisters.

The members of this rebellious faction took up the great processional cross, and, each one carrying a candle, formed lines to process out of the Convent through the lower choir and into the presence of the Bishop. One of them assured the others that she had the keys to open the doors.

"When the others see us in such formal procession," they said, "they will become fearful and will not dare to stop us. Thus we will be able to carry out our plan. We must make this attempt now, or we will have to continue on as we are. Even Mother Valenzuela is no longer with us. So let us go ahead."

They formed the procession in two rows and began to pray the Rosary, since the lay sisters did not know any other prayer. Hearing their voices, Mother Valenzuela left her cell to see what was happening. Astonished, she asked the meaning of the procession.

---

55. The lay sisters are religious occupied solely with manual labor and the secular affairs of a convent. As a rule, the lay sisters, who can have provisory vows, wear a habit different from that of the contemplative sisters. Usually their prayers consisted of the Rosary or a certain number of *Paters, Aves* and *Glorias*.

But no one responded. All the religious were wearing veils, including the lay sisters, so she could not see their faces. But one of the devotees, who had been brought into the Convent by Mother Valenzuela, replied that they were going to see the Bishop.

Overcome by holy indignation, Mother Valenzuela grabbed this devotee by the arm and pulled her into her cell. There she asked her what they were doing. The poor girl, having already received one blow and trembling with fear to see Mother Valenzuela raising her hand again with the discipline, told her everything.

Mother Valenzuela took away her veil, headdress, and scapular. Giving vent to her anger, she told the frightened sister, "I am locking you in here for now until I return. Tonight I will give you what you deserve, and then put you out of the Convent." Locking her in the cell, she went to look for her Abbess, whom she could not find anywhere. Tired and disstressed, her face deathly pale, she continued her search.

### The "Little Patroness"

When the Founding Mothers and observant sisters heard a group of voices praying aloud, they also came to ask what was happening. But no one in the procession would respond with even one word. The praying figures all appeared so pious that nothing could perturb them.

Finally, they found Mother Valenzuela, who told them, "Mothers and sisters, help me find the Mother Abbess, for these mad women say that they have the key and are going to process through the lower choir, leave the Convent, and go to speak with the Bishop. The outcome of the meeting does not worry me, but what causes me great concern is the consequence for the souls of these imprudent women."

They all began to anxiously search for the Abbess, but she could not be found. Mother Valenzuela then called the Founding Mothers and observant sisters to the lower choir, where they would wait for the non-observant sisters in order to stop them from leaving, by force if necessary. They gathered together there, weeping and imploring assistance from the Statue of Our Lady of Peace:

"Oh! Mother of Peace, who was brought from Spain by Our Founding Mother, save us in this crisis. Oh! Founding Mother, rise up from this sepulcher and subjugate these imprudent women." [56]

As they prayed, they saw close to the grille their Mother and Abbess, who was there praying in silent contemplation. No one dared to interrupt her until Mother Valenzuela, hearing the sound of the approaching procession, nervously approached and said, "What is this, Mother? Rise up and see these imprudent sisters who are leaving the Convent. We must take quick and forceful action to stop them. Your Reverence, as Abbess, knows what must be done. Here is a discipline." And she handed her Abbess a thick, strong discipline.

### Mother Mariana Confronts the Non-Observant Sisters

The Holy Abbess gave a sigh that penetrated the very depths of all their hearts. After kissing the ground, she stood up, and the sisters gathered around her. Looking at them with affection, she said, "Why do you fear? Do you not know that God lives in Heaven and in the Most Holy Sacrament?"

Taking the hand of Mother Valenzuela, which trembled with fear, she pressed it to her heart, kissed it, and said, "Mother, the situation would have been much worse but for the merciful intervention of God. Your Reverence knows that there are two keys to the grille doors. I have one, and the non-observant sisters have tried to obtain the other through cunning and guile. However, our good God permitted them only to procure a false copy. Now you will see what will happen."

---

56. The Statue of the Virgin of Peace, called the "Little Patroness" by the Conceptionists, was brought from Spain in 1576 by Mother Maria de Jesus Taboada, Founder and first Abbess. This wood statue, 31 inches tall, was highly prized among the sisters, and the Little Patroness worked many miracles in the Convent's first days when it was displayed for public veneration in the Church. During these times of internal turmoil and division, Our Lady of Peace was brought inside the cloisers at the special request of the Founding Mothers. The small statue was set in a finely carved niche in the lower choir near the locked gate separating the Convent cloisters form the Church Sanctuary. The Spanish Founding Mothers would often go there to pray before her and lament the loss of the Franciscan Friars who no longer had jurisdicition over them.

Hearing this, Mother Valenzuela became a bit calmer. In another moment, the procession of those poor blind souls came into sight. Reverently they processed in, walking steadily toward the iron gates.

Stepping in front of the first grille door, Mother Mariana gravely addressed them: "Where are you going, my sisters? Whose cadaver do you carry and to where? [referring to the processional cross that bore the crucified Christ]. Better said, you are the cadavers."

The non-observant sisters and their captain trembled with terror to hear these gravely spoken words. Rallying strength, they curtly replied, "Your Reverence, do not impede our procession. We are going to the Bishop so that justice might be done."

"You will not go," the Abbess said in a severe tone. Violently pushing her aside, some of the non-observant sisters reached the iron grating of the first door. Finding they could not open the lock with the key, they broke it.

### The Miracle of the "Little Patroness"

Without saying a word, Mother Mariana raised her eyes to the Virgin of Peace while Mother Valenzuela, with incredible strength, physically restrained the non-observant sisters. She tore the candles from their hands and threw them away from them. The Abbess quietly gave a command for the observant sisters to gather up these burning candles, extinguish them, and put them in a pile.

Realizing they could not break the lock [of the second door] to the Church, and feeling themselves cornered by Mother Valenzuela, the non-observant sisters heard a sound that left them terrified. They turned around and saw the Little Patroness, who was turning her back to them.

The holy statue then spoke these words: "Unfortunate women, what are you doing? Go, then, if you so desire, but you will have no place to which you may return, for I will return to Spain with the Founding Mothers and the observant sisters. Too late will you weep for your follies. And so that this house might forever remember this day, I will always remain like this, with my back turned toward you, as a warning and lesson to those who will follow you."

Raising their eyes in the direction of the holy statue, they saw the Little Patroness illuminated by light, her face pale, her countenance severe. They tried to speak, not knowing what to say. Instead they all fell to the ground unconscious, like cadavers.

Mother Mariana, Mother Valenzuela, and the rest of the observant sisters, terror-stricken, knelt directly before the holy Image, contemplating her face. This blessed and miraculous statue fixed upon them a sweet gaze, full of affection and warmth. With a loving smile, she raised their timid spirits and restored calm to their hearts. They rose up without further delay to try to make the guilty sisters, the lay sisters, and the devotees return to consciousness. The ensemble was a considerable number.

This scene seems to re-enact the arrest of Christ Our Lord in the Garden of Olives when the guilty soldiers fell to the ground, while the Apostles remained standing. The soldiers represent all the rebellious sisters, and the Apostles represent Mother Mariana and all her faithful observant sisters.

### The Tears of the Virgin of Peace

Mother Francisca of the Angels hurried back and forth with remedies to bring the stricken sisters to consciousness. They had begun to moan and emit a foam from their mouths and noses; their bodies remained cold like cadavers. Mother Valenzuela and the observant sisters were weeping in their distress and fear. Only Mother Mariana and the Founding Mothers remained serene and calm, applying the remedies to their poor guilty sisters who had been struck down by the Hand of God.

The holy Abbess then commanded the sisters to pray three Hail Mary's to the Holy Virgin of Peace with their arms in a cross. When they finished, she approached the non-observant sisters, raised them to a sitting position, and blew on them. With this, their bodies returned to life. When all were restored enough to stand, they turned their eyes with dread toward the Little Patroness and saw that she had turned her back to them. Filled with fear and confusion, they did not know what to do or say.

Mother Mariana then ordered them to leave. They walked with great difficulty and, as the group passed before the holy statue, they saw her face become pale and her expression severe. This was also noticed by the observant sisters. Then, from her eyes fell three large tears that slowly rolled down her cheeks.

### THE LAY SISTERS ARE FORGIVEN

The whole group of weakened, guilty sisters left the lower choir like a defeated army. The lay sisters did not know how to make reparation for their fault, for they were there to serve the nuns and not to insolently rise up against them. They believed, and with good reason, that their holy Abbess would rightfully chastise them for their rebellion against their humble position.

Sick as they were, some of them said, "After committing such a fault, how can we go to bed to be assisted by Mother Francisca? Let us continue to serve and do our work, for this is the purpose for which we entered this Convent." And, shamefacedly, they tried to return to their daily work, but were too weak to carry it out.

Mother Mariana, who was observing the scene unnoticed, unexpectedly presented herself before them. The poor lay sisters began to tremble, for they had a great respect and love for her. They knelt before her, awaiting their punishment.

But the holy Abbess, with that amiability proper to her grand soul, raised them up, saying, "My sisters, you need to recover your strength. I order each of you to go to your bed. I will find Mother Francisca of the Angels so that she can attend to you. Go, then, and tranquilly restore your physical strength. At the same time, repair your souls. Enter into yourselves and beg God mercy and pardon for your sins with contrite hearts. He will receive you with open arms just as the prodigal son was received by his good father. For, in truth, you are prodigal daughters. Now, rise up and return to your paternal home."

These poor lay sisters, prostrate at the feet of their Mother Abbess, were weeping and trembling in fear. In voices broken by sobs, they begged her pardon. The holy Abbess comforted them, assuring them that they were pardoned and that she would forget that grave fault. She ordered them, however, not to speak to anyone until the excommunication they had incurred would be lifted by the Bishop.

She added, "Some of you should prepare yourselves to die, for your hour is arriving. And to assure you of the truth of my words, you will see with your own eyes that the candles you carried in that foolish and blameworthy procession have changed into bones with your names imprinted on them."

Obeying the order of their Abbess, these non-observants set out at once for their cells after receiving her blessing and kissing her hands, feet, and scapular.

The charitable Abbess went in search of Mother Francisca of the Angels, whom she found in the lower choir praying before the Virgin of Peace. She told her, "My daughter, the Most Sacred Hearts of Jesus and Mary are active volcanoes of divine love, and they will not turn away even our guilty sisters. Go now to assist our poor lay sisters whom I have commanded to rest in their beds because of their extreme weakness. First, make a good quantity of anise water and give them this to drink. Then you can decide what is better for them. You already know that you should not speak to them except for what is absolutely necessary until the Bishop lifts their excommunications. Afterwards, you should comfort their fearful and timid spirits, since this is your vocation."

Kissing the ground in obedience, Mother Francisca rose to carry out her obligation of charity toward her poor sick sisters with the grace, goodness, and winning sweetness that characterized this angelic soul.

### The Plot of the Non-Observant Sisters

Early the next morning, the Abbess visited each of the poor lay sisters, giving them all her blessing and ordering them to rise at dawn. They assured her that they were much better after taking the anise water and remedies administered with such charity by Mother Francisca.

The non-observant sisters and their leader, however, continued to stir up trouble over the election, which would take place on the following day. The whole day, these malcontent sisters strove to provoke arguments and disputes. They approached the lay sisters again to induce them to be their spies. These lay sisters, however, turned them away. They told the non-observant sisters that they deplored their former rebellion and would never take part in anything like that again, for now they realized the great injustice of the non-observant sisters, especially on the serious matter of disavowing the merits of their Abbess, whose behavior was a mute voice proclaiming her sanctity. They also reminded these non-observant sisters that because they had listened to them before, they were now excommunicated, although they hoped to be absolved in order to carry out their humble duties.

"Let me remind you, sisters," added one of the lay sisters, "that you, like us, are also excommunicated and that you should correct your behavior so that God does not punish you here and in eternity."

The non-observant sisters blushed to hear the firm resolution of the lay sisters. Addressing them with a few disparaging words, they withdrew.

The holy Abbess and the rest of the Community occupied the day begging God and the Blessed Virgin Mother for a remedy to cure the difficult situation and to send a ray of divine light to enlighten those poor sisters who walked in such complete spiritual blindness. For these intentions, they increased their customary penances. In the refectory, some kissed the feet of the other sisters; others ate on the ground with cords around their necks and without their veils; still others remained prostrate on the ground while the others ate.

They performed these and other edifying penances that are customary in the Seraphic family, which, by the grace of God, is characterized by penitence, humility of heart and of understanding, following the example of our Father, the Seraphic Francis.

### Yet Another Election

The next day the Bishop came to preside over the election. Again the votes were divided. The non-observant sisters all wanted the captain as Abbess. The observant sisters divided their votes among the various Mothers, all good, admittedly, but this in itself made a decisive election difficult. Since the election was secret and there was no opportunity to make them understand this problem, the situation steadily worsened.

The non-observant sisters, who were not that numerous, strove to influence the observant sisters, who could not reach a concensus. The latter ignored them in silence. What was certain was that the spirit of division was reigning.

At midday the Bishop sorrowfully retired to his house to take his repast, saying that he would return three hours later and if they would not elect an Abbess then, he himself would name the religious whom he judged more capable of governing. He would choose one who would govern with a demonstrated wisdom, sanctity, prudence, and extreme tolerance.

The Community went to the refectory. The holy Abbess, without her veil and with a cord around her neck, kissed the feet of the religious and ate on the ground. How edifying it was to see this beautiful creature, self-effacing, making these acts of humility. Her cheeks rosy red, she blossomed in the simplicity of her love of God, Whom she begged for a solution to this crisis in her beloved Community.

Mother Valenzuela and the rest of the Founding Mothers, following her example, also ate on the floor. But the non-observant sisters only mocked and laughed at them, providing these good creatures with the opportunity to practice patience. Mother Valenzuela charitably rebuked them, telling them to be silent and cease their insolent behavior.

### STILL NO DECISION

At mid-afternoon, the Prelate returned. Before the votes were cast, he addressed the sisters shortly and severely, making them see the bitter times through which their recently founded Convent was passing. He ordered that the election should take place and said that he would not intervene unless he judged it convenient. Should no decision be reached, he himself would name the religious who would govern for three consecutive years. He would not allow any complaints or arguments over his choice.

The voting began, and again there was no decisive result. Weary, the Bishop again warned, "If you persist in this, I will make my own choice, which will be the right one." And he opened proceedings for another election. In this one, only a few votes were lacking to re-elect Mother Mariana. The Prelate said he would take a short break before the next vote.

The holy Abbess asked Mother Valenzuela to help her prepare something to drink for the Bishop. In the meantime, one by one, the religious approached their Abbess to make sure that she was not angry with them. This saintly creature received them all with the same goodness and imperturbable spirit that she displayed in every situation.

Mother Valenzuela, however, took the opportunity to address them with seriousness and authority, "My sisters, why do you want to destroy this Convent? See where your caprice has led us? Use good sense and unite your spirits. Another Abbess like the one we now have cannot be found."

"Mother," the humble Abbess replied in kind, "Your Reverence can govern this Community much better than I. Remember, my sisters, that the holy Rule says that a Superior can only govern for three years. Here, instead, you have Mother Valenzuela, a person most fit to govern."

### The Bishop's Solution

After drinking his cordial, the Prelate returned and reassembled the group to begin the voting. This time, only two votes were lacking for Mother Mariana to be elected.

At this point, one of the non-observant sisters spoke out, saying, "We do not want Mother Mariana to govern another term. She is unacceptable to us all and has many defects. Narrow-minded as she is, she wants us all to conform to her impossible standards. We would like a little more liberty, and, for this reason, we choose Mother X," naming the leader of the non-observant sisters.

The captain then spoke, "Your Excellency the Bishop, to stop the tears of these sisters, I will accept the Abbacy, for it is true that life is unbearable under these Spaniards who require an iron fist while the rest of us need kid gloves.

"Your Lordship well knows that the letter of the law kills, and it is only its spirit that gives life. With the Rule in their hands, these Spaniards want to fulfill it to the very letter, thinking that we can do all that they can. Thus, we take advantage of this opportunity and we all beseech you that the Spaniards either return to their own land or else be permanently imprisoned. Only in this way can we be left free and at peace."

As soon as this impertinent sister finished speaking these words that manifested her limited understanding and complete lack of virtue, the Bishop indignantly replied: "These criollas are a miserable people, ignorant, vicious, and lacking all discernment. I order in the name of holy obedience that this sister should be immediately imprisoned so her ungoverned tongue might be restrained. As for her companions, I annul their votes for this election, which will now depend on the nobility of heart of the remainder of the Community. Only in this way will the election proceed in peace and according to the desire of God.

"Moreover, the Abbess who is elected must keep this mad, pretentious woman in prison and rule the rest with a firm hand, giving them the lowest and most humble offices and imprisoning whoever resists her orders. Now, take this sister to the prison, for the voting will not proceed until this order is carried out."

The captain was struck speechless by this strong public rebuke. She wanted to respond, but could say nothing. Nor could her imprudent companions, who were also struck mute, just as Aman was stuck dumb when King Ahasuerus rebuked him before his enemy, the Jew Mardechai (cf. Esther, 6, 1-12).

Mother Valenzuela took it upon herself to carry out this order. Rising from her seat, she bowed her head to the Prelate. Then, taking the arm of the captain, she said, "Walk quickly to prison, and leave us in peace. Obey the order of the Bishop, since you always boast of knowing what to do."

As she started to lead her away, the Bishop said, "Mother, your behavior pleases me, and I will begin the new vote as soon as you have returned and given me the prison key." Saying this, he pounded the table.

### A Vision Showing the Eternal Destiny of the Non-Observant Sisters

The unhappy captain trembled in anger and shame because, for a proud soul like this, humiliation deals a mortal blow and inconsolable suffering.

In fact, unknown to the Bishop and other sisters, something extraordinary was taking place while this poor sister was speaking to the Prelate. For as she rose to propose herself as Abbess, Mother Mariana saw that she was surrounded by monkeys emitting fire from their mouths, eyes, and noses. These flames passed to the leader's heart and the hearts of her non-observant companions. To the measure that this fire overpowered their hearts, the passions of anger and envy seethed in them against the Abbess and the Spanish Mothers, extinguishing the fire of the love of God. Further, she saw that these souls, empty of good works, were weighted down by many sins, bearing grave consequences for eternity.

Mother Mariana saw that this poor captain would not be saved, nor would many of her followers who had been led astray by her bad example. It would have been better for these souls to have remained in the world than to have entered into religion to lead such lax and dissipated lives. For they had introduced agitation where there should have been silence, peace, fraternal unity, charity, detachment, mortification, and humility, with the exact observance of the Rule, whose daily practice is easy for a good religious.

What this sister said about the letter of the law killing and the spirit giving life is not in conformance with any of the Rules of monastic institutions, because the eternal life of a religious person depends upon the literal observance of the Rule. We have a practical example of this from our Father Saint Francis, to whom God Himself directed these words concerning the practice of the Rule: "To the letter, to the letter, to the letter; without comment, without comment, without comment."

The sophistic reasoning of this poor sister revealed her bad spirit and total lack of virtue.

Let us continue, however, with the vision of Mother Mariana. She saw that the captain, along with various of her followers, would not be saved because of the blatantly relaxed life they were leading. The divine graces that pour torrentially on good religious in their cloisters were transformed into venom for these deplorable creatures, blinding their souls despite the vibrant light around them and making them die of thirst despite the fountain of living water in their midst.

She saw how they would fall from one abyss to another the rest of their lives, at times placing the Convent at risk and leading yet other religious sisters astray by their bad example. For the infernal serpent was using them as subtle instruments to carry o his plan to destroy the work of God and of Mary Immaculate the foundation and preservation of this Convent.

## THE HOLOCAUST REQUESTED BY OUR LORD

The soul of this charitable spouse of Jesus grieved to s this series of disasters for her beloved Convent, for which she w disposed to give her life should it be necessary. She was also w ing to offer her life to prevent the loss of the souls of the religio her sisters, who had cost the Divine Redeemer so dearly. Te ran down her cheeks, and her fervent and silent prayer rose up Heaven like the smoke of an exquisite incense burning in the te ple of her pure heart and in the thurible of her profound humili

Then, Our Lord Jesus Christ appeared to Mother Maria as He was in the Garden of Olives, kneeling in mournful, ard prayer. She was given to understand the most bitter sorrow t overpowered His Sacred Heart in those moments when, feeli the tedium of life, He said, "My Father, if it be possible to t from Me this bitter chalice, do so ... but not My will, but Th be done." She saw that the greatest interior torments of the S cred Heart of Jesus were the ingratitude and indifference of th souls who, chosen among millions to be His spouses and mir ters, abandoned Him in the most absolute solitude. This, desp the fact that He would live under the same roof with His spou and descend into the hands of His priests at the simple call their voices at the most solemn moment of the Consecration of Holy Host and Chalice.

Mother Mariana then heard the Beloved of her soul claim in His sorrowful agony, "Alas, I look for those who mi console Me, and I find none. I created sons, and they ignore despise Me! And you, my spouse, what will you do for Me, sin I have done so much for you? Oh! how much these religious so have cost Me! Snatch them from the throat of the infernal wo How it pains me to lose them!"

Immediately, the heroic Conceptionist responded: "I Beloved, what dost Thou desire? What dost Thou request of n Until now Thou hast denied me nothing, and I am resolved to n er deny Thee anything – even to my last breath. Tell me, my go ness: Dost Thou desire that I live and die in prison, in absolute isolation from creatures, abandoned by all, suffering double what I have endured until now in those times when I have been Thy faithful companion? .... I willingly accept. I do so not in an impulse of momentary fervor, but with mature reflection upon what is being asked of me. Here I am before Thee. I will release my guilty sister and remain to suffer for her... My nature withdraws in horror, but my spirit is ready for the sacrifice, relying as it does on the fire of Thy ardent love, which inflames my weak heart."

Our Lord responded: "It is not your life, nor your health, nor imprisonment that I desire of you, My beloved Mariana. Rather, I ask that you suffer for the period of five consecutive years the punishments of Hell that the soul of this poor sister would have suffered for all eternity. I have chosen five years in memory of the five Wounds impressed on My body during My sorrowful Passion. Understand, My daughter, that during those five years, I will absent Myself from your earthly eyes and deprive your spirit of every consolation and relief amid your suffering, for it will be similar to what the soul of your poor sister would have endured in the obscure prison of Hell. Be certain that interiorly I will be with you, fortifying you, for otherwise neither you nor the holiest of mortals could tolerate such suffering for even a minute. I ask you, do you agree to My request?"

Then the Divine Master showed her those five years, which seemed not a handful of years to Mother Mariana, but an eternity. Her body quivered even to the bones, and she felt her heart compress so tightly that she would have died from the violence of her pain if God, prodigious in His grace and mercy, had not miraculously preserved her life.

### Mother Valenzuela Is Elected Abbess

Undetected by anyone in the room, she fell into a swoon. Her sisters, as well as the Bishop, only perceived that she was trembling fiercely. Attributing this reaction to shock over the rigorous punishment that he had imposed upon the captain of the non-observant sisters, he gently admonished her: "Valor, Mother, valor! It is necessary to punish the guilty to give an example to the others. I am absolutely inflexible in this matter." And he ordered her to temper her sorrow. Immediately, her trembling ceased, and she awakened as from a dream.

Mother Valenzuela roughly led the guilty sister to the prison. The other non-observant sisters remained in their places, mute with fear. Several of the sisters told them that they should leave, but they took no heed of their words. Mother Valenzuela went to the Bishop, placed the prison key on the table, and said, "Now we can vote in peace. If things had remained as they were, God would not be with us." Then she raised the non-observant sisters by their arms and expelled them, one by one, from the room. Sprinkling them with holy water, she told them, "Go in peace, rebellious sisters, and weep for your sins." After the last one had filed out, she firmly closed the doors.

The Bishop thanked her and praised her energy. They then invoked the Holy Ghost, Our Lady of Wisdom, and the Seraphic Francis and made up a new voting sheet. The ballots were cast and counted, and Mother Magdalena of Jesus Valenzuela was elected with five votes more than Mother Mariana, which was the necessary majority.

The Bishop and those present were quite satisfied and content with the results, remarking among themselves, "If only we had eliminated the guilty sisters earlier from the vote, we would not have lost so much time. But all is well now, and those difficult moments were worthwhile, for the majority of the sisters are observant and united. Let the troublemakers remain where they are, and, above all, their captain, who is so lacking in good sense!"

### DESCRIPTION OF THE PRISON

This place, so necessary and so sacred to all religious communities, was never lacking in those that were truly observant. The prison in the Convent of the Immaculate Conception of Quito is located in the lower cloisters and adjoins the lower choir. From the outside, the prison has a strong, double door. On the outside of it are two large bars. After the bars are set in place, the door has a bolt that is locked with a key. This makes the door virtually impossible to open – even with great violence.

Above the door is a small window with crossed iron bars covered with a wire screen, which permits light to enter the prison, not profusely, but enough for some manual work to be done, as well as for reading and praying the Breviary. However, it is impossible to pass any paper, however small it might be, through the tight screen. Across from the door, about 15 feet away, is a small 1 x 1-1/2 ft. window with bars that also provides light for the prison.

### The Interior of the Prison

To the left of the entrance is a small niche on the wall where a crucifix hangs to remind the guilty sister that the Holy Cross is the wood of salvation and the life-giving bed where the Spouse of just souls rested, inviting her to do the same. It also provides a reminder that under the cross, one reposes in complete security.

To the side of the cross and a little behind it, there is a large cavity imbedded in the wall with a stone bench inside it, which serves as a bed for the repose of the imprisoned religious. The whole prison measures about 30 x 15 feet. Along the wall across from the door and bed, running from one wall to another, are stone benches about five feet long.

The small window above the door that opens to the cloisters has thick bars of iron, and can be closed from inside the prison by a small wooden door to keep out the damp night air. This small door is painted on one side with a picture of the Archangel Gabriel announcing the sublime mystery of the Incarnation of the Word to the Holy Virgin. Below this picture these words are inscribed in large, clear letters: "Remember the four last things and you will never sin." This small door always remains open during the day.

On the other side of this small door, which can be seen at night when the window is closed, is a beautiful picture of Our Lord Jesus Christ imprisoned and wearing heavy iron chains. Two weeping angels watch Him tenderly and under His divine feet are roses and lilies. This picture is very moving; in it Christ inspires tenderness, love, and repentance for all the sins one has committed. Under this picture are large letters reading, "One dies as one lives," followed by this stanza:

> See that God watches you.
> See that He is watching you now.

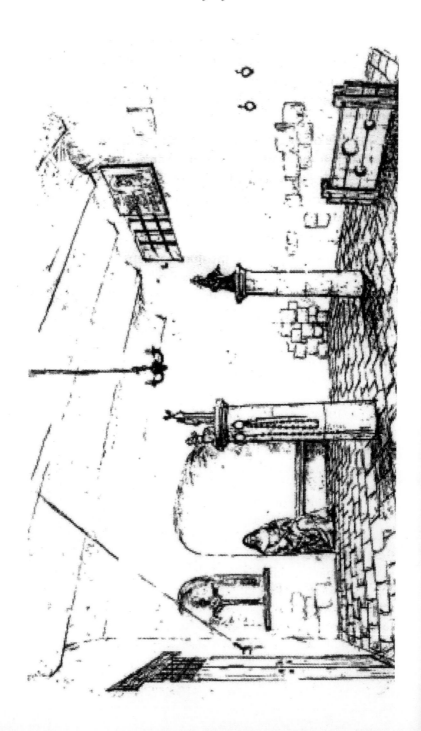

See that you must die.
See that you know not when.[57]

Hanging from the ceiling in the center of the room is a simple, heavy curved candelabra that holds three candles to provide light at night.

### THE TWO COLUMNS

Four feet in front of the bench is a thick column of stone in the form of a circular pillar, 5-1/2 feet high, and topped by a round wooden platform 2-1/2 feet in diameter. Like a small altar, it holds a precious statue of Christ Our Lord imprisoned and bound to a column upon which a rooster perches. At the feet of Our Lord is a moving figure of Saint Peter the Apostle repenting after Christ fixed him with His gaze. Weeping over his sin of denying his Master, he inspires guilty souls to contrition as well as love and confidence in the goodness of Christ Our Lord.

The statue of Christ is touching. Looking at it, one's heart fills with tenderness and love. To the innocent and the just, it seems to say, "Look what I suffered to give you an example and to give you strength." To the guilty, it says, "Beloved soul, I keep you company in this place where you justly atone for your faults. Turn to Me and, with unlimited confidence throw yourself at My feet like My penitent Apostle and weep for your faults. Study Me well: I have allowed My hands to be bound to this column to pay the punishment due for your sins. Give Me your love and tears so that they might intermingle with Mine and be presented before My Celestial Father, Who will grant you full pardon."

On one side of this stone pillar there are three metal rings or irons from which hang three long iron chains. At the end of each chain is a kind of handcuff that can be locked on the feet, hands, or waist of the prisoner. These handcuffs are of various sizes, so that they can be applied to the guilty sister according to the need or nature of the faults committed.

The other side of this column is smooth. The prisoner can bind herself to it voluntarily, if she so desires, to make penance

---

57. Mira que te mira Dios. Mira que te estamirando. Mira que debes morir! Mira que no saves cuando.

and pray with the sorrowful and suffering Christ. The floor around this column was often found stained with blood from the penances that Mother Mariana and the Spanish Mothers made there on the various times they were imprisoned.

Eight feet away from this column is another one, also of stone and similar to the first. On top of it is a beautiful statue of Our Lady of Sorrows. The image is very moving and captivating. It inspires love, tenderness, compassion, and sorrow for one's sins. Her eyes, turned on high as if she were gazing up at the Child of her love and sorrow, are filled with compassionate tears. Like the other, this column has the same shackles and chains on one side, while the other side is smooth.

The prison also has a stock, fetters, and chains. It lacks nothing, and is a most respected place. One who enters it is filled with a holy fear and dread of occupying it. However, in it the innocent have suffered, as we see in the story of Mother Mariana de Jesus Torres.

To the right of the entrance, there are more of the same limestone tile benches. In the middle of them is a long closet that holds the food provisions, sewing supplies, books, and instruments of penance. The stone bench then continues, extending from the end of the closet to the next wall, which has the small barred window that has already been described. The floor is of tiles, and the room is dry.

Fathers Isquierdo and Jurado, both Friars Minor, zealously designed this venerable place. Father Isquierdo personally directed the making of the statues of Our Lord and the Virgin. He provided exact instructions for the sculptor, Francisco de la Cruz de Castillo, about how to make them so that they would be appropriate for such a place, communicating that mystical unction which Our Lord imparts to attract souls to Himself – the guilty souls, by means of repentance, and the just souls, by means of love and gratitude.

This, then, is the prison in the Convent of the Immaculate Conception in Quito. It is a necessary place, as we have said, given the weakness of human nature. Yet it has been sanctified by the fact that more of the innocent rather than the guilty have suffered there.

### Considerations

Oh! If it were possible for me to be in this very place occupied by Mother Mariana de Jesus Torres, the place where, through the benevolence of the Queen of Heaven, she received such extraordinary graces that this place of suffering was transformed into a Heaven rather than a place of penance! Our sisters, the religious of the Immaculate Conception, should consider themselves most fortunate in possessing such a sacred place in their Convent and should love and respect it, as well as preserve it with veneration.

When, through the course of time, it should happen that someone should occupy it, that person should consider herself fortunate, for it is a holy place. If she is guilty, she should mourn her faults, convert, and change her life. If she is innocent, she should remember Mother Mariana de Jesus Torres and the Founding Mothers and how they transformed this prison into a Heaven, and then imitate their conduct. Thus will she perfect her soul and draw to it, to her Convent, and to this city so laden with sins, the mercy and grace of God that only holy and humble souls can attract. That God resists the mighty, and converses and unites Himself with the humble of heart is a truth that will remain throughout the centuries until the end of time.

I have the certainty that even if all mankind, however good they might be, should try to close the Convent of the Immaculate Conception of Quito, prevailing on every viable means, they would not be able to do so. For this blessed place is consecrated with the most exquisite incense of elevated prayer and with the oil of the blood of innocent virgins, who, lacerating their blameless bodies with blows from severe disciplines, thus consecrated the walls of this beloved place.

For this Convent is built upon the profound foundation of admirable humility and is constructed with the stones of solid virtue – from the virtue of its saintly Founding Mothers up to that of the final holy sister who will live here. For I am certain that these great and hidden souls will not be lacking throughout time. They will be sculpted from within the very bosom of their Community by the sufferings imposed by the hands of their sisters, all the more painful and sorrowful than if made by the hands of strangers.

A thousand times blessed art Thou, my God, Who hast made the Seraphic family a mother fecund with holy sons and daughters.

Immaculate Daughter, hidden in the womb of your mother Saint Anne, thou wert the delight of God and the terror of demons. Blessed art thou for making the daughters of the Immaculate Conception an integral and fruitful branch of the Seraphic family.

And you, angelic creature, Saint Francis of Assisi, my Father, blessed art you for corresponding with perfection to the divine call, founding a mendicant Order that spread throughout the entire world and attracted many souls to God by means of humility, meekness, and poverty. To this Order I belong, the least of your sons, yet I desire to exceed all of my brothers in loving you and imitating you, fulfilling to perfection the holy Rule that you gave us.

But since my virtue is small and my strength only that of a weak child, I pray that you yourself, my holy Father, ignite in my heart the ardent fire of the love of God. For your heart was the blazing volcano that inflamed your sons and daughters throughout time. Bless your sons, the Friars Minor, and your true daughters, the religious of the Immaculate Conception of Mary Most Holy, so that one day all your sons and daughters, united with you in Heaven, might sing in praise the goodness and perfection of our God: "*Ecce quam bonum et jucundum fratres habitare in unum.*" [Behold how good and pleasant it is for brethren to dwell together in unity]. Amen.

\* \* \*

## Chapter 26

The Bishop confirmed the election of Mother Valenzuela with great satisfaction. Immediately the solemn act of the Community rendering obedience to the new Abbess took place. Mother Valenzuela told the Prelate that to proceed with peace and harmony, the imprisoned captain and the other guilty sisters should also render her obedience and the excommunication should be lifted from them.

The Bishop readily acceded to this request, ordering Mothers Mariana de Jesus, Francisca of the Angels, and Lucia of the Cross to go and release the guilty leader from prison and bring her and all the others into his presence.

With that docility characteristic of grand souls, Mother Mariana went with her companions in search of the guilty sisters to tell them that the Bishop had requested their presence to free them.

Seeing them, the captain arrogantly asked, "What do you want? If you have come to take my place, then you are doing the right thing. For the real saints chose to take the place of those who were imprisoned."

The Mothers replied serenely, "Sister, the Bishop is calling for you to lift the excommunication. Then you can also render obedience to the new Abbess who was elected, Mother Magdalena de Jesus Valenzuela."

Finding a ray of hope in this news, the captain was encouraged. "Let us go then," she said.

Standing before the Bishop, the non-observant sisters felt somewhat fearful. He addressed a brief sermon to them to make them realize their bad behavior and terrible consequences it would have for eternity. He lifted their excommunication, but then ordered that the captain should return to the prison, which was done after she kissed the scapular of the new Abbess.

### Happiness Returns to the Convent of the Immaculate Conception

After the Mothers had accompanied the captain to prison, the ceremony of rendering obedience began. One by one, following the order of precedence, each sister pledged her obedience to the new Abbess. At the end of this solemn act, the Bishop made a magnificent speech, exhorting them all to the love of God and the practice of mutual charity. Then he publicly manifested his will that Mother Mariana should retain all the privileges of Abbess and Founder, and that the present Abbess should not resolve any matter, however small it might be, without first consulting with her and receiving her approval. She would also retain full rights to punish and imprison the insubordinate non-observant sisters. Then, blessing them, he left.

A great happiness fell over the Convent of the Immaculate Conception of Quito as the sisters celebrated the election of their new Abbess. The only one not rejoicing was Mother Valenzuela. Weeping and disconsolate, she kept Mother Mariana constantly at her side, for she looked upon her as the guardian angel of her Abbacy. With profound humility and charming sweetness, Mother Mariana attempted to console the Abbess. The very soul of the happiness of her sisters, this angel of innocence began to play her harp, singing divine canticles that inspired her sisters with new fervor. Only the non-observant sisters were somewhat downcast and withdrawn.

When Mother Mariana stopped singing, the sisters began to converse about the beauty of Heaven and the happiness of the blessed, who enjoy eternal and holy harmony in their possession of the heavenly Fatherland. Other sisters left to help the lay sisters who were preparing the meal. Every time that the bell of the call box rang, Mother Mariana would answer it. She always returned with more food and gifts, for she was greatly loved inside and outside the Convent.

When the meal was ready, Mother Mariana herself went to the refectory to serve it. Taking the portion reserved for the prisoner, she asked the Mother Abbess for the key so that she could bring her the meal.

When this miserable sister saw Mother Mariana, she spared no words of abuse, telling her that she had fooled the Bishop with her hypocrisy and tricks so that she could continue to tyrannize the sisters. But the day would come, she threatened, when she would have the consolation of seeing Mother Mariana imprisoned again. Then she would be happy.

Mother Mariana said nothing to all his. After embracing the embittered captain, she left to rejoin her sisters.

During the three days of festivity, Mother Mariana glowed. It seemed as if God Our Lord had further enhanced her normal beauty. Her cheeks were full and rosy, her blue eyes shone with greater brilliance and charm.

When the festivities ended, Mother Valenzuela - from now on we will refer to her simply as the Abbess - communicated to Mother Mariana her decision to call together the sisters to assign them their various offices. She told her that she desired that Mother Mariana be Vicar Abbess, or Novice Mistress. But this humble sister, shying away from every office of dignity, protested that since she had just been Abbess, she needed time to recollect herself after so many hours of distraction that were necessarily a part of that office. The two of them discretely distributed the various offices in charity, peace, and unity, which is no cause for surprise since one of the members of that fortunate council was a saint.

### THE MYSTERIOUS CONTENTS OF A BOX

The offices were distributed, and each one who was chosen took possession of her function. The non-observant sisters, however, were given no positions. They went to visit the new Abbess and tried to win her to their side with sweet words, as is the habit of shameless persons lacking character.

They would also speak highly of their imprisoned captain, insisting that this sister was suffering now only because she had been so good. If she spoke as she did in the chapter, they explained, it was not from pride, but from holy zeal. Since Mother Valenzuela had always acted as their mother, they pleaded, now she should free the captain and put in her place the insupportable Spanish Mother who had abused her Abbacy and whose behavior demanded chastisement.

"One day, Mother, she carefully hid for herself a three-square-foot iron chest that she ordered specially made not long ago. It is filled with precious jewels given to her by the donors who admire her. She sends the jewelry to Spain, and eats the sweets and drinks the liqueurs, while she pretends to be mortified in front of the Community.

"What is worse, Mother, is that she hides this box in the lower choir, daring to eat and become drunk there at will without being noticed, before His Majesty in the Sacramental Species. This is why she emerges from the lower choir so rosy-cheeked and inebriated, pretending sanctity with such hypocrisy. It seems that it is time to expose this Spaniard and make her fall."

Hearing this, the Abbess was interiorly distressed, fearful that this might be true and dreading to discover it to be so. She replied, however, by stating that she could not believe that such evil could exist in one so obviously humble, mortified, and patient, but that she would investigate the matter.

The non-observant sisters retorted, "Yes, Mother, but do so very cautiously and quietly so that she will not perceive you are watching her. Then we can catch her by surprise and she will have no way out!"

### Candles Change to Bones

With this suspicion in the back of her mind, the Abbess tried to follow Mother Mariana everywhere she went, especially to the lower choir. As her office of Abbess did not permit her to remain there as long as Mother Mariana did, it never happened that they would both leave at the same time. The Abbess noticed, however, that Mother Mariana always sprinkled the iron chest with holy water.

Her distress increasing, the Abbess finally told herself one morning when Mother Mariana was praying in the lower choir, "Today I will order her to reveal to me the contents of this box that has made the other sisters so suspicious. If, by some chance, what they have said is true, I will tell no one, but will guard the secret in my heart. For I love her so much. She is still young, and her nature might crave sweets, poor sister. And even if it is true, she is still an angel."

Entering the lower choir and finding herself alone with Mother Mariana, the Abbess called to her and said, "Mother, what does Your Reverence have in this box? Perhaps some instruments of penance or some other such private thing? I would like to see what it contains. Perhaps Your Reverence has forgotten to tell me about it. Now, while we are alone in the presence of the Blessed Sacrament, I want to see what it is."

"It is neither an oversight nor a secret, Mother," the creature gravely and humbly responded, "for it is not fitting that a subject should have secrets from her Abbess. I had a great desire to show you its contents on the very day you were chosen by God to govern this Community. I did not, however, want to embitter the days of celebration. Day after day, I have deliberated on whether to reveal to Your Reverence the contents of this box, but seeing you suffering so much and your health so precarious, I have not done so. Even today I do not feel it would be prudent for you to see it."

This explanation roused the concern and curiosity of the Abbess, who told her, "It does not matter, Mother, that I am suffering. I have decided to see it."

"Very well, Mother," responded the obedient religious. "But first, ask the Lord for fortitude and strength."

Approaching the box, Mother Mariana said, "Mother, do you remember the shameful procession that our poor sisters made with lighted candles as they tried to cross through this blessed door?"

"I remember it well," the Abbess replied. "And I became so indignant that I seized them violently, took the candles from their hands, and threw them far from them. But what does this have to do with the contents of the box?"

"Mother, all those candles were transformed into the shin bones of the dead," said Mother Mariana, "and here they are, each one with the respective name of the religious who carried it marked on it. For this reason, I, Mother Francisca of the Angels, and Mother Lucia of the Cross carefully picked them up and secretly guarded them. A short time afterward, I ordered the box to be made so that this event would be preserved and passed on as a lesson for those who follow us. For in every age, Satan will wage a fierce war to demolish our beloved Convent, and this grave event will serve to check our younger sisters."

"We will see, Mother," said the Abbess with a trembling voice. Opening the lid of the box, she looked in, tried to cry out but could not speak, and fainted.

Catching the body of her Abbess, Mother Mariana gently eased her to the ground near the box, carefully supporting her head all the while. As she did so, she prayed to the Sacramental Jesus to send one of her sisters to help her revive the Abbess.

### THE ABBESS CALLS TOGETHER THE COMMUNITY

While this scene was taking place, Mother Francisca of the Angels and Mother Anna of the Conception were heading to the lower choir to visit the Prisoner of Love. Hearing the cry of their Abbess, they hurried their pace. Entering, they saw the Abbess stretched out on the floor with her head supported by Mother Mariana, who said to them, "Come quickly!"

"What has happened?" they asked.

"You know that the candles from the procession changed into bones and that we kept them here so that they would be preserved for all times," explained Mother Mariana. "The Abbess insisted upon seeing the contents of this box. Unable to withstand the shock, she fainted. Now, Mother Francisca, go quickly and bring wool to burn so that she can smell it and return to her senses, and also a cup of anise water for her to drink. Mother Anna of the Conception and I will massage her. Also, tell the others that we are here."

Mother Francisca of the Angels hurried away. Seeing her haste and concerned expression, the other religious, one after another entered the lower choir and found their Abbess on the floor in a swoon next to the box.

With smiles on their lips, the non-observant sisters said, "Poor Mother! She had an attack when she saw with her own eyes such great hypocrisy."

The rest of the sisters did not understand the meaning of these words, but God Our Lord revealed the secret of their malicious hearts to His gentle spouse Mother Mariana, who saw how they had calumniated her to the Abbess. She pardoned these poor, blind sisters and prayed for them, begging that they receive light, mercy, and forgiveness.

Mother Francisca of the Angels returned with the remedies and applied them. Returning to consciousness, the Abbess took a deep breath and, squeezing the hand of Mother Mariana, kissed it with tenderness and love. The latter, meanwhile, pressed her to drink the anise water.

The non-observant sisters quickly approached the Abbess. Addressing her in tones of honey, they said, "See, Mother, what we have told you is true. Mother Mariana has caused this illness, for you had this attack because of the shock of what you have seen. Now you know the terrible hypocrisy that has been going on for such a long time. We implore you, then, that Mother Mariana be justly chastised and imprisoned, and that you release the captain, who has been unjustly imprisoned."

Hearing these words, the Abbess was taken by a holy impatience and cried out, "Get out of this holy place, you liars and slanderers. Soon you will receive your punishment."

Meanwhile, Mother Mariana fixed her eyes on the ground and, without the least change in expression, continued to administer to her Abbess to restore her completely.

The fury of the Abbess increased as the non-observant sisters drew yet nearer and insisted that she show everyone the contents of the box. Her countenance severe, she replied, "Yes, you will see with your own eyes the fruit of your sins. Examine your consciences and ask God for pardon."

Hearing these words, the non-observant sisters drew back, somewhat concerned and no longer certain of what they were going to see.

### The Community Gathers Together Again

Fully restored, the Abbess gave an order to her secretary to ring the bell, calling the whole Community together in the lower choir. In the meantime, she consulted with Mother Mariana, saying it was her opinion that the hour had arrived to reveal to the whole Community the transformation of the processional candles into bones inscribed with the names of the guilty sisters. The humble religious responded that God so desired it, and that it was also His divine will that a detailed account of this terrible and extraordinary event be written and preserved for posterity in the same box that guarded the bones. She had known that this was the will of God when she ordered the box to be made.

Presided over by the Abbess and her worthy counselor, the Community gathered together. The Abbess gave an order to Mother Lucia of the Cross to accompany her to the prison and bring out the prisoner so that she might also be present. The two left together and entered the prison, which was located next to the lower choir.

Seeing them, the prisoner rushed forward to greet the Abbess, speaking with sweet cunning, "Welcome, my Mother. I hope in your charity you will release me from this place where I suffer innocently, and that Your Reverence will place here instead the guilty one, Mother Mariana, the sole cause of all the disturbances in the Community."

The Abbess told her: "You, sister, are the sole cause of all these things. Make a true conversion if you want to save yourself. Agitated, rebellious, disobedient, ambitious – your example leads many imprudent sisters astray, just like Lucifer who swayed to his side one-third of the Angels. As for me, I would like to have you imprisoned permanently or put out of this Convent so we might be left in peace. Putrid member that you are, you need to be separated so that you do not infect the others.

"Now I will conduct you to the lower choir where the whole Community is gathered. There you will see with your own eyes what God has done on behalf of the innocent and holy Mother Mariana, and to reprove your rebellion and pretentiousness. Let us go."

### Mother Mariana's Innocence is Avenged

With the captain walking ahead of them, they returned to the lower choir and took their respective places. The Abbess assigned the prisoner the last place behind the lay sisters and on the floor.

Closing the door, the Abbess then spoke: "Mothers and sisters, God Our Lord gathers us together to avenge the innocent Mother Mariana, so calumniated for a long time and always so unjustly persecuted and punished. The rebellious sisters told me that here, in the lower choir, in this iron-plated box that you see, she was keeping various jewels to send secretly to her family, along with sweets and cordials that she took to become drunk and please her senses, all the while pretending to virtue with great hypocrisy. I refused to believe this. Nonetheless, a cruel doubt crept into my heart, and I suffered unspeakably until, surprising her unawares, I found her here and demanded to see the contents of the box. Unable to bear the shock of what I saw, I fainted.

"As soon as I recovered, my first desire was for the whole Community to see its contents and tremble to realize what has taken place among you. Let the guilty ones implore God for mercy and atone for the many sufferings they have caused Mother Mariana, who was an innocent victim during her Abbacy. Nonetheless, she always pardoned and loved her guilty sisters. The worthy daughter of our unforgettable saintly Founder Mother Maria, Mother Mariana valiantly carries out what her aunt, upon leaving this earth, entrusted to her and to all her daughters so that we might be happy in this life and eternity.

"Now, Mother Francisca, Mother Lucia, and Mother Anna of the Conception, accompany the prisoner and the non-observant sisters and bring this box to the center of the choir."

Discontent, the non-observant sisters helped to carry the box to the place designated by the Abbess. The three Spanish sisters, however, were in peace.

Mother Valenzuela descended from her place, telling the prisoner and the non-observant sisters that she would open its lid for them to see the contents. They approached quickly, thnking that their slanders might be proved true.

The Abbess raised the lid, saying, "See, sisters, the candles that you carried in your hands during the procession you made only some days ago. They have changed into your bones inscribed with your names. Read each one. You had the presumption to calumniate your innocent Mother and sister. Now take the jewels, cordials, and sweets that you said were concealed here. Enjoy them yourselves if you so desire."

When they saw the contents of the box, the screams of the sisters filled the whole Church. The Abbess ordered the three Mothers to empty the contents of the box on the ground. The guilty religious, trembling and stupefied, wept in fear.

The ones who had taken part in the procession from coercion or lack of character wept and cried out: "Most Holy Mother of Peace, have mercy on us! Beloved Little Patroness, mercy! We have sinned! Mother Mariana of Jesus, pardon! A thousand times, pardon! Our intentions were not bad. We were dragged along out of human respect. Beg mercy from God for us that we might never again take part in such mutinies! Sister X [the captain] is responsible for all this. She won us over with threats and promises. Mercy! Mercy!"

Weeping, each one publicly confessed her misdeeds.

The lay sisters said, "Have mercy on us, Lord! For we are only poor lay sisters who, according to the holy Rule, should serve our mothers with humility. Yet we, won over by Sister X, went against our innocent Mother and Founder, Mother Mariana de Jesus, causing her to suffer. Pardon, Lord, pardon! Our dear Little Patroness, forgive us and erase our names from these bones, for it was an unfortunate hour when we took those candles into our hands. Have mercy on us!"

Amid these cries of confusion and fear, the prisoner and the calumniators said nothing. They were very upset and even had they wanted to hide their fear, God would not permit it, for their faces were livid and they trembled uncontrollably.

### How the Non-Observant Sisters Reacted to this Chastisement

The Abbess ordered Mother Mariana to come down from her place and indicate to whom each bone corresponded according to the name written on it. Then, after the name was read out, the Abbess placed the bone in the hands of the guilty sister to whom it belonged. The captain and the calumniators wanted to protest, but when they tried to speak, they were unable to make a sound. They fell unconscious over the bones upon which their names were written.

Mother Mariana, whose compassionate heart could not bear to see her sisters suffer, re-collected the bones and put them back on the floor in the center of the choir. Then she hurried to help the fallen sisters, who had become like corpses, unwillingly clutching the bones in their hands. Perhaps it was the finger of God acting.

She took the stiff bodies of these sisters into her arms and vigorously rubbed their faces and arms, while Mothers Francisca of the Angels, Anna of the Conception, and Lucia of the Cross hurried to get anise water and wool to help bring them back to consciousness. With this assistance, one by one, they gradually came to themselves.

The first person they saw upon opening their eyes was their benefactress who was assisting them. They were shamefaced and large tears rolled down their cheeks. Fearfully, they cast away the bones, which were picked up by one of the Mothers and placed on the floor in the center of the choir.

The last to return to consciousness, and this only with great difficulty, was the captain, who was thought to be dead. The Abbess regarded her with severity. When she revived, she saw herself in the arms of the humble Mother Mariana. Still holding the bone, she fearfully threw it aside and disdainfully gestured away the holy sister who was helping her, saying, "Imposter!"

All were scandalized at such ingratitude. The Abbess, whose temper was fierce, approached and threatened to give her a blow, exclaiming, "Insolent women!" But Mother Marian intervened and forestalled the blow that the captain would have otherwise received.

### A Written Account Is Made of the Incident

Fear, confusion, and shame filled the room, as some of the sisters cried out loudly and unceasingly for mercy from God, the Little Patroness, and Mother Mariana. The Abbess ordered silence, and all became calm.

She then spoke to them, exhorting them to union, peace, and charity, and advising the guilty ones to convert so that their souls might be saved. Some of the non-observant sisters rushed to embrace Mother Mariana, who received them most amiably, extending her arms to them. They apologized profusely for their misdeeds and kissed her feet in their penitence. Others, however, including the captain, said nothing, although they remained quite perturbed.

Accompanied by Mother Lucia of the Cross, the Abbess returned the captain to the prison, locking her in and leaving her without saying a word.

Then, returning to the lower choir with parchment and ink, the Abbess instructed the secretary to write down all that had taken place. She told her to add to the account that the box with all its contents should remain forever in the lower choir as a lesson for posterity.

After the Abbess, her council, the secretary, and the whole Community had signed the document, she placed the parchment, along with a small metal crucifix, in the box and ordered it locked. This box, like the prison, is a precious treasure that belongs to our sisters, the religious of the Immaculate Conception of Quito.

### APPARITION OF THE VIRGIN OF PEACE TO MOTHER MARIANA

The next day, Mother Mariana was in the lower choir making her customary meditation when her heart stirred and her sensibilities became alert. She heard a soft murmur that came from the niche where the Virgin of Peace stood, and then the melodious voice of her Most Holy Mother, who told her, "Child of my Heart, I am the Queen of Peace and the Mother of Fair Love. Prepare your heart and expand your spirit so that your heroism might save the soul of your imprisoned sister. For you must either sacrifice yourself for her, or her soul will be lost. How I suffer from the loss of a religious soul!"

And large tears rolled down the beautiful cheeks of the Queen of Peace, whose precious image had come alive to speak to her beloved daughter.

Mother Mariana became inflamed with the love of God and Mary Most Holy, and a strong desire to save souls consumed her being. She offered herself for all that God desired of her, without recalling what Our Lord had already asked of her and what she had accepted – five years of Hell to save the soul of her sister.

### FIVE YEARS OF HELL FOR THE SOUL OF THE CAPTAIN

Continuing her prayer, she then saw Jesus Christ anguishing and crowned with thorns. Large drops of blood flowed from His forehead and fell onto His face. Our Lord gave a touching sigh, and said, "My spouse, the time has arrived for you to fulfill the offering that you made to Me to save the soul of your sister – suffering five years of Hell so that she will not suffer it for eternity. You must now fulfill your word, or Divine Justice will fall upon this guilty soul. See her even at this moment…"

Mother Mariana then saw that the captain was out of herself in a state of despair. Dissatisfied with life because of the terrible remorse of her guilty conscience, she was trying to find something with which she could kill herself. At her side were two huge black creatures who were taunting her to greater despair. They were whispering in her ear that there was no other way out for her, and that either she should kill herself and finish with such a sad life, or else leave and go into the world where she could enjoy herself and find some pleasure in life.

In the world, they told her, she could live more freely and without such oppression, for it would be intolerable to live her whole life imprisoned, all the more so because the Spaniards were all her enemies who, with their lies, had turned the spirit of the whole Community against her. In the Convent, she would henceforth be regarded with hatred and horror, like a diseased member. With these words, the black creatures strove to make her lose her soul.

Accosted by these ideas, which all seemed to be true to this poor sister, she began to run back and forth in the prison like a madwoman, wishing herself dead. She fell to the ground, foaming at the mouth and shrieking. Then she ran to the door of the prison and tried to tear it down.

Seeing this, Mother Mariana suffered indescribably and prayed with great fervor for her poor sister. She then recalled the vision that she had experienced during the election in the chapter hall, and the formal promise she had made to Our Lord to suffer Hell for five years to save this soul.

Our Lord showed her again what these five years – which seemed more like centuries – would entail, letting her see the full intensity of the painful suffering she would take on in a state where she would be without relief or divine consolation, much less human consolation, which is futile in this type of suffering. Again, Our Lord allowed her to freely accept or refuse such torments, and to choose whether she would sacrifice herself for the salvation of this soul.

For the captain, who was spiritually dead, needed a human victim who, united to the Divine Victim, would do violence to Heaven to snatch her from the claws of the Devil, who already considered her in his possession because of the many sins she had committed for so many years in the religious life.

The religious life is most charming in its essence: sweet, consoling, filled with indescribable peace and divine pleasures. The faithful soul feels the grace of her divine vocation like a torrential rain falling on the pleasant garden of the cloisters. However, for the dispersive, unfaithful soul, this same downpouring of graces become poison, leaving her increasingly languid, dry, and remarkably indifferent. Such souls are not attracted by the moving mysteries of Calvary, the Holy Eucharist, and Bethlehem, nor do they feel the tenderness that faithful souls enjoy in these mysteries. Poor souls! May God forbid that this type of soul ever again occupy the Convent of the Immaculate Conception of my beloved sisters!

### THE HEROIC SACRIFICE

The heart of Mother Mariana shuddered and vacillated upon seeing the intense agony she would have to endure. Then she recalled the unspeakable sufferings of Jesus Christ in the Garden and on the Cross when He saw that a great number of souls would be lost, making no use of the copious graces of the Redemption. She also saw the ingratitude and perfidy of those who called themselves His friends and of those souls chosen by His love to be called His beloved spouses. Then, such a great love for her Divine Spouse took possession of her heart that she considered herself fortunate to be able to suffer and unite herself to Jesus and save souls – especially the soul of her poor sister separated from Christ who had not combatted the pride in her heart in its first manifestations.

In her amorous fervor, she said: "My Divine Redeemer and Beloved of my soul, I, the favored daughter of Thy love, had forgotten the generous resolution and offering I made to Thee in order to save this sister's souls. But today, gazing again at Thy Divine Heart, I ask Thee to allow me to save souls, especially this one. I offer myself to suffer this five years of Hell so that she might attain eternal happiness.

"Well do I understand the bitter and terrible suffering this resolution encompasses. I fear and shudder when I consider my weakness and little virtue. But confiding in Thy divine strength and in the love that Thou hast for me, I not only accept, but, humbling myself in Thy presence with my forehead on the ground, I implore Thee in Thy charity to allow me to suffer these five years of Hell so that my poor unfortunate sister can be saved. For she, like a sheep gone astray, has separated herself from the flock of the Divine Shepherd.

"Uniting myself to Thy internal and external sufferings, making Thy merits mine, and relying on the favor of my Immaculate Mother and my Seraphic Father Saint Francis, I do not fear.

"How difficult it is to think of myself deprived of Thy presence and suffering such a grievous separation! Since Thou didst also suffer that loss of the condemned souls during those three hours of Thy Agony on the Cross, Thou knowest from Thine own experience what this sorrow is. I hope and pray, therefore, that Thou wilt sustain me."

Our Lord accepted this generous offering of love and said to her, "I desire hearts like yours, My beloved spouse, for the salvation of souls. And such hearts I will always find in this, My beloved Convent.

"Have no fear. I will be your secret strength. You will suffer the five years of Hell, and in exchange, the soul of your sister is already saved. She will first suffer a severe illness, during which time you will take care of her in order to win and convert her. You will have much to suffer in bearing the severity of her abusive treatment. Then she will be cured. After she stands before the Judgment Seat and realizes her bad life, then your Hell will begin."

Mother Mariana understood, then, all that she would suffer during this sickness of her sister. She saw how her abnegated and loving service would be received with ingratitude and roughness. She also saw the Judgment through which this religious would pass, and how she would be condemned to remain in Purgatory until the day of Final Judgment. However, by virtue of her heroic sacrifice, the soul of this guilty sister would be saved.

### Strange Voices Coming from the Prison

The Abbess, who vigilantly watched over the whole house and habitually passed by the prison, would hear strange noises and screams coming from it that frightened her very much. She was by nature fearful, and for this reason, never entered the prison alone. The Mothers and sisters who frequented the lower choir to visit the Blessed Sacrament and pray – for at that time the fervor of the religious was very great – told the Abbess that they had also heard these noises.

One day, the Abbess and Mother Mariana were walking together to the lower choir when they heard the raucous shouts and ugly voices of persons inside the prison.

The Abbess became exceedingly frightened and asked, "Mother, do you hear that? My Lord and my God! What is happening in there?"

Mother Mariana sighed, saying, "Mother, this poor sister is a victim of the Devil. We should have zeal for her soul and go to visit her and remove her for a short time to the lower cloister so that she will not despair."

The Abbess replied, "Mother, it would be better if she were to leave the Convent so that we were completely rid of her, for I believe that she has gone mad."

"No, Mother," replied Mother Mariana. "If she leaves the Convent, this poor sister will lose her soul. We must instead win her for God."

"If Your Reverence is strong enough to accompany me," returned the Abbess, "then I will do as you say. Otherwise, no."

"Yes, Mother, I will take care of everything."

"And if you are attacked?"

"I will embrace her and hold her to my heart. Fortunately, she is a very small person," Mother Mariana concluded.

Crossing themselves, the two religious opened the door to the prison and entered.

Seeing them, the prisoner ran to them, shouting, "I am dying! Dying! And the Devil is carrying me away!" She ran to and fro in the prison, beating her head against the walls.

The Abbess looked at Mother Mariana, who was quietly praying for her poor sister, renewing her offer to suffer Hell so that she might be saved. Her prayer was heard, and the prisoner suddenly fell unconscious in front of the column with the statue of the scourged Christ atop it.

"Let us go to help her, Mother," exclaimed Mother Mariana, directing herself to her superior, who was trembling.

The Abbess replied, "Let Your Reverence go by yourself."

Mother Mariana went to her poor sister and raised her up.

The captain was lying face down, spewing foam from her mouth and blood from her nose, her face fixed with a fearful expression. She charitably cleaned and rubbed the captain, trying to make her regain consciousness.

The Abbess, who remained standing in the prison doorway trembling with fear, said, "Mother, if she returns to herself, I am going to rush out of here."

Mother Mariana wept, and her tears fell on the forehead and face of the poor captive. From time to time she was shaken by strong convulsions, after which she would cry out and her body would start. Meanwhile, Mother Mariana continued to hold her head and torso in her lap.

Turning to the Abbess, she said, "Mother, it would be good to ask Mother Francisca for anise water and wool to burn. Tell her that there is a seriously ill person here so that she can come with others to assist our poor sister."

"I will go tell Mother Francisca this. But what will you do here by yourself if she regains consciousness while I am gone?"

"Do not worry, Mother. Jesus and Mary are here with me."

### THE EXORCISM

The Abbess quickly took her leave. While she awaited assistance from Mother Francisca, Mother Mariana continued to do all she could to revive her poor sister. As she attended her, she saw the two black creatures, who were timidly pressing themselves against the wall as if to hide themselves.

Seeing them, Mother Mariana cried out: "Vile and abominable beasts, what are you doing here? Return to your own wicked abode, for this is a holy place, a house of prayer and penance. All your efforts to take the soul of my sister will be in vain! Jesus Christ died for her and, in spite of you, she will be saved!

"I order you now, in the name of the mysteries of the Most Holy Trinity, the Divine Eucharist, and the Divine Maternity of Mary Most Holy and her glorious Passage and Assumption body and soul into Heaven, that you immediately leave this holy place, never again to return to torment with your abominable presence any of my sisters, be they justly or unjustly confined here!"

Before the humble religious had finished pronouncing her last word, a dreadful roar was heard. The earth trembled and horrible howling sounds could be heard. The Abbess was returning at that very moment with Mothers Francisca of the Angels, Anna of the Conception, Lucia of the Cross, Magdalena of St John, and Catherine of the Conception, who were bringing the remedies. All were quite frightened, especially the Abbess.

The religious recovered their courage and said to the Abbess, "Mother, have no fear. Something diabolical must be taking place in the prison. But Mother Mariana is very good, and the devils have no power over her. Let us enter without fear and with haste. We will see what will happen. Besides, Sister X is small and thin, and she would not be able to attack Mother Mariana, who is tall and strong."

The Mothers pressed forward to learn the cause of the dreadful commotion, but the Abbess, terrified, followed at a distance. Mother Francisca entered the prison with the other religious and saw that the room was darkened with a thick smoke.

They called out to Mother Mariana, who replied, "Come quickly. One of you go tell the Abbess to bring holy water and the incenser."

Mother Lucia of the Cross found the Abbess in the cloister hallway and told her Mother Mariana's request, which they both hastened to carry out.

When they returned, they saw that the prison was still obscure with smoke. On Mother Mariana's orders, Mother Lucia burned the incense while Mother Magdalena of Saint John sprinkled holy water around the prison, including on its walls. With this, the smoke dispersed and all could approach the poor sick sister, whom Mother Mariana was holding, half-dead, in her lap. They rubbed her, shook her, and fanned her. Finally, she opened her eyes and suddenly sat up.

### THE INGRATITUDE OF THE PRISONER

Finding herself among the good Spanish Mothers whom she despised, the captain seemed somewhat ashamed, and said, "I do not feel well."

Mother Mariana brought to her lips the cup of anise water and made her drink it, making the Sign of the Cross over her.

The Abbess approached and said, "Let us take her outside for a while to take some sun."

"Thank you, Mother," the prisoner responded. They raised her up, but she lacked the strength to walk, even with the support of the religious.

Consoling her like true Mothers and sisters, the religious visited her and provided her companionship throughout the day. The next day, the Abbess entered the prison with Mother Mariana and Mother Francisca. The prisoner, glowering at the Mothers, directed her attention only to the Abbess. Gravely, the Abbess addressed her, "Sister, you should be grateful to these two good and charitable Mothers who have come to take you outside for awhile so that you might get some fresh air."

"I will go, Mother," responded the prisoner. Supported by the two Mothers, she left the prison for the cloisters, where they helped her to stroll for a good length of time.

When an hour was up, the Abbess said, "Return, daughter, to prison, where you will remain until, contrite of heart, you amend your life and ask a public pardon of the Community for your bad example, and especially of Mother Mariana de Jesus, who loves you and has only compassion and tenderness for you."

The poor sister, weeping, returned to the prison. That night she suffered much, battling with her guilty conscience. But the envy in her heart was so deep-rooted that she could not bring herself to ask pardon and love the humble Mother Mariana.

### The Revelations of Our Lord Begin to Be Fulfilled

The next morning, the prisoner woke with great pain, a high fever, and symptoms of pneumonia. Seeing her in this state, the Abbess sought the counsel of Mother Mariana. Hearing the news, Mother Mariana sighed and large tears ran down her rosy cheeks.

She responded without hesitation, "Mother, I am going to the infirmary to advise Mother Francisca to prepare a comfortable bed for her, for she can be cured with care. Poor little thing, she is our sister and a soul redeemed by the Precious Blood of Our Divine Redeemer."

"If you deem it convenient, then do so. As for me, I would prefer she be nursed in the prison itself," responded the Abbess, who drew near the captive.

Mother Mariana took her leave so she might forewarn Mother Francisca about their sick sister and the need to bring her to the infirmary and nurse her with diligent care.

"Blessed be God, Who, by this, allows us an opportunity to practice charity with our adversary," said Mother Francisca. Together, they prepared the bed and everything necessary for transporting the sick sister. As they spoke of the prisoner, large tears rose in the eyes of Mother Mariana.

Taking note of them, Mother Francisca exclaimed to her, "Courage, my Mother and sister! The hour of your heroic sacrifice has arrived, for by your unspeakable suffering, this poor soul will be saved."

She continued, "Your Reverence should know that today, while I had Our Lord in my heart during Communion, He communicated to me the sacrifice that He had asked of you for this soul and the heroism with which Your Reverence accepted. Further, He told me that you were a most precious jewel which He possessed in the arid desert of this Spanish Colony, placed here in order to save souls and to placate Divine Justice, angered by the many crimes of its inhabitants.

"He asked that I encourage and console you in your arduous suffering. He revealed to me that this agony would not begin while the poor prisoner is ill. When she recovers, you will suffer the pains of the Hell that she would have suffered eternally. The duration of your suffering was not revealed to me. I hope that you do not turn away your sister who wants to share your sufferings and alleviate your pains."

"Ah, my sister!" exclaimed Mother Mariana with tears in her eyes. "No mortal can alleviate my five years of suffering in Hell. Five years where, for me, each day will be centuries. Have pity on me! Ask Our Lord to give me strength, valor, and humility so that I do not weaken, for I am a weak and miserable creature in a human body. I ask only that you do not tell this to anyone, not even to the Confessor."

"The Confessor and the Community do not know," replied Mother Francisca. "However, Mothers Maria of the Incarnation, Anna of the Conception, Lucia of the Cross, Magdalena of Saint John, and Catherine of the Conception already know, for Our Lord spoke to them also during Communion. They said nothing, for each thought it to be only an illusion. Even should it be true, each one is thinking to herself, they could not bear to see such an innocent and blameless creature suffer like that. Each one is waiting for the other to mention the matter, but none have done so since they are all uncertain of the truth of this distressing fact. I never doubted it for a minute, and, because I believed it, I suffer and tell you all this."

The two embraced and, weeping together before a crucifix, Mother Mariana offered herself again as the expiatory victim to save the soul of the poor sister.

### Who Will Nurse the Sick Sister?

After preparing the infirmary room, Mother Mariana told Mother Francisca, "Call the Founding Mothers so that we can go down to the prison and transfer our beloved sister here. I will go ahead, for the Abbess, who is fearful by nature, is there alone with her. We cannot allow her to suffer alone."

When the Abbess saw Mother Mariana, she exclaimed with relief, "Mother, enter immediately! You were so long in coming!"

"What is it, Mother?" Mother Mariana asked. "I was delayed because I went to prepare the bed in the infirmary where our sick sister will be cured." And she told her all that she had done.

The Prioress embraced Mother Mariana, saying, "Mother, your humility enchants me, but I fear that you debase yourself too much!"

To this, she responded, "Jesus Christ, our Master and Model, humbled Himself more than we do. Since we are His spouses, we should imitate Him closely. After having done all that our strength permits, we should still say, 'We are useless servants, because we do not do what we should, but only what we can.'"

At that moment, Mother Francisca and the other Founding Mothers entered the prison, greeted the Abbess, and asked her blessing. They approached the prisoner, addressed her fondly, and expressed their sympathy for the violent sickness that assailed her. Trying to encourage her, they told her that she would soon be better. To hasten that day, they said, they had come to carry her to the infirmary, where everything was prepared for her. They wrapped her in a warm covering, placed her on the litter, and transported her to the infirmary.

During the transit, the eyes of the Founding Mothers were fixed on Mother Mariana, who manifested profound sorrow, yet, at the same time, remained unperturbed, so characteristic of that great soul, whose physical beauty was just a weak reflection of the beauty of her soul.

Arriving at the infirmary, they called the doctor, who diagnosed her sickness as pneumonia complicated by another infectious virus that had caused the fever. He gave a prescription for medicines and warned that the sickness was very serious and contagious. He recommended that none of the sisters, and especially the younger ones whose health was more vulnerable, should enter the sick room, and that those who attended her should number no more than three. These sisters should nurse her in rotating shifts and take the greatest precautions, since anyone who was contaminated - young or old - could lose her life.

Because it was most grave, he recommended that, as a prudent precaution, it would be better for a woman from outside the Convent - middle-aged, better thin than fat - be engaged to come into the Convent and care for her. Otherwise, they could run the serious risk of one sister passing the virus to another, transforming the Convent into a hospital, which would be a most lamentable situation.

"It is nothing," said the doctor, "if only one sister dies. But it is quite another matter should all of the sisters in this Royal Convent be taken."

The doctor also advised that the sick sister not be kept in the infirmary, which was near the service room. He asked permission to look through the Convent to find a better place. The Abbess and Spanish Mothers walked with him through the Convent until he found a room of regular size, isolated and well-ventilated.

"The sick sister should be brought here," he decided, "although it will be most troublesome to nurse her because of the distance from the rest of the Convent. She should be assisted by two women, as I already indicated. One is needed to attend her quite closely. The other, without entering the room, should bring the first all that is necessary for the patient's cure. But this must be done immediately, for it is an urgent matter." And he took his leave.

### CONSULTATION WITH JESUS IN THE BLESSED SACRAMENT

The Abbess called Mother Mariana aside and said, "Mother, I pity this sister, but I am very worried that she might contaminate me. I know that as Abbess, I should be the one to attend her at close quarters. Yet despite the violence I make against myself, I cannot conquer my fear. My nature will not permit me to do this. Therefore, I have decided I will renounce the office of Abbess.

"Then it will be the duty of the new Abbess to find the two women whom the doctor advised should nurse this sick sister, for I cannot do this. For to introduce complete strangers into the Convent does not seem fitting to me.

"In face of all this, let this sister die. We will not miss her. On the contrary, without this revolted person, we would enjoy peace. Since God Himself wants to free us of this burden, why should we try to cure her with such zeal?

"What does Your Reverence think about this? What should we do? I ask your advice, Mother, first, because I know your virtue, judgment, and prudence, and second, because you are the Founder, and the Prelate directed you to give me counsel and to command in the Convent."

Mother Mariana prudently replied, "Mother, this matter is most delicate. Your Reverence is right in part about this. But, along with abnegation and humility, charity is a fundamental virtue of religious life. So that we do not err in this matter, let us go together to the lower choir for a half hour, and there, in silent prayer, we will speak intimately with the Eucharistic Jesus at the foot of the Sacrarium. Let us ask Him with filial confidence His divine counsel, and we will do what He tells us. Our Lord is very good and will not be deaf to the humble supplications of hearts that love Him."

"Very well, Mother," responded the Mother Abbess. "Let us go, but I ask that you beg Him most emphatically to manifest

His will to us. For I have a great fear of introducing strangers into the Convent."

Together they went down to the lower choir and prostrated themselves at the feet of the Divine Prisoner of souls, Who, day and night, remains with His beloved ones, watching over them with a truly paternal solicitude. During the half hour of prayer, the Abbess glanced from time to time at Mother Mariana, who seemed absorbed in sweet, heavenly contemplation, far removed from this miserable earth of sorrow and tears.

Seeing her so beautiful and holy, she said to herself, "Ah! How happy are the truly good souls! Surely she is a saint! How many sufferings this beautiful soul has borne! I would not be capable of suffering so much and with such serenity! My God, I beg Thee to consider her merits and enlighten me and give me discernment in this matter!"

At the end of the half hour, the Abbess touched the arm of Mother Mariana, saying, "Let us go, Mother. The half hour has passed." Upon hearing the voice of her Superior, the obedient religious tranquilly left her sweet prayer and, kissing the ground, accompanied her outside.

The Abbess asked her, "Mother, what was the response of the Sacramental Jesus? Do not conceal it from me."

"And to Your Reverence, what did He say? As Abbess, it is your right to speak first."

"Mother, Our Lord did not inspire me with any definite resolution," responded the Abbess. "I float on the waters of tribulation. To refuse any treatment for this sister would be a blatant lack of charity that would displease God. To introduce strangers from outside does not seem fitting to me. I do not have the courage to sacrifice some religious, ordering them to take care of the sick sister. Thus I resolved that, after consulting with you, I would present my resignation to the Bishop, for my health is certainly quite broken. My heart causes me great pain and needs to be calm. This is impossible for a poor Abbess. Does it not seem, Mother, that this would be a sensible and godly thing to do? Answer me, Mother, I beseech you."

### Mother Mariana Proposes her Solution

Mother Mariana gave a deep sigh and large tears ran down her rosy cheeks. Drying them, she responded, "Mother, the Sacred Heart of our Divine Redeemer is a furnace of ardent charity, and these conquering flames cannot remain in the divine sphere, but want to transmit their fire to creatures so that this charity might live in them and for them, as Our Lord did in His mortal life. It is not, therefore, the divine will that you should renounce the Abbacy, for this would show that you do not want to carry the cross with Christ, our Divine Spouse. Much less is it the will of God that outsiders should be introduced into the closed garden of the cloisters, for the spirit of secular women in domestic service would be injurious to the delicate spouses of the Lord. Nor does His divine will want us to abandon this poor sick sister.

"The will of our Divine Spouse is that I assume the duty of closely nursing this sister, who is sick in soul and body. I will be assisted by Mother Francisca and the Founding Mothers, but by none of the other religious. Be assured, Mother, that none of us will catch this sickness from the patient, for this is the will of God. Moreover, in this way, we will save the soul of the poor sister."

She had not finished speaking when the Abbess exclaimed in surprise, "How can Your Reverence accept such conditions from Our Lord? Such heroism is beyond my understanding. Reflect well, Mother, on what you will have to do and what you will suffer from the rudeness of such a creature."

"I see everything, Mother, but I also see that my self-love is different from that of my Lord Jesus Christ, who prayed for His very persecutors, executioners, and calumniators. He died for them, offering His precious life. Moreover, He would still be disposed to die again, if it were possible, so that all His souls might be saved. And I, who am completely insignificant in this world, a nun unknown to all, how can I bargain with my God over small sacrifices? Heaven is costly, my Mother! Why should we not labor arduously while we still see the light of day, before the night of death arrives when the time for all labor will be ended?

"The Founding Mothers and I need nothing more but the blessing of Your Reverence and your formal command to proceed so that all might be done meritoriously. Do not be fearful that one of us will catch this sickness. As for the personal apprehensions of Your Reverence, do not worry, for they result from your own sickness. Keep yourself calm and do not go near the sick patient. I, or one of the Founding Mothers, will inform you minutely of all that takes place with her. Mother Francisca, a religious of great virtue and soul, will tell you the things needed for the cure of this sick sister so that nothing will be lacking to her."

The Abbess responded, "Mother, how can I impose such a harsh order upon the Founding Mothers? They do not know that this is the will of God and, with reason, they will resent me for ordering this of them."

"Mother, the Founding Mothers already received a forewarning that this is the will of God and are only awaiting the order from Your Reverence to convince them entirely of its truth. They will then go joyfully to serve their poor sister. For they are magnanimous souls and live only to sacrifice themselves. To obey this command will be sweet for them since they will see it as a formal mandate from God Himself. Indeed, they do not know resentment, for they live a life of the spirit on this earth."

Mother Valenzuela was simultaneously admiring, confused, and edified to see this degree of heroism in the Founding Mothers, who, by right of their position, should be excused from such humble offices. This is the way the proud world thinks because, in its crass ignorance, it lacks the higher light of the spirit. Only souls that live in the refulgent light of the Most Sacred Heart of Jesus Christ can see, clear and unveiled, the valor of humility. They know that the higher the place a creature occupies in the House of the Lord, the greater should she humiliate herself in order to strengthen the foundation of her perfection. For those in religious life should aspire to greatness in Heaven by solidifying their virtue while on earth.

What great edification and love of virtue are inspired when one sees how those who occupy offices of authority and dignity behave with humility and suavity with their subjects. By reprimanding them in private, they achieve a swifter correction of sinners, and they infuse in them a healthy shame for their bad behavior. On the contrary, daily experience shows that the abuse of authority damages many subjects and vocations.

"Mother," continued the Abbess, "Will Your Reverence herself arrange for the Founding Mothers to come to me so that I can impose this command upon them under the law of obedience? I will do this with timidity and sorrow. Seeing such humility greatly edifies me, even while I lament my own lack of virtue in governing the Community, where I should be the example. Pray for me to God Our Lord."

"I will ask them to come to Your Reverence immediately," Mother Mariana replied, "so that as soon as possible we can begin to cure our sister, for it is a most urgent matter."

She quickly rose and left the presence of the Abbess, who never tired of admiring such great virtue in a person so young and beautiful. For God Our Lord, Who was so munificent in conceding to her the gifts of nature, was still more generous in communicating to her the gifts of grace.

### The Joy of the Founding Mothers

Mother Mariana did not delay in finding her sisters in religion and virtue. Calling the Founding Mothers together, she revealed what Our Lord had manifested to her: that He desired they should all take upon themselves the task of curing their poor sister. She told them that she knew that Our Lord had made this known to each of them during the morning Communion and that they were only awaiting the formal order from the Abbess to confirm the truth of this and render their immediate services to the poor, sick patient. She invited them to appear before the Abbess to inquire about their sick sister and offer themselves to do whatever their Abbess might deem necessary to help this sick member of the Mystical Body of Our Lord Jesus Christ.

The Founding Mothers replied, "What you have said is correct, dear Mother and sister. Our Lord also communicated to us how much you will suffer at the hands of this poor sister and the Hell that you have accepted in order to save her soul. We are deeply moved and offer ourselves to share in your suffering to alleviate it in any way that we can.

"How admirable is the goodness of God! He gives us pleasure, allowing us the opportunity to help cure this poor sister. You can count on our good will and the fraternal affection that unites us, since we are all daughters of the same mother. In effect, if our unforgettable Mother Maria de Jesus Taboada, our Founder and your aunt, were still living, how she would suffer from seeing you suffer. But since she is now in Heaven resting from all her earthly labors and enjoying the reward of her virtue, we who remain here, loving each other and desiring our mutual sanctification, will keep you company, and participate in your joys and sorrows.

"Now, accept our warm embraces, and then we will go before our Abbess to joyfully receive this much-desired command."

After each one embraced Mother Mariana, these human angels directed themselves to make their heroic sacrifice. The angels in Heaven, undoubtedly astounded, contemplated this cortege of virgin spouses of the Immaculate Lamb who on earth rivaled the angelic inhabitants of the celestial Jerusalem!

### THE SPANISH FOUNDING MOTHERS ACCEPT THE COMMAND OF THE ABBESS

Filled with that holy joy proper to just souls, the Founding Mothers greeted the Abbess and inquired about their sick sister, saying, "Mother, it is our duty, as Founding Mothers, to attend and serve this sick patient, who is our sister. What can we do to help our poor sister who is so gravely ill? Let Your Reverence command whatever she deems convenient, and we will be quick to obey, convinced that from the lips of the Abbess, God Himself speaks to us. We ask you, then, to command us with full liberty." All of them, together with Mother Mariana, knelt to receive her order.

How edifying a sight were these young religious whom God Our Lord had favored with every gift of nature and grace, who knelt to receive from their Abbess the command to begin their sacrifice, as if they were receiving the order to do some agreeable thing.

The Abbess wanted to kneel also, but they said, "Mother, we will not allow this! It is for us, the subjects, to be on the ground, and not Your Reverence. Do us the favor of either standing or sitting as you impose this command."

Blushing, the Abbess stood up and said: "Beloved Mothers and sisters, the holy will of God asks of you a sacrifice, and your Abbess asks of you a favor. By the power of holy obedience, I command that all of you, together with Mother Mariana de Jesus Torres, take care of our poor sick sister and nurse her, diligently accepting the bad with the good, thus imitating your Divine Spouse. Be certain that He will protect and guard you. And I, with tears in my eyes and a heart filled with tenderness, I bless you and ask that you pray for me to the Lord Our God."

The sisters bowed their heads and kissed the ground, and then the feet and scapular of their Abbess, saying, "Thank you, Mother, for having considered us worthy to render our services to this poor sister. We owe her much, for she provides us with an efficacious means to acquire great merit for Heaven. We joyfully accept your order, and now we leave to serve and nurse our sick sister with dedication."

The Abbess embraced each one of the Mothers, who, tranquil and happy, headed to the room of the sick sister.

Arriving there, they prayed a Hail Mary and approached the patient, who rudely upbraided them and asked why they had left her without the care the doctor had prescribed. She told them they had an obligation to cure her as soon as possible since it was because of their insidious schemes that she had been imprisoned and suffered so much. Moreover, she added, it was her desire to get well so that she could again obtain their imprisonment, for only this would make her happy.

The humble Founding Mothers, with unchanging expressions of edifying serenity, only replied, "Be patient, dear sister. We will now apply all the remedies. God Our Lord and the Most Holy Virgin, Who are goodness itself, will make you better, healing not only your body, but also your soul."

### The Marquesa's Dream

After arranging the bed, which had been disheveled by the agitated movements of the impatient sick sister, the Founding Mothers prepared what the doctor had ordered for her cure. While the others were doing this, Mother Mariana and Mother Francisca arranged to administer the prescribed treatments, one of which was to take a bath in a tub of very hot water. The Convent, however, had no tub, so Mother Francisca went to explain the problem to the Abbess, who was also at a loss as to what to do.

At that moment, the sister-porter came in to tell the Abbess that the Marquesa wanted to greet and speak to Mother Mariana. The Abbess called for her, and they both went to speak to the Marquesa.

This lady, in great agitation of spirit, recounted to the Mothers a disturbing dream that she had experienced the night before. In it, she saw and recognized Mother Mariana, so beautiful, smiling, and gracious, laboring untiringly for a sick woman whom the Marquesa did not recognize. The patient, miserable and under the power of two huge black creatures with eyes of fire, abused Mother Mariana in both word and deed, even to the point of physically attacking her several times.

On one of these occasions, Mother Mariana fell dead, her soul leaving her body in the form of a beautiful white dove carrying a rich bunch of grapes toward Heaven. The holy Mother said to the Marquesa, "Thank you, thank you, good lady, for the favors that you have done for me. Now I entrust to you my Convent and ask that you bestow your alms on it. From Heaven I will watch over you and reciprocate your kindnesses." Hearing these words, the Marquesa screamed and awoke.

Her maids quickly called for her nurse, for the Marquesa, in her perturbation over this dream, could not speak. They called the doctor, who came quickly and applied various remedies. Regaining her senses, she nonetheless remained most grieved and anxiously awaited the morning so that she might speak with Mother Mariana and assure herself that she were still alive. For the Marquesa could not resign herself to the death of her holy friend, who, by her counsels and prayers, had done her many spiritual favors and sustained her in many battles of the spirit. Describing the dream, the Marquesa sobbed inconsolably.

"Do not cry, my good lady," Mother Mariana comforted her. "One should not believe in dreams. You can see that I am still living in order to give you whatever happiness I can. I still have many long years of life on this earth. Alas, my exile will last for many years yet to come. On another day, we can converse more; now I have to go for I have an urgent occupation. I assure you of my affection and gratitude, and, since you are so kind, I will ask of you a favor."

"Mother, what do you want? My greatest joy and happiness is to be able to please you. What do you need?"

"I will tell you, gracious lady, that one of our sisters is gravely ill. The doctor prescribed a warm bath in a tub, but we have no tub in the Convent. Perhaps Your Grace could provide one for us?"

"Considering myself most fortunate in being able to serve you, I will most happily and without delay send you a tub. I also give you 30 sterling pounds for the cure of the sick sister. I only ask one thing, that you come to me first to ask for anything else that is needed for this holy patient."

The Marquesa asked the blessing of the Mothers, then took her leave. Since this good lady knew nothing about the guilty sick sister, she had called her holy, for she was convinced that all the sisters were like the saintly Mother Mariana.

### The Enormous Patience of the Spanish Mothers

After this providential conference, Mother Mariana hurried back to her place of sacrifice. She found Mother Francisca before a fire heating the water.

The latter asked, "Mother, what shall we do about the tub? As you can see, the water is almost hot enough."

"My beloved sister! God is so good! Even while I received the call to speak with the Marquesa, He had already prepared the gift of a tub. For that good lady will provide this for our poor sick sister and is sending it immediately."

Soon, she received a message saying that the tub had arrived. Mother Mariana and Mother Magdalena of Saint John went to get the tub. After everything was prepared, Mother Francisca said, "The water is ready now. Let us bathe our sick sister."

Entering the sick room, they said, "Dear sister, the water and everything necessary for your bath are ready. Prepare yourself."

To this, she responded, "I am ready. Do you think I am as stupid or retarded as you are? All you have to do is pick me up and let me down into the tub, since I am not strong enough to do this myself. Besides, this is a job most fitting for you Spaniards."

Mother Mariana and Mother Francisca approached her bed, took her in their arms, carried her to the tub, and let her down into it with great charity and kindness. Meanwhile, the other Mothers made her bed, prepared towels for after her bath, and helped her to wash herself.

"This water is boiling!" the sick sister exclaimed. "The doctor did not order it to be like this. These Spaniards are trying to kill me!" And she threw water into the face of Mother Mariana.

This water entered her eyes and brought forth an abundant stream of tears. Seeing this, the impatient sick sister said, "The water is ice cold. It feels as if it had never been heated. And Mother Mariana is proof of this, for she is crying because her guilty conscience is accusing her of her negligence. She is so proud and self-indulgent that she does not know what suffering is." Again, she threw water in her face.

Mother Francisca told her, "Sister, be quiet. You should act as a religious at least once. This way, you will not get well. Time is short."

"You are lazy," retorted the patient. "You are the ones who should do something at least once." And she twisted and turned in the tub, making as much work as she could for the Mothers, who suffered all this with an edifying patience and charity.

After she had finished her bath, they removed her from the tub with great difficulty, for she acted like a stubborn child. They placed her in her bed and began a hot massage over her whole body. As Mother Mariana rubbed her, the captain threw out blows and harsh words at her. This miserable creature, undeserving of the name of sister, screamed and cried in rage, saying that she was being treated with unspeakable harshness. The good and charitable Mothers passed the whole night without sleep taking care of her.

### THIRTY DAYS

The fever and pneumonia rapidly became worse. In her delirium, the sick patient would address the Bishop accusing Mother Mariana and demanding her imprisonment.

"Only then," she said, "will I be at peace. For she is repugnant!"

When the doctor came to visit, she complained that nothing he had ordered had been carried out. On the contrary, she said, the sisters did whatever they thought best, and, because of this, she was worse. Because of the hatefulness and stupidity of the Mothers, she was being left to die. She asked that he arrange with the Abbess to have them replaced by someone who could cure her.

"While I was suffering from thirst and pain," she continued, "the Spaniards were sleeping soundly."

The doctor, who knew the Mothers well and, above all, Mother Mariana, whom he venerated, reprimanded the patient severely for her words, but the Mothers excused their patient, attributing everything to the delirium of fever. The doctor gave new orders and left, quite shocked by the ingratitude of the sick sister, and most edified at seeing such virtue, charity, and abnegation.

The Spanish Mothers prepared the medicines. When Mother Mariana administered them, she received them back in her own face, spit there by the rebellious sister. With holy patience and a sweet smile, she would dry herself off and embrace the patient, making her take a new dose. Often the sick sister would spit the final mouthful out at her. At other times, the captain would call Mother Mariana to attend to her bodily necessities, which were more frequent because of the medicine. When she raised herself, she would fling her filth upon Mother Mariana, soiling her.

Without altering her expression or uttering the least word of complaint, this holy religious would change her own clothing and then continue attending to the patient for the love of God. It is impossible to describe how much this unconquerable and blameless creature suffered from this sick sister, whose illness lasted thirty days and nights.

### DEATH, JUDGMENT, AND ...
### THE CONVERSION OF THE GUILTY SISTER

On the thirtieth day of her illness, the captain became much worse and appeared to be dying. Her face was pale, distorted in terror and agonizing despair. Her short hair stood on end and her eyes seemed to jump out of their sockets.

She screamed and writhed, calling out, "It is too late for me now. I cannot love or pardon her. I want to save myself, but, in my present state, I cannot. If those black creatures would only go away! Help me, Spaniards, since they are carrying me away with them!"

She threw her arms around Mother Mariana, who silently shed a torrent of tears over the head and face of her sick sister. With this healing bath, her panic subsided somewhat, and she said, "Keep applying this fresh liquid that is giving me relief. This is what the doctor has been ordering. These Spaniards have finally been moved to compassion and are providing me with some relief."

They called the confessor, who, frightened, did not want to remain long in the room. He told the Mothers, "This poor sister is dying impenitent. I will not return to see her. Do not call me again. She should confess and repent for the sins she has committed in this life. But she is impenitent. How much have I labored in vain for her! You must forgive her and pray, for she is entering her last agony."

Mother Mariana held her in her arms, praying to the Divine Majesty that He would not permit this soul to be seized from her arms and carried into Hell. Reminding Him of her offer, she again renewed it. As she prayed, the sick sister began to have strong convulsions, her body shaking violently. Her death agony began, which lasted for two painful days. Finally, she gave a cry, opened her eyes and mouth, which was expelling foam, and her body fell limp.

Since Mother Mariana was holding her in her arms, the Founding Mothers told her, "Mother, she had already died. Do not continue to hold her corpse. We have exhausted every means possible to cure her, soul and body. How often did we counsel her! But it has been to no avail."

Mother Mariana replied, "My sisters and Mothers, do not forget so quickly the offer that was accepted to save this soul. Pray to God for her. Now she is standing before the judgment seat of God and realizing all the evil for which she was responsible. She will return to life and amend her life. Do not be frightened and remain calm.

"Later, she will die, but she will save her soul, even though her Purgatory will last until the Final Judgment Day. Our Lord has revealed this to me even now."

As she finished speaking, the sick sister quivered and returned to consciousness. Her eyes moved around the room, as if she were looking for one in particular. Her gaze came to rest upon Mother Mariana, who was holding her in her arms. She pressed her hand and tried to speak, but her voice would not respond. Her eyes were streaming with tears. The charitable Mother Mariana dried them with the love of a mother and spoke tender words to her, infusing a great confidence in the goodness of God and making her feel how much He loved her.

The saintly religious asked Mother Francisca for a little anise water and, with her fingers, she moistened the dry lips of the captain. Finally, she made her drink. Regaining her strength, the recovered sister reported that she was returning from eternity, that she had become a better person, and that she understood who Mother Mariana was.

She seemed to be ashamed, but the charitable Mother Mariana told her, "Do not become disturbed, my little sister. You need to remain quiet and calm so that you can make your general confession with a Franciscan Friar. For this, we must first cure you and rebuild your strength. You must love and have much confidence in the good God. Courage, for all your sisters love you and wish you both physical and spiritual health."

## Reparation and Penitence

From that moment on, the captain became a model patient. Her docility was like that of a child. She received everything prescribed with appreciation and holy shame, manifesting her profound gratitude to Mother Mariana, whom she always wanted near her, as well as to the other Mothers who attended her. She continued to improve and, in one month she had completely recovered.

She then asked that they call the Abbess, who came, fearful of catching the sickness.

"What do you want of me, sister?" the Abbess gravely asked her, "Are you the same as before – or worse?"

The poor religious flung herself at her feet, saying, "Pardon me, Mother, for my bad behavior. And may the Founding Mothers and the whole Community pardon me for the scandalous life that I have led until now. Above all, may my dear Mother Mariana pardon me and have compassion on me."

"It is not enough that you humble yourself and ask pardon here. You must do this before the Community and then return to the prison where you will stay until you die," replied the Abbess.

"Yes, Mother," responded the poor sister. "Your Reverence is right to command this. Well do I deserve to remain in prison forever, for now, through the mercy of God and the prayers of dear Mother Mariana, I am free from the eternal prison of Hell. I will return to prison today if Your Reverence so orders it, and there I will do penance for my sins. When I left this mortal life, I received a severe but just reprimand from our Founding Mother, but she did not turn me away from her feet. I am truly the prodigal son."

And the poor sister began to cry inconsolably. Here it is fitting to describe her features. Small of body, her color was neither brown nor white. Her eyes, nose, and mouth were large. She had black hair, and was more thin than fat. Her illness had weakened her considerably so that she appeared quite pale and feeble.

Seeing her so confused and contrite, Mother Mariana and the Founding Mothers spoke on her behalf to the Abbess. Because her state of soul was so improved, they argued, it was no longer necessary to imprison her. Further, because of her weakness and broken health, she needed to remain free. They promised that they themselves would answer for her conduct.

Mother Valenzuela conceded, although somewhat reluctantly, to ask the Bishop to release the captain from prison. However, she would do this only to please the Founding Mothers. If this sister committed the slightest fault, she would imprison her forever and allow no intercession on her behalf, for justice and reason would demand this.

From that day forward, this sister enjoyed freedom. The first thing she did to atone for her past was to accuse herself of her faults in the refectory with a cord around her neck. She also asked for a penance for her past scandalous deeds.

The Abbess reprimanded her severely. She applied the discipline to her before the full Community, and ordered her to kiss the feet of the religious and eat on the floor of the refectory for nine days. The contrite sister carried out all of this with humility, and often, Mother Mariana would accompany her.

## The First Year of the Abbacy of Mother Valenzuela Ends

All this took place during the first year of the Abbacy of Mother Valenzuela. At the end of the year, the captain was completely recovered, saved because of the heroic sacrifice of Mother Mariana. Working together with the Abbess, Mother Mariana then began the process of obtaining permission from the Bishop for this sister to make a general confession to a Franciscan friar, the very one whom Mother Mariana consulted.

After this permission was granted, the sister made her general confession. The friar heard her calmly and charitably. He took pity on the many sufferings of this poor lamb who had strayed from the flock of her Divine Shepherd. He absolved her and gave her pardon for her sins, thus freeing her from this enormous weight and leaving her reconciled with God, Who, with the Angels of Heaven and the just on earth, rejoiced at the return of the prodigal son who had so imprudently abandoned the paternal home to fritter away his inheritance. Having squandered everything and being reduced to entire misery, his hunger drove him to eat the remains of the acorns left by the pigs...

How valuable it is to overcome the passions that assail us in life at their very inception and while there is still time. For when we accede to them, virtue and religious perfection fade. Farewell, then, to our vocations and to Heaven. Religious persons in particular should fear letting themselves be carried away by their passions, for they should be as Angels on earth. By their virtue and hidden lives of sacrifice, such holy men and women in religious communities hold back the hand of Divine Justice and avert the punishments merited by the traitors and guilty persons.

\* \* \*

## Chapter 27

One day at the end of the first year of the Mother Valenzuela's Abbacy, Mother Mariana and the happy converted sister were praying in the lower choir, when the holy Mother fell into ecstasy and saw Jesus Christ.

Sorrowful and loving, He gazed at her, saying: "My beloved spouse, the time has arrived for you to suffer the five years of Hell that you accepted with heroic charity to save the soul of your poor sister. Pray insistently to the Holy Ghost to prepare your soul for this and fortify your spirit with the gift of fortitude. Confidently embrace My loving goodness and enclose yourself in the Wound in My side that was opened to shelter My chosen souls, and place yourself under the maternal care of My Virgin Mother.

"Further purify your soul with the grace of absolution, which you should receive tomorrow with great faith and humility. I will remain with you in Communion until the Sacramental Species has been consumed, and then your Hell will begin."

Blessing her, Our Lord, the Prisoner of Love, again concealed Himself in the Sacrarium. Returning from her ecstasy, Mother Mariana pondered with the keen intellect given her by God these future sufferings. She trembled at the sight of them, but was happy to offer this suffering to save one religious soul from the eternal fires of Hell.

The next morning she spoke with the Franciscan friar who directed her and told him all that had passed. He heard her confession, as Our Lord had instructed, and gave her absolution. Throughout her life, this saintly soul committed no sin save the slight imperfections that are bound to occur in this mortal life. The whole day she prepared herself to receive her God in the Eucharist, as if it were to be her last Communion. She experienced most ardent sentiments of love, gratitude, and faith and was filled with a deep and pervading joy the whole day.

### After Communion, Hell...

The next morning as she approached the Table of the Angels to say farewell for the long period of five years to the intimate union she enjoyed with her God, she felt as if her heart were being ripped asunder. She tried to conserve Him in her heart as long as possible, but the hour for her sacrifice had struck.

After the Sacramental Species had been consumed, Mother Mariana felt a sorrow so intense that it seemed to wrench her heart violently from her breast. At that moment, she became completely insensible to her God. She felt a tedium toward Him, and even more, she experienced a type of hatred and despair that did not permit the least ray of hope.

She tried to reflect upon the heroic sacrifice that she had made to save the soul of her sister. However, instead of receiving relief, she felt fury, despair, and a total suspicion with regard to God. She wanted to remind herself that the Divine Heart loved her to the point of delivering Himself for her sake to cruel torments and infinite humiliations, but she only felt the weight of the Blood of Christ, shed in vain for a condemned soul! She reminded herself of all the sublime mysteries of Christ on earth and of His Virgin Mother, pure and immaculate from her conception, but these thoughts were only a perpetual source of unending rage and despair. She still felt herself to be a daughter of the Immaculate Conception – but now, a condemned one.

The notion of the five years vanished from her mind, and she could only foresee from then on an eternity of affliction.[58] She wanted to encourage herself by thinking that some day this Hell would end, but she heard rough, terrible voices taunting her without any order, saying: "Eternity! Eternity! Forever! Forever! In Hell, the Redemption has no meaning. Oh! religious who squandered the time given to you on earth, who wasted countless graces, you deserve the unspeakable torments and horrible sufferings of the punishment of perdition."

### THE TORMENTS OF THE FIVE SENSES

The terrible chastisements of the senses fell upon Mother Mariana. Her body would feel a fiery heat, as if it were a living coal

---

58. In the years 1760-1770, Fr. Bartolomé Ochoa de Alácano y Gambo, O.F.M., published *The Vida Admirable of Mother Mariana de Jesús Torres*, providing dates and copious documentation. This venerable Franciscan, who served various terms as Provincial of Saint Paul Monastery in Quito, attested to this heroic act of charity carried out by Mother Mariana in favor of the revolted sister (Cadena y Almeida, *Apariciones*, pp. 154-6).

that burned without being consumed. Then, following this extreme heat, she would experience a coldness impossible to express or describe, more intense than if she were buried under a mound of snow. Her breathing was constricted by the immense pain caused at times by fire, and at times by the frigid cold.

Before her eyes appeared horrible infernal visions. Her ears were tormented by the appalling blasphemies made by the condemned souls and devils. Repugnant odors permeated her sense of smell, worse and more intense than if she were surrounded by the filth of all mankind. Her sense of touch was tormented, and she felt as if she were lying on a hard bed, hard with the hardness of Hell, a bed lined with sharp nails that penetrated to her very depths. Her palate was tortured by a horrible taste, worse than anything she had ever experienced. In addition, the devils forced her to swallow molten hot sulfur and dealt her strong, harsh blows that drove her mad and incited her to fury, despair, and blasphemy.

In face of these unspeakable trials, she never opened her lips to say the least word whatsoever to her Community about the sufferings transpiring in her soul. Only the Franciscan friar who directed her knew of them.

## THE REJECTION OF GOD

During these long years of her trial, her memory was afflicted by the remembrance of graces received from the loving goodness of God and Mary Most Holy, Whom she seemed to have lost forever. It was especially painful for her to think of the grace of the religious vocation and the joys of conventual life. For while she had suffered many hardships in her religious life, these now seemed like veritable pleasures to her, for then at least she could love her God, and this was denied to her in her present condition.

Her mind understood perfectly and with the greatest clarity who God and Mary Most Holy were, and she recognized the existence of Heaven and the eternal delight of the blessed who inhabited it. But hopeless, she felt that it was absolutely unattainable for her. Her will was no longer free to do either evil or good, as it was in her mortal life, for she was a prisoner suffering the rigor of Divine Justice. She wanted to have recourse to mercy, but from the depths of her tormented soul, she heard voices that echoed through her being, "It is too late for you. Everything is over. Now the only thing that remains for you is eternal punishment. The avenging justice weighs over you. Hell ... for all Eternity!"

"Oh! unfortunate time given to me," she would say to herself. "Now I see how I strayed from the pathway of truth."

Mother Mariana took upon herself the guilt of all the sins of her sister, suffering as if they were her own sins. These sins tormented her with their weight and their memory. She entertained not the least hope of relief and even less of pardon, for she saw God unhappy and irritated with her. Mary Most Holy, as well as her Founder Mother and all her celestial friends, showed themselves completely indifferent to her cries.

She was convinced that this punishment was just, for the sins of the sister for whom she was expiating were numerous. She no longer had any memory of how she was a favored soul beloved by God, or that she was suffering for a span of five years in an heroic sacrifice to save a sister's soul. All this was lost to her memory, and only the conviction that she was condemned forever lived in her. These dark, dismal shadows that were in her spirit constituted the worst part of her Hell.

She wanted to love God and raise her spirit to Him, but she felt repelled by Him. When she thought of God and His infinite beauty that had been lost to her forever, she fell into an anguished despair so great that she wanted to end her very existence. The thought that the soul is immortal filled her with fury and despair, for such a suffering is incomprehensible and inexplicable. In short, for this suffering creature, there was not the least consolation, the least respite to her sorrow, or the least type of physical or moral relief.

All creatures without exception became for her sources of great torment. The attentions and kindnesses of her Abbess and the Community only augmented her suffering. She considered herself interiorly abandoned and irremediably lost, living and breathing in an atmosphere of hatred.

### Our Lord Enlightens the Founding Mothers about her Sufferings

This holy creature suffered all these torments – and unspeakable others – every minute of the day and night, in all times and places. At the same time, throughout these years of harsh expiation, she appeared to all around her as a model of sweetness, humility, and meekness in her exact observance of the Rule. She was for her fellow religious a mirror: Looking at her, they could see a faithful and exemplary model to imitate.

Although her expression remained serious, dignified, and sweetly amiable, there was, nonetheless, something in it that manifested a profound sadness that caught the hearts, affection, and attention of her Community. Yet no one dared to question her as to the source of her sorrow.

On one of the first days of her Hell, the Founding Mothers, surprised to see her great affliction, asked themselves, "What could it be? Has her time in Hell begun?" And they prayed to the Lord that He would enlighten them.

Our Lord did not delay in responding to this question of His faithful spouses. One day, after they had all received Communion, he manifested to them that Mother Mariana, His beloved and faithful spouse, was already suffering the Hell that she had accepted for five years to save the soul of her guilty sister. He made them understand that she suffered without the least relief, and that no one could help alleviate her pains.

He showed them the heart of Mother Mariana, which He was protecting, hidden in His own Sacred Heart and safeguarded by His Immaculate Mother. During her time of Hell, she would remain without a heart, thus being deprived of the power to love Him and enjoy intimate communion with Him. On the other hand, the keenness of her senses were sharpened and quickened, so that she would suffer both physically and morally the pains of this loss, and experience the feeling of being a condemned soul.

Thus, in face of the many great sins committed during this epoch in the Colony, this heroine held back the hand of Divine Justice from burying this Spanish possession under the ashes of the Pichincha Volcano, whose strong tremors periodically shook that guilty country.

### The Suffering Leaves its Mark

Enduring this great suffering and pain of loss, Mother Mariana's health rapidly declined. She lost the beautiful rosy color of her face, which was now sallow; her eyes became hollow and sad. Her whole physiognomy expressed a private, profound suffering.

Noting this, Mother Valenzuela, who loved Mother Mariana dearly, said: "Mother, what is wrong with Your Reverence? Why have you declined so rapidly and lost your natural color? If you are sick, it is best that you see the doctor so that he might cure you as soon as possible. I cannot bear to think that you might die and leave me alone on this earth. Nor can I help but suspect that the sickness of our sister has passed to you, for you nursed her closely and breathed all that foul air. I had wished for her to die, but now it will be you who will perish. You will die, and she will live. The hope of the Convent will die, and the obstacle will remain. This thought is with me day and night and prevents me from sleeping.

"For the love of God, my Mother, take care of your health. You must have a complete rest in order to recover. The cool dawn and damp night air are damaging your health. Arise later and go to bed earlier. Do not fast or do any penances, for already you are a living corpse!" And, weeping, Mother Valenzuela embraced her.

"Besides, you had assured me," continued the Abbess, "that no one would catch this sickness. It seems to me that Your Reverence took the illness upon yourself to prevent it from spreading to the others. If I had foreseen this, I would not have permitted you to assist the sick sister. I would have forbidden you to go near her to even ask how she was."

Mother Mariana responded with her customary calm and sweetness, "My Mother, how I appreciate your care and concern. But be assured that I most absolutely did not catch the virus of my poor sister, but that it is God Our Lord Who is punishing me for my ingratitude. It is His most holy Will that I suffer the rigor of Divine Justice – and I will do so.

"From you, my Abbess and Mother, I pray and beg for myself what I most need. There is no sufficient reason to exempt me even in part from the observance of the Rule since I am not suffering from any physical illness. Remain tranquil concerning me and freely dispose of me for whatever Your Reverence desires."

This response quieted Mother Valenzuela's fear that Mother Mariana had caught the contagious sickness. But she continued to suffer intensely as she watched Mother Mariana wasting away day after day. She would send her more nourishing food, and this humble and obedient religious would eat and drink everything that her Abbess ordered given her. The Abbess's admiration increased to see this prompt acquiescence to her orders and her irreprehensible behavior, as well as Mother Mariana's regular and exact obedience to the smallest details of community life.

According to her reports to her spiritual director, it is known that her daily meditations, instead of being a consolation, relief, and support, as they used to be, constituted a cruel Hell.

Those who study mystical theology understand the step Our Lord takes to purify and refine the souls He wants to raise to high degrees of perfection. We, however, know it only from study, and not from our own experience. We cannot describe, therefore, the kinds of interior sufferings endured by this Conceptionist sister, a martyr of fraternal charity. Either she herself would have to return to earth to give us an account of it, or we ourselves would have to suffer something similar for us to have an idea of the profound, intense sorrow she suffered. There is no other way.

### THE CONVENT'S CONFESSOR AUGMENTS HER INTERNAL TRIALS

During this time, she continued to receive the holy Sacraments of Penance and the Eucharist. Her director testifies that despite her interior state, which only he knew, the purity of her beautiful soul shone admirably and that she committed no sin that required absolution. She, however, was convinced that she was the worst of sinners for having abused such singular graces that Divine Goodness had conceded to her.

The confessor of the Community, who was not a Franciscan, remained ignorant of the state of purification of this heroic soul. Augmenting her sufferings, he reprimanded her severely:

"How you have changed, Mother! Why is this? Before you were a simple soul without any dissimulation, and now it is difficult to understand you. I do not know what you are saying. I fear that some hidden sin is the cause of this transformation. Examine your conscience well and place yourself in the presence of God. If we lose our innocence, we can still save ourselves through the

Sacrament of Penance. I do not understand the present state of your soul. I cannot enjoin you to receive Communion, for I am afraid to stand responsible for your soul. Examine yourself to see if you can or cannot approach the Holy Table to receive the God before Whom the Heavens and the Earth tremble."

The Confessor never ordered her to receive Communion. However, her spiritual director, a Franciscan friar, obliged her under holy obedience to receive the Communions prescribed by the Rule, an order that this docile and abnegated creature obeyed without a word.

She would prepare herself for Communion with the most profound humility. But when she received Communion, she felt neither the love nor the sweetness she had formerly experienced. Also, she did not sense the presence of her beloved Creator. During these moments, however, the fury and despair would abate, although she continued to feel an indescribable darkness and desolation of spirit that caused immense interior suffering to this seraphic soul. In the ardent depths of this victim soul, the fire of divine love burned strongly, her outward spiritual state being only a thick layer of ashes that kept it hidden from sight.

### THE CONVERTED SISTER

Meanwhile, the captain mended her ways, although the Mother Abbess still treated her with severity and even harshness. At times, the non-observant sisters, who were reduced in number, sought out their old leader in hopes of plotting new revolts. When Mother Mariana died – for her health was rapidly deteriorating, the Convent would finally be free of her influence, they told her. Now, they insisted, was the time to set in motion a plan to elect the captain as Abbess and finish with the Spaniards.

Sometimes this religious would simply turn a deaf ear to the seducing voices of these revolted sisters who wanted to shipwreck her again in the dangerous sea of her former laxity. On other occasions, she treated them with scorn and contempt. There were also moments, however, when she would weaken and feel inclined to accede to their demands. When this happened, she would run to Mother Mariana, her refuge and support. Confessing everything to her, she would ask for her counsel, prayers, and courage.

With admirable calm and sweetness, as if nothing unpleasant were passing in her soul, Mother Mariana would listen to her charitably and give her sound practical advice. After receiving this counsel, the captain's fears would dissipate, her spirit would be strengthened, and her will to persevere in her conversion would be sustained.

### AMID THE SUFFERING, THE FESTIVITIES FOR THE NEW ABBESS

So the years of the Abbacy of Mother Valenzuela passed. She suffered so much that her heart became worse, and she experienced frequent painful attacks. When they would occur, she did not want Mother Mariana to leave her side, because only she could give her consolation. On the other hand, her sorrow increased to see Mother Mariana's worsening state of health. The latter, always humble, sweet, and discerning, would try to distract the Abbess who loved her so greatly.

The time for a new election arrived. The non-observant sisters voted for their old leader, the captain, who was far from accepting any change. Along with Mother Valenzuela and some of the others, she voted for Mother Mariana. But her state of debility and almost complete collapse was causing fear within the Community, and the majority of the votes fell in favor of Mother Inez Zorrilla, who was confirmed as Abbess. The others rendered her their obedience and celebrated her election with joy and elation.

In these Community celebrations, Mother Mariana took an active part, even while she suffered such indescribable and profound torments! Weakened and desolate as she was, she entertained the Community at this celebration with her harp and melodious voice, which seemed to have taken on celestial timbres in her profound sorrow.

Even as she diffused this happiness in her beloved Community, her soul felt not the least personal consolation. Alone in her interior desert, she suffered her cruel Hell, feeling hatred and despair as well. What is most admirable and incomprehensible is that she showed no sign of these feelings that overwhelmed her soul, but rather displayed toward her sisters only sweetness, amiability, and endless goodness.

Mother Inez Zorrilla loved her greatly, but Mother Magdalena de Jesus Valenzuela surpassed all the others in her affection for this holy creature. When her attacks would come on, she would beg insistently to have Mother Mariana with her. The Abbess would ask Mother Mariana if she would be willing to stay with the former Abbess. This docile creature, as if she were a newly professed sister, would obey immediately whatever she was asked. Even more, she would try to foresee the desires of her Abbess and carry them out promptly. Mother Valenzuela's love and profound gratitude continued to grow, and Mother Mariana would render her every possible service, as if she were a maidservant.

\*

What an inimitable example! If we were suffering such interior trials, we would have found ourselves unable to render such delicate services to our fellow brothers. Even if we possessed great virtue, we would at least occasionally have manifested our impatience and anger, conceding to forces outside our power to contain.

This young Conceptionist heroine surpassed the greatest masters of the mystical science. As for her virtue, the way she conducted herself during this cruel suffering should have sufficed for the Holy Church to raise her to the honor of the altars even in her own time. She was, indeed, a matchless religious following an extraordinary pathway, which no one, without being called by God, should imprudently venture to travel lest she go astray. But we can all imitate her in her humility, obedience, sweetness, silence, prudence, and charity, virtues that attract others and move them to draw nearer to God. They either convert from their bad path and relaxation or they become more perfect, more faithful to the grace.

Happy the Convent of the Immaculate Conception in the city of Quito, which sheltered within its walls such a creature!

Happy the religious of all times, who, called by God, will reside in this blessed place, sanctified by such a creature!

Happy the Seraphic family who counts this heroine among its ranks, and a thousand times happy am I, who, being a Friar Minor, have such a sister!

## THREE MORE YEARS PASS

The three years of the Abbacy of Mother Zorrilla passed. These years saw some laxness in fidelity to the Rule due to lack of prudence on the part of the Abbess rather than bad will. This, however, is not the place to discuss these matters, since this is the story of the life of Mother Mariana de Jesus Torres, which we thus continue.

By the end of Mother Inez Zorrilla's term, the health of Mother Valenzuela had improved since she had been relieved of the heavy duties of the office of Abbess and the worries that accompany it. The state of Mother Mariana, on the other hand, had worsened considerably. Without exaggeration, she was nothing more than a living corpse.

When the day arrived to elect a new Abbess, Mother Valenzuela again found herself with a majority of votes and was confirmed in the office by the Bishop. She was very reluctant to accept such a responsibility, which, for her, was an enormous burden.

But Mother Mariana spoke these few words to her, "Mother, accept it, for it is the will of God. Soon, all your earthly concerns will be over."

These were prophetic words, for after only three months of her term of office, Mother Valenzuela left this earth for eternity.

## MOTHER MARIANA LEAVES HELL

After the sisters officially rendered obedience to the new Abbess, the festivities began. Mother Mariana, as always, took upon herself the task of offering entertainment to her Community; all the while her Hell continued.

On the fifteenth day after the election, she was making her early morning meditation along with the Community when she suddenly cried out and fell unconscious to the ground. Mother Valenzuela ran to her, took her in her arms, and rubbed her face and hands, trying frantically to bring her to her senses. The face of Mother Mariana expressed a distress that touched her to the quick of the soul.

"She is dying!" cried the Abbess, sobbing like a child. "My

God! Do not take away my consolation! Let her remain here so I can die peacefully, having her close to me!"

Mother Zorrilla, along with the Spanish Founding Mothers, hurried to bring remedies. They returned a short time later and told the Abbess that prudence demanded that they take Mother Mariana to the dormitory so that she might receive attention there. She gave the order for this to be done, and the Mothers promptly transported her there and began administering to her. The Abbess sat next to Mother Mariana, who was inert, as if dead, and would not permit anyone except the Spanish Mothers to touch her.

They bathed her in warm water and applied poultices. After four hours had passed, her condition still had not changed, and the doctor was called. After examining her, he shook his head, saying, "What a pity! I will do my best, but if she has not returned to consciousness in an hour, then it is certain that she is no longer with us."

Mother Valenzuela took this much harder than the others. Weeping inconsolably, she embraced Mother Mariana, who was already nothing but skin and bones. Forty-five minutes later, Mother Mariana slowly opened her eyes, finding herself in the arms of her Abbess.

She lifted her head slightly and, seeing her Superior so distressed, said to her, "I am sorry to have caused you such grief, Mother." Clasping the hand of the Abbess to her breast, she exclaimed, "Enough tears! No more! How good and worthy of love is our good God!"

Turning to Mother Francisca of the Angels, she said, "Mother, I ask that you would have the charity to bring me a little anise water, for you know that this is an excellent remedy for all ailments."

### THE SURPRISE OF THE PHYSICIAN

The humble religious asked the blessing of her Abbess and permission to drink the water, which she drank with unusual pleasure. This, however, worried and distressed the Mother Abbess, who feared she was drinking too much after such a severe attack.

Noting this, Mother Mariana told her, "Mother, do not worry. I feel such thirst because I am now well - for the greater glory of God and the consolation of Your Reverence, whom I will serve with filial love."

Taking the hand of her Abbess, she brought it to her lips and kissed it, bathing it with her tears.

When the hour had passed, the doctor returned to find Mother Mariana not only alive, but recovered and well with a strong pulse. In admiration, he said, "Human science cannot begin to understand the divine will. There is nothing for me to do or prescribe. I am very happy that this holy creature has not been taken from us. I rejoice for you, and also for me. I remain always at your disposal." And he took his leave.

After drinking the anise water, Mother Mariana turned to her Superior, "Mother, the hour for choir to praise the good God is drawing near. In the refectory, God, our good and loving Father, has already set the table and today He will serve us a most excellent bread."

No sooner had she spoken these words than a knock sounded on the door and a sister arrived carrying in some large, very fine bread sent by the Marquesa, who had ordered it made that day specially for her beloved Community of Conceptionist sisters.

Mother Valenzuela sat in a kind of dazed state. The unexpected recovery of her beloved Mother Mariana seemed like a dream to her. She would repeatedly ask how she was feeling.

"Well, Mother," was the invariable response.

## THE SPANISH MOTHERS EXCHANGE CONFIDENCES

The hour for choir arrived, but the Abbess feared that her recently recovered daughter would not have the strength to go to prayer after all that had occurred.

She told her, "Mother, I do not want you to go to choir today. When we have finished, I will return to you and we will go to the refectory together."

This humble religious responded, "Mother, I feel well enough to join my sisters at choir, but if it pleases Your Reverence that I remain here with Mothers Francisca and Magdalena, who will also be unable to participate, I will remain, for it is my pleasure to obey you."

The Abbess confirmed her command, "Yes, Mother, today

you will not go. We will see each other in the afternoon. We have the whole day before us."

With the tranquility of the obedient soul, Mother Mariana remained, praying with the two religious.

The two Mothers, who realized that her time in Hell had come to an end, addressed her, "Mother and our dear sister, how joyful we are that the time of your agony has ended! Your soul is marked with the indelible seal of divine charity. During Communion today, our good Jesus manifested this to all the Spanish Mothers, in the same way that five years ago He revealed to us the sufferings you would undergo. How much we suffered before Communion in the fear that you had left us alone and orphans, but when it was given to us to see your glory, our sorrow gave way to rejoicing.

"During these five long years, we have accompanied you in your sufferings. United in spirit, we never ceased to assist you with our prayers, sacrifices, and penances, begging strength and valor for your tormented soul."

Then they embraced her.

### Prophecies about the Future of the Convent, the Sisters in Purgatory, and the Return of the Friars Minor

Mother Mariana returned their embraces, saying: "Alas, my sisters! How terrible Hell is! No words can describe it! Only by seeing it can one know what it is! But, also, how ineffable are the delights of the glories of Heaven, where I was taken by the hands of our Most Holy Mother, the Virgin Mary. As you know, I have spent the past morning there!

"I will tell you a secret that you should keep from everyone, for I know I cannot hide it from you. Our sister, for whom I atoned, will die in one month, and our good Mother Abbess after two months and 15 days. Our Abbess will have to pass a century in Purgatory, and we will be unable to alleviate her sufferings. Our sister will remain in Purgatory until the Day of Judgment. However, we and our successors can mitigate her sufferings to a certain point. She will also receive some relief when, after a long time, the Franciscan friars return to administer to our Convent. From Heaven, I will give assistance to the Convent.

"I will live yet many more years and will bury all of you. Know also that many of our sisters will remain in Purgatory so long as our Convent is subject to the Ordinary. They will rise to Heaven only when jurisdiction has returned to the Franciscan Friars. A long time will pass before this takes place. We will see it happen from Heaven, and we will help our daughters to attain this grace, after they have been tested by great tribulations, which will come from hands inside this Convent as well as from outside.

"And do you know why our sisters will remain in Purgatory until the return of the Friars Minor? Because upon them will weigh the guilt for the relaxation of the Rule that will be introduced and will last for a long time in our beloved Convent. Upon them will weigh this laxity, and also the trials and tears of those, who, with upright hearts, will strive to carry out the Rule to its very letter and who, for this reason, will suffer humiliations, scorn, and calumnies.

"However, these souls will be blessed by Our Lord, Who will flood their souls with torrents of divine grace, engendering a great and hidden sanctity. I recognize these sisters and they give me much consolation, for they will sustain our beloved Community through certain times of agony.

"Woe to those hypocrites and lax sisters who are stubborn in their infidelities! Their number will not be great, but they will always exist, just as there will also always be saints. The unfaithful ones will carve the crowns for the latter, just as some non-observant sisters did for us. Our sufferings were well spent to build and sustain our Convent. Blessed are the efforts of our Founding Mother, who from Heaven blesses all her faithful daughters, our daughters also, and our sisters for eternity."

The Community prayer had ended and the Abbess hurried back to Mother Mariana, whom she found quite well and cheerful, already having lost that deathlike pallor. Together they went to the refectory where they took some nourishment. The poor captain outdid herself in showing every kindness to Mother Mariana, who treated her with the sweetness and love of a mother, for she had cost her soul much suffering. She was truly the daughter of her interior sorrows, and, for this reason, she loved her most tenderly.

## Our Lord Returns the Heart of Mother Mariana

The next morning, Mother Mariana approached the Holy Table radiant with happiness, her countenance manifesting the glory of her soul. The evening before, she had spoken with her Franciscan director and told him all that had passed during her long swoon.

During that Communion of her first day of glory, she saw Our Lord Jesus Christ take from His Sacred Heart her own purified heart, which, during those five years of trial, He had safeguarded under the maternal care of Mary Most Holy. Our Lord and His Blessed Mother then returned Mother Mariana's heart to her bosom and again took possession of it. With her heart, all her tender and loving affection returned, further augmented.

The holy religious also noted that the devils and all Hell trembled at seeing her escape their clutches. They wanted to newly assail her but were unable to do so, for her simple presence sufficed to shame and scatter them. Thus would they be impeded from doing any more great harm in the Convent where she lived and died, and where her remains, although still hidden, are preserved to this day. For, upon her humble request, God permitted that she be buried under one of the arches of the Convent for which she had sacrificed herself.[59]

This Convent will be persecuted throughout time by the good and the evil, who will ignore the advantage of having this blessed cloister in the heart of the city to act as a deflector for the many private and public crimes committed by persons of both sexes and in every condition of life in this sinful city.

Woe to Quito should this Convent be lost! Rightly should its inhabitants shudder!

---

59. The body of Mother Mariana de Jesus Torres was exhumed in 1885, 271 years after her death. Her body was found whole and incorrupt. She was wearing a white habit with a black veil. Her face retained its natural color with a rosy hue in the cheeks and lips. Through her slightly parted lips, the tongue could be seen. The eyes were closed, but preserved, as well as the eye lashes. The ears were flexible. The hair was red. The whole body exhaled a perfume of lilies. Some tools of penance were found in her pockets, as well as some personal objects. These objects were placed there by the Friars Minor with the permission of the Abbess Mariana de San Domingos and the Convent Council. They were removed and are conserved in the archives of the Convent.

The bodies of the other Founding Mothers were also discovered incorrupt, and are preserved today in the Convent.

## The Converted Sister Dies

From this day on, Mother Mariana began to regain her health as if by magic. Her countenance recovered its joy, the rosy color returned to her cheeks, and life and vigor returned to her whole being. The Abbess, on the other hand, was steadily weakening, and the captain went to bed with a very high fever. In her delirium she called for Mother Mariana.

The Abbess forbid her to attend this sick sister. But Mother Mariana told her that it was the will of God, and that this poor sister would never rise again from her bed.

The Abbess, who watched over Mother Mariana with solicitous care, acceded to this request only with great reluctance. Constantly she checked on the sickroom to be sure that the captain was treating Mother Mariana well. When she saw that Mother Mariana continued her recuperation and that the sick sister was treating her with love and respect, she was more at ease. But she did not let up in her vigilance.

Finally, the last hour of the captain arrived. She made a very good confession, devoutly received the Last Sacraments, and asked pardon for her faults and bad example. Then, with Mother Mariana at her side, she died on a Thursday at 3 p.m.

Mother Mariana saw the judgment of this sister, who, standing before the throne of God, finally realized that five years of Hell suffered by an innocent soul had been the price for her salvation. For this, throughout eternity, she would be profoundly grateful. Frequently in Purgatory she would recall the heroic sacrifice made for her, and she would continue to rely on her benefactress to alleviate her sufferings through prayers, Communions, and penances.

Mother Mariana always showed the greatest charity for the soul of this converted sister, and, until the end of her life, she sought to alleviate her pains and console her. Then, as time passed, this unknown soul was forgotten. She will remain forgotten until the day when a kindred soul who will be very close to God will assist her again. This soul, who will know various secrets and communicate with those in Purgatory, will obtain great relief for this soul and for many others. And this, according to the words of Mother Mariana, will take place in the 20$^{th}$ century.

## Death of Mother Valenzuela

As the days and weeks passed swiftly by, the fragile heart of Mother Valenzuela weakened more and more. She had turned the government of the Convent over to Mother Mariana, who cared for her Abbess day and night without leaving her. Finally, after just three short months of her Abbacy, she received the Sacraments in her last agony and closed her eyes to this earthly light, opening them again only to the light of eternity.

Mother Mariana wept copiously. She herself prepared the body of the Abbess, arranging flowers around it on the stretcher, which the Convent kept for this purpose and which Mother Mariana had ordered made when she was first elected Abbess. This stretcher was used for the first time to carry the venerable body of Mother Maria de Jesus Taboada. It was used throughout time to carry the bodies of all the Founding Mothers and other religious, including the body of Mother Mariana de Jesus Torres herself. With filial affection, this religious mourned the death of Mother Valenzuela, for they had loved one another dearly.

\* \* \*

## Chapter 28

After the death of Mother Magdalena de Jesus Valenzuela, who had governed for only three short months of her Abbacy, Mother Mariana notified the Bishop so that he could specify what should be done.

The Prelate sent a private note to Mother Mariana de Jesus Torres, making her the presiding Abbess for three years. When the humble religious read these lines, she immediately sent back a reply, pointing out to the Bishop the advantages of allowing the Convent to choose a new Abbess. The spouses of Christ, she argued, should be able to elect freely the one whom they would lovingly obey. For this practice prevents resentments and fears, which can cause so much turmoil in communities, she noted.

### Mother Mariana Is Again Elected Abbess

The Prelate accepted the reasoning of the humble and selfless religious, whose great virtue he once again recognized. He arranged to come to the Convent to preside over the election.

The first vote was split between Mother Mariana de Jesus, Mother Magdalena of Saint John, Mother Anna of the Conception, and Mother Inez Zorrilla. The second vote was divided between Mother Mariana de Jesus and Mother Magdalena of Saint John. In the third ballot, Mother Mariana received the majority. The Prelate joyfully confirmed the election, exhorting the sisters to love and obey her as the mother and head of the Community. In his presence, the religious rendered their obedience to Mother Mariana. After the Bishop left, the community celebrated the election.

The non-observant sisters, as usual, were not pleased, but since they lacked a leader, they could do nothing. On the contrary, they made an earnest attempt to appear happy, but in fact, it was the depths of their hearts that appeared on their exteriors. Despite the false front they presented, what was passing in their hearts was seen by the humble Mother Abbess, who loved them dearly. She would even think that their bad behavior was caused by her poor dedication to the service of God. For this reason, these daughters were the favored souls of her maternal love. In her effort to win them to the service of God, she would assist them and relieve their every need even before they could make it known, for she knew better than they themselves what they wanted and needed.

### The Intransigence of Mother Mariana

When, however, it was a matter of some relaxation or fault against the Rule, she would immediately call the offenders to her cell or she would go to theirs. With disarming sweetness, she would make them see the temporal and earthly happiness of the observant religious who followed the Rule even in its most minute details. She would then tell each one the fault she had committed, embrace her tenderly, and humbly demand that she not repeat the offense. After praying a Hail Mary with the guilty sister, she would kiss her feet.

Thus she provided the example of true humility and attracted the souls of her daughters by the sweetness characteristic of the spouses of the meek and humble Jesus, with Whom they live united by the strong and indissoluble bonds of divine and heroic charity.

### The Most Holy Virgin Comes to Complain to Mother Mariana

It was the beginning of the year 1610. Each day of this happy year was one of an uninterrupted sequence of supernatural communication of God and Mary Most Holy with Mother Mariana.

During this period, Our Lady often admonished her favored daughter about the delay in ordering her statue to be made. She told her that she wanted her statue of Our Lady of Good Success to be placed above the abbatial chair, where, as absolute Mistress, Mother, and Abbess of the Convent, she would govern her beloved Community until the end of time. She threatened Mother Mariana that if this were not done, she would withdraw her graces and favors from her and give them to another more worthy soul, who would correspond and carry out the request that she had made some years ago.[60]

---

60. In the second vision of Our Lady of Good Success to Mother Mariana on January 16, 1599, she had commanded that her statue be made and had given her the measurement for her height.

The heart of this humble religious was inflamed anew with divine fire and, like a penitent child, she begged pardon of her Most Holy Mother. She told her that she did not think it was possible to describe the dazzling beauty of her queenly features to the sculptor, who, regardless of his skill, could never do them justice.

In addition to this, she feared that she would not be believed by the Bishops and priests, and that this revelation might destroy her beloved Convent, which had been founded upon and conserved by the suffering of her aunt, the Founding Mother, who now enjoyed eternal happiness in Heaven, as well as by her suffering and that of the other Founding Mothers.

However, she begged the Queen of Heaven and Earth, who knows all the events of the future, to show her the way to obey and please her, for this was her only ambition on this earth.

### END OF VOLUME I

*In Volume II, Fr. Manuel Sousa Pereira tells how the miraculous statue of Our Lady of Good Success was made by an artist and miraculously completed by Saint Francis of Assisi and the Archangels. It was solemnly consecrated and installed in the Convent in the Abbess' chair on the Feast of the Purification, February 2, 1610.*

*Our Lady of Good Success appeared again to Mother Mariana on February 2, 1634 and described the great crisis in the Church and society in the 20th century. In the last apparition of December 8, 1634, Our Lady warns about the corruption of customs and loss of purity in priests and religious.*

*In Volume II, the author also recounts many miracles inside and outside the Convent worked through the intercession of the saintly Abbess, Mother Mariana. It includes her last words to her sisters on her deathbed, and her Last Testament, a moving document that transmits the spirit and virtue of religious life.*

\* \* \*

# *BIBLIOGRAPHY*

**Luis León Acosta & José Conde Castillo:**

*El Ecuador y sus Santuarios*. Quito: Editora Luz de America, 1992.

**Luis E. Cadena y Almeida:**

*Apariciones de María Santísima del Buen Suceso a la Sierva de Dios Sor Mariana Francisca de Jesús Torres y Berriochoa (O.I.C.)*. Quito: Libreria Espiritual, n.d.

*A Spanish Mystic in Quito: Sor Mariana de Jesús Torres*. Mount Kisco, NY: Foundation for a Christian Civilization, 1990.

*La Mujer y la Monja Extraordinaria – Mariana Francisca de Jesus Torres y Berriochoa*. Quito: Libreria Espiritual, n.d.

*"La Violeta de los Andes" – Mariana Francisca de Jesus Torres y Berriochoa*. Quito: Libreria Espiritual, 1990.

*Madera para Esculpir la Imagen de una Santa*. Mount Kisco, NY: Foundation for a Christian Civilization, 1987.

*Memorial Historico de la Coronacion Canonica a la Sagrada Imagen de Maria Santisima del Buen Suceso*. Quito: Libreria Espiritual, 1991.

*Mensaje Profetico de la Sierva de Dios Sor Mariana Francisca de Jesus Torres y Berriochoa*. Quito: Libreria Espiritual, 1989.

**Marian Therese Horvat:**

*Our Lady of Good Success – Prophecies for Our Times.* Los Angeles: TIA, 1999.

*Stories and Miracles of Our Lady of Good Success.* Los Angeles: TIA, 2002.

*Novena and Prayer Booklet of Our Lady of Good Success.* Oconomowoc, WI: Apostolate of Our Lady of Good Success, 2003.

**Mary Maxwell Scott:**

*Gabriel Garcia Moreno – Regenerator of Ecuador.* Oconomowoc, WI: Apostolate of Our Lady of Good Success, 2004.

**Carlos de la Torre Reyes:**

*Treasures of Quito.* Columbia: El Sello Editorial, 1990.

\* \* \*

# MORE ABOUT OUR LADY OF GOOD SUCCESS

## BOOKS & BOOKLETS

***THE ADMIRABLE LIFE OF MOTHER MARIANA*** - Fr. Manuel S. Pereira (Volume I) Additional copies can be purchased for **$16** each.

***THE ADMIRABLE LIFE OF MOTHER MARIANA*** - Fr. Manuel S. Pereira (Volume II) Many more apparitions and prophecies 358 pp. **$20** each.

***OUR LADY OF GOOD SUCCESS - PROPHECIES FOR OUR TIMES*** - MARIAN HORVAT. A summary of the extraordinary revelations of Our Lady to Mother Mariana, including her 1634 vision of the sanctuary light being extinguished in the 20th century and the five causes for this. 72 pp. **$7**

***STORIES AND MIRACLES OF OUR LADY OF GOOD SUCCESS*** - MARIAN HORVAT. More marvelous stories about how the miraculous statue was made and completed by the Archangels and St. Francis. 102 pp. **$8**

***OUR LADY OF GOOD SUCCESS NOVENA AND PRAYER BOOKLET*** - An old and blessed novena with daily meditations - written for the cloistered sisters in the Quito convent - and many other prayers. Handy pocket size. 48 pp. **$6**

## CDs

***PROPHECIES OF OUR LADY OF GOOD SUCCESS*** - How these 17th century prophecies confirm & complete the message of Our Lady at Fatima. 50 min. **$6**

***THE SUFFERING OF MOTHER MARIANA*** - The story of the miracle of the Little Patroness and its application for our times. 50 min. **$6**

***A SOLDIER CONVERTS*** - The conversion of the soldier Manuel Pereira, who wrote the biography of Mother Mariana. 50 min. **$6**

***PROPHECIES FULFILLED!*** - A record of the perfect accuracy of Mother Mariana's prediction of future events. 50 min. **$6**

## SET OF 5 QUALITY COLOR PICTURES

Four color postcard-size pictures of Our Lady of Good Success and one of Mother Mariana de Jesus. Set - **$2.50**

Large 9" x 12" color photo of Our Lady and the Christ Child - Each **$7**

Christ child Crucified Holy Card. 3" x 4" - **5/$1  50/$8   100/$15**

### SHIPPING AND HANDLING:

U.S. orders: If your total is less than $15, add $3.50;  $15 to $29, add $4.50; $30 to $49, add $6.50;  $50 to $99, add $8; $100 or more, add 10%
Canadian and International orders: Call 323-725-0219 or Fax 323-725-0019

## TRADITION IN ACTION, INC.

P.O. Box 23135 - Los Angeles, CA  90023
Phone: 323-725-0219     Fax: 323-725-0019

**Order online at www.TraditionInAction.org**